# BODYWORK & PAINTING

# BODYWORK

# & PAINTING

Hearst Books
The Hearst Corporation
New York, New York

Other
titles
from

BASIC CAR CARE ILLUSTRATED
TUNEUP & TROUBLESHOOTING
CAR CARE GUIDES
  *Chevy*
  *Chevelle*
  *Cutlass*
  *Nova*
  *Vega*
  *Ford*
  *Pinto*
  *Torino*
  *Dart*
  *Valiant*
  *Datsun*
  *Toyota*
  *VW Beetle*
  *VW Rabbit*

Library of Congress
Catalog Card No. 79-66360

Soft Cover ISBN No. 0-87851-514-3
Hard Cover ISBN No. 0-87851-515-1

Printed in the United States of America

Designed and produced by: For Art Sake, Inc.
Automotive Books Division, 36 West 89th St., New
York, New York 10024

The information herein has been compiled
from authoritative sources. While every
effort is made by the editors to attain
accuracy, manufacturing changes as well as
typographical errors and omissions may
occur. The publisher and the editors cannot
be responsible nor do they assume responsibility for
such omissions, errors or changes.

## ACKNOWLEDGMENTS

The editors are grateful for the assistance provided by the following individuals, manufacturers, and organizations.

Michael Beazley
Saunders Technical School, Yonkers, NY

Glen Bradshaw,
Marson Products, Chelsea, MA

Carl Caiati

Joe Carra, Mutual Spray
Equipment Corporation, NY, NY

Central Auto Glass, Yonkers, NY

Larry Ciancio, Ditzler Automotive Finishes

Andy Cooper, Ditzler Automotive Finishes

Pat Donnelley

John Drummond, General Motors
Research Laboratory, Warren, MI

Tom Fitzpatrick, Fitzpatrick Auto Body,
Yonkers, NY

General Motors Research Division,
Warren, MI

Walter Gerber, Central Auto Glass

Gerald Hopkins, Board of Cooperative
Education Technical School, Carmel, NY

Hunts Point Auto Wreckers

David Lewis and the staff of the
MOTOR Crash Estimating Guides

Virginia Meeker, A-Design Group,
Badger Air Brush Company, Oak Brook, IL

Claude Milot, Assistant General Manager,
MOTOR Publications

Tod Mitzman

Daniel Oates, Production, POPULAR MECHANICS

Olinville Auto Body, Bronx, NY

Jim O'Sullivan

Wilfredo Otiz

PPG Industries, Ditzler Automotive
Finishes Division, Detroit, MI

Prestolite Company, Toledo, OH

Rinshed-Mason Products, Inmont
Corporation, Detroit, MI

Mike Sack, Ditzler Automotive Finishes

John Samanich, Auto Trade School,
Automotive Books Division, Brooklyn, NY

William Schipper, Ford Training and
Publications Department, Dearborn, MI

Fritz Schmidt

Dr. Steve Schwabe, Devilbiss Company,
Toledo, OH

Ira Smithheimer, Sears, Roebuck & Company,
Hicksville, NY

Mary R. Strahlendorf, Public Relations,
Sears, Roebuck, and Company, St. Davids, PA

Alex Vida

# CONTENTS

# PREP TALK

Would you like to hold on to your present car but are ashamed of how it looks?

Do you know what it feels like when the deductible on your car's collision insurance policy reads $250 and the bodywork estimate for fixing a parking lot scrape reads $280?

Are you beginning to wonder whether anyone knows how to do a job right anymore—and deliver it on time? That's when do-it-yourself begins to look worth the effort.

We decided it was time for a reliable book that could show a Saturday mechanic how to repair the kind of auto body damage that doesn't require costly tools and technical training. Fortunately, that includes most kinds—from fixing parking lot scratches to replacing an entire front assembly. So we arranged for some smart, experienced bodywork and painting pros to show us how to do the jobs that come up most often. We assigned a photographer to look over their shoulders with a lens while our writers asked the obvious, smart, naive and practical questions that anyone working on his car in the street would need answers to.

**Bodywork doesn't require the years and years of training in metalworking that it used to.**

Can you spackle a crack, a dimple, or a hole in Sheetrock before you paint over it? That's how a lot of bodywork is done these days—with plastic fillers you mix up like spackling compound. You don't need to coax the sheet metal back to a perfectly smooth contour the way a few of the old-time masters still do. The secret is this: once you get the metal pounded out close to its original shape, the new fillers take you the rest of the way. Or if you've got an accordian crunch on your hands, unbolt the part and bolt on an identical one purchased from a salvage yard. (Those operations perform a real service by organizing their inventories of spare body parts better than "junkyards" did in the old days.)

**This book is designed for people who have to work on their cars in the street or their home garages or driveways.**

A Saturday mechanic can do a lot of bodywork jobs very well under street conditions, but there are some he can't do. For example, if you are like most nonprofessionals, you probably won't be able to paint your car's hood, roof or rear deck perfectly because you can't control the weather or the dust and bugs that can settle on the wet spray. And, it's silly to go out and buy hydraulic frame-squaring equipment for one job (you probably couldn't even fit the equipment into your garage). Most of us could get into serious trouble trying to cut away a quarter panel with an acetylene torch and welding a new one back on. These are jobs the pros should get paid for. This book includes separate sections called "How the Pros Do It" that show how most of these specialized jobs are done, but we don't recommend that amateur mechanics tackle such jobs without professional training.

## How to Get the Most Out of This Book

**Get the big picture first.** The first three chapters can make your job a lot easier. The chapter called "Sizing Up the Job" tells how to evaluate the damage to a car and decide what it will take to repair it. One car may look hopeless, but is easy to fix because it's just a lot of little jobs that are easy to do; another car may look easy and be impossible. Sometimes you are better off replacing a section altogether.

The chapter on "Replacement Parts" explains how salvage yards work and how to identify the exact part you need for your make, model and year. Check the "Tools" chapter. You may be surprised to learn that you already own most of the things you need.

**Read through chapters that look as if they might have something—even a little bit—to say about your problem.**

At the beginning of each how-to chapter, you'll see a page full of photos illustrating the different kinds of damage we show you how to fix in that chapter. The "Job steps" drawings on the facing page give you a brief run-through by showing *generally* what steps are involved before you get into the detailed instructions on the pages that follow. As you read through those instructions, try to picture yourself doing the work on your own car. In fact, it's not a bad idea to take the book out to your car and do your reading there. We

loaded this book full of photographs for that reason—so you can compare your damage to the illustrated instructions in the book and see where they match best. Once you start to work, the less you have to refer to the book the better.

**"If all else fails, read the instructions,"** as the saying goes. If you take only a quick look at a rust spot, a sprung hood, even a simple nick in the paint, then jump to a few fast conclusions and tear into the job, you could end up doing that job a couple of times before you get it right. At the very least, you should read about the job you want to do *before* you start spending your hard earned money on tools and materials.

Take the section on "Surface Damage," for example. It tells you to look at the damage very carefully first, then feel it, and, if you can reach it, put your hand up behind it to see if it is worse than it looks. That will tell you the type, extent, and depth of the problem. Then find the pages that give you the step-by-step "how-to" for fixing that specific kind of damage.

So the payoff reason for getting the whole picture first is money—the money you save by not having to do the job twice because you got halfway through it before you realized you should have "frittered" the "framish" before you started. Read the labels on the cans, boxes and kits you buy but don't rely on them to give you the whole picture. Sometimes they make the job sound too easy. Since it's your body, you obviously want it to look good, but you also want it to last.

# TYPICAL BODY PANELS ON CONVENTIONAL FRAME

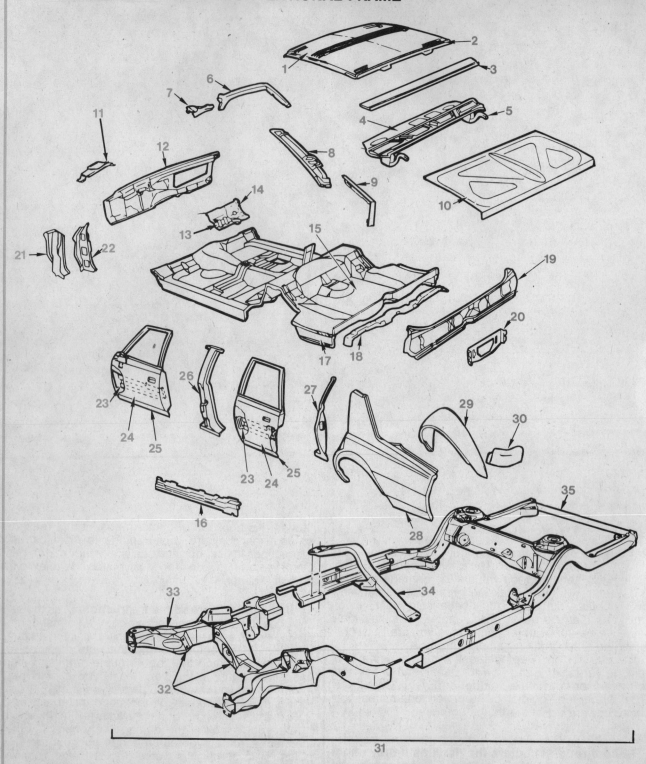

| | | |
|---|---|---|
| 1 Roof panel | 13 Front outer rocker panel | 25 Door assembly |
| 2 Rear window roof rail | 14 Floor to rocker filler | 26 Center pillar |
| 3 Upper body panel cover | 15 Rear floor pan | 27 Quarter panel lock pillar |
| 4 Seat to rear window reinforcement | 16 Rocker panel | 28 Quarter panel |
| 5 Trunk lid hinge | 17 Floor to quarter panel extension | 29 Wheelhouse |
| 6 Side frame and reinforcement for windshield | 18 Rear floor cross bar | 30 Tail pipe shield |
| 7 Lower frame brace for windshield | 19 Rear body panel | 31 Frame assembly |
| 8 Roof inner side rail | 20 License plate mounting panel | 32 Front side members and cross member |
| 9 Roof outer side rail | 21 Lower hinge pillar | 33 Front side member |
| 10 Trunk lid | 22 Lower hinge pillar reinforcement | 34 Transmission support |
| 11 Fender mounting plate | 23 Door reinforcement | 35 Rear cross member |
| 12 Dash panel | 24 Door outer panel | |

# TYPICAL FRONT SHEET METAL ON CONVENTIONAL FRAME

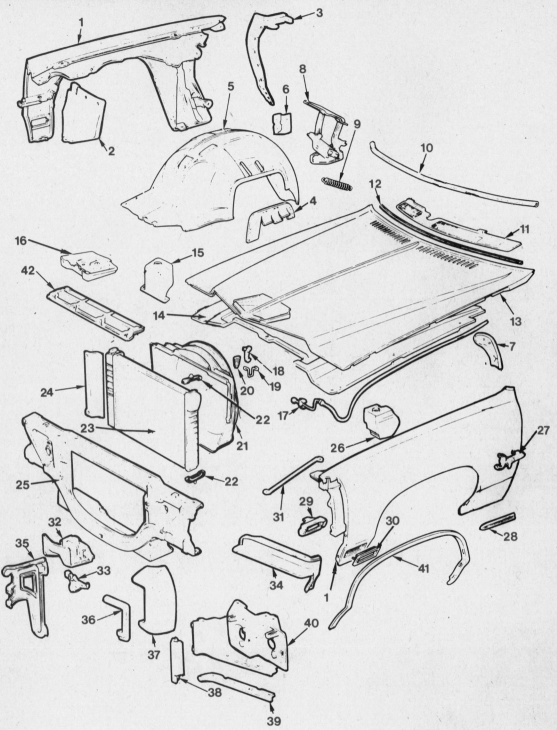

| | | |
|---|---|---|
| 1 Fender | 15 Coolant recovery tank | 29 Side marker lamp |
| 2 Dust shield | 16 Battery tray | 30 Side marker lamp bezel |
| 3 Seal to body | 17 Hood lock cable | 31 Fender skirt brace |
| 4 Dust shield | 18 Hood safety catch | 32 Hood lock plate |
| 5 Skirt | 19 Hood lock striker | 33 Hood lock |
| 6 Dash panel brace | 20 Hood pop-up spring | 34 Bumper to fender filler |
| 7 Dash panel brace | 21 Fan shroud | 35 Hood lock support |
| 8 Hood hinge | 22 Radiator retainer pad | 36 Fender extension molding |
| 9 Hood hinge spring | 23 Radiator | 37 Fender extension |
| 10 Hood molding | 24 Radiator air baffle | 38 Vertical headlamp housing molding |
| 11 Top vent screen cowl | 25 Radiator support | 39 Lower headlamp housing molding |
| 12 Hood to cowl seal | 26 Windshield washer bottle | 40 Headlamp housing |
| 13 Hood | 27 Name plate | 41 Wheel opening molding |
| 14 Hood insulator | 28 Lower side molding | 42 Radiator mounting panel |

# TYPICAL BODY PANELS ON UNITIZED BODY

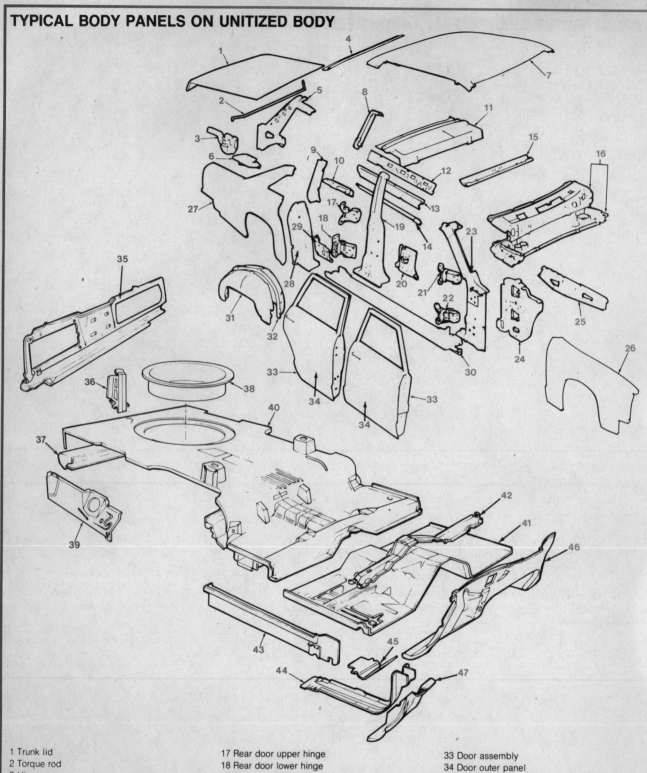

| | | |
|---|---|---|
| 1 Trunk lid | 17 Rear door upper hinge | 33 Door assembly |
| 2 Torque rod | 18 Rear door lower hinge | 34 Door outer panel |
| 3 Hinge | 19 Center body pillar | 35 Rear body panel |
| 4 Rail above rear window | 20 Center body pillar extension | 36 Rear body panel support |
| 5 Rear roof rail | 21 Front door upper hinge | 37 Rear floor cross member |
| 6 Quarter window reinforcement | 22 Front door lower hinge | 38 Spare tire well |
| 7 Roof panel | 23 Hinge and windshield pillar | 39 Extension from quarter panel to floor |
| 8 Roof rail extension | 24 Cowl inner side panel | 40 Rear floor panel |
| 9 Rear quarter upper lock pillar | 25 Front fender reinforcement | 41 Front floor panel |
| 10 Quarter panel reinforcement at belt line | 26 Front fender | 42 Front floor panel support |
| 11 Upper rear body panel | 27 Quarter panel | 43 Inner rocker panel |
| 12 Inner roof side rail | 28 Rear quarter panel lower lock pillar | 44 Front sidemember |
| 13 Outer roof side rail | 29 Lock pillar reinforcement | 45 Front sidemember reinforcement |
| 14 Center roof side rail | 30 Rocker panel | 46 Dash panel |
| 15 Windshield header panel | 31 Outer wheelhouse | 47 Gusset to dash panel |
| 16 Cowl top panel | 32 Inner wheelhouse | |

# TYPICAL FRONT SHEET METAL ON UNITIZED BODY

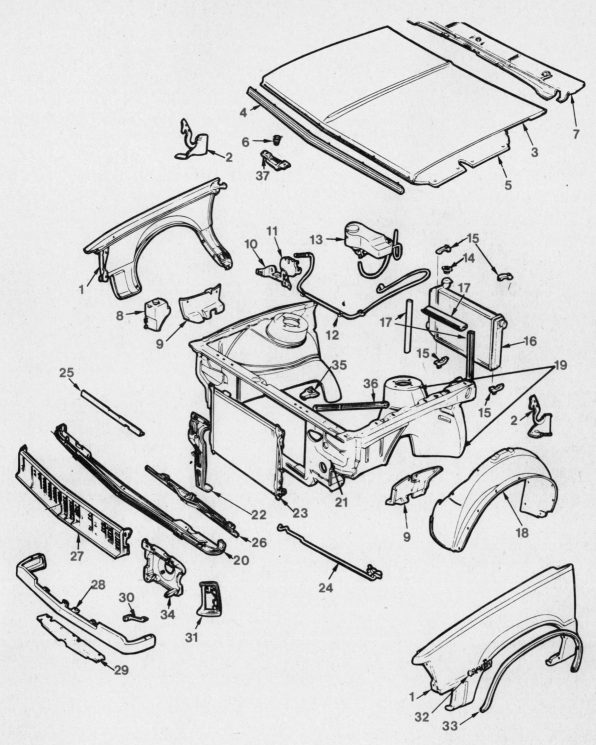

| | | |
|---|---|---|
| 1 Fender | 14 Radiator cap | 27 Grille |
| 2 Hood hinge | 15 Radiator pad | 28 Valance panel |
| 3 Hood | 16 Radiator | 29 Radiator air deflector |
| 4 Hood molding | 17 Radiator air seals | 30 Valance panel brace |
| 5 Hood insulator | 18 Fender skirt | 31 Side marker lamp bezel |
| 6 Hood pop-up spring | 19 Fender wheelhouse and spring mounting panel | 32 Name plate |
| 7 Top vent panel cowl | 20 Tie bar | 33 Wheel opening molding |
| 8 Radiator overflow reservoir | 21 Side baffle | 34 Head lamp mounting panel |
| 9 Dust shield | 22 Hood lock support | 35 Head lamp mounting panel brace |
| 10 Hood lock mounting bracket | 23 Air conditioner condenser | 36 Wheelhouse to tie bar brace |
| 11 Hood lock | 24 Hood support rod | 37 Hood lock striker |
| 12 Hood lock cable | 25 Front hood seal | |
| 13 Windshield washer bottle | 26 Air conditioner condenser seal | |

## THIS BOOK BELONGS TO:

**MAKE OF CAR:**

| MODEL: | | MODEL YEAR: |
|---|---|---|
| Body Color # | | Name |
| 2nd Color # | | Name |
| Vinyl Top Color # | | Name |
| Interior Material Color | | |
| Repaint History— | | |
| Year | Area | Paint Type |
| Year | Area | Paint Type |
| Year | Area | Paint Type |

# WEEKEND SHAPEUP

**Before** we began our weekend shapeup, the car looked like this: scratches and dents, broken trim, and a finish that was strictly dullsville. The looks alone had us longing for a brand-new model.

**After** the shapeup, who needs a new car? With the repairs made and the broken parts replaced, we're proud to be seen tooling around town in this beauty. The car is worth more, too.

## Checklist

On the following pages you will find, in outline form, a dandy way of spending next weekend: shaping up your car.

Why, you ask, would anyone want to spend those two swell days between Friday and Monday patching, pulling, and bending metal into shape? Well, there are a couple of compelling reasons. For one thing, a shapeup increases the value of your car. These repairs will do as much for your car as a tuneup.

Second, the work isn't too demanding. It's as easy to do body-work as it is to get at the last spark plug on a modern engine.

Third, think how good you'll feel on Monday.

What you'll see in the next nine pages are photos arranged in sequence showing how to repair scratches, chips, and dents; how to replace lights and other exterior parts; and how to give your whole car a thorough cleaning so that it will shine as you never thought it would again. Take the sample car, a 1974 Capri. We had to wash it just to find out how bad it was. But by the time we were finished. . . .

Bright and early Saturday morning, we started in on the dents. By dinner time (repeat, dinner time) everything was primed and ready for painting.

On Sunday morning, we cleaned the inside of the car and lubricated a sticking lock. Then we masked and wiped in preparation for painting. By late afternoon, it wore a beautiful coat of paint where dents and rust and scratches had once been. The results were good to look at and value-enhancing. And we felt really great on Monday morning.

# Body language

**Accordion crunch.** The name for the crumpled metal that results from a front- or rear-end collision. This damage is difficult to repair. Replacement parts or power equipment is needed.

**Buckles.** The ridges or high spots seen in metal that has been forced back.

**Bumping.** Hammering metal back to its original shape using a body hammer and a dolly.

**Color sanding.** The final wet-sanding of the top coat of paint before buffing and polish-blending.

**Dollying it out.** Hammering from the underside of the metal using the dolly (see Chapter 5) as a hammer.

**Featheredging.** A sanding technique that creates a tapered edge that blends two areas together. You sand from the center toward the edges.

**Georgia undercoat.** Specks of tar and oil picked up when driving on hot or soft pavement. This is a common problem that soap and water won't solve, but gasoline will. Minimize buildup by cleaning regularly with gas, then rewax.

**Getting good cover.** Achieving paint coverage so the primer or base coat doesn't show through.

**Giving it tooth.** Roughing up a surface so the next coat of material will adhere. When the surface is rough enough, it "has tooth."

**Grater shaving.** Using a cheese-grater file to take off high spots in plastic body filler.

**Grit.** The size of particles on sandpaper. It is determined by a grading process in which particles are forced through a series of screens. Each screen has a certain mesh. For example, only #400 grit particles could pass through a screen numbered 400, while #280 grit particles would be blocked.

**Holiday.** An unflattering term for a missed spot in one or all of the paint coats.

**Mud-slinger.** One who applies body filler too heavily and without shaving and smoothing it.

**Open coated.** Paper which has 60–80% grit coverage on the surface.

**Road haze.** The layer of film your car picks up over a period of months. Actually, it's tiny, almost imperceptible scratches in the wax, plus film from sun and pollutants. You can't get it off with soap and water. It requires polishing.

**Roughing it out.** The first step in straightening sheet metal. You start from the back of the panel and use a heavy hammer or dolly.

**Seeing with the hand.** Feeling a surface lightly with the bare palm of the hand or while wearing a white cotton glove. This helps locate the highs and lows.

**Shooting color.** Spraying successive coats of paint onto the car's surface.

**Tacking.** Removing dust and foreign particles with a chemically treated cloth just before painting.

## Getting your tools together

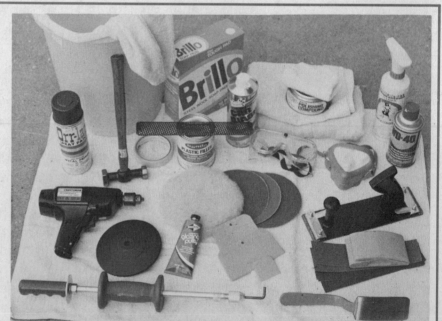

Here are the tools we used for the Weekend Shapeup. Some we found around the house: steel wool soap pads, a pail, sponges, and plenty of clean rags (preferably cotton).

The ½-inch variable-speed drill turned out to be the handiest tool of all. By simply changing attachments— from bit to sandpaper disc to buffing pad—we used this tool every step of the way from preparation for dent pulling to the final waxing.

Coaxing crumpled contours back to their original shape is the forte of the dent puller, the body hammer, and the small spoon. Remaining imperfections were smoothed with plastic body filler applied with spreaders.

Smoothing the surface was necessary at various times, and the tools shown—"cheese grater" file (on top of the filler can), sanding block, and flexible sander—met our needs very well.

To prepare surfaces for painting, we purchased primer, glazing putty, and a roll of masking tape. And no shapeup would be complete without fixing all those annoying sights and sounds that occur when a car starts to show its age. Silicone cleaner/protectant and penetrating/lubricating oil restored the glow of youth to our car. Finally, no job should be started without the proper safety equipment: in our case a pair of goggles and a mask with replaceable filters.

**"First, we washed the car to get a good clean look at the damage."**

*8 am Saturday: There it was! We finally couldn't stand it any longer and resolved to "do something" about the family car to ship it into shape before the end of the weekend!*

*June 2. Crawled under a barbed wire fence — with the car.*

*December 5. Bobsledding on Rt. 22 without snow tires.*

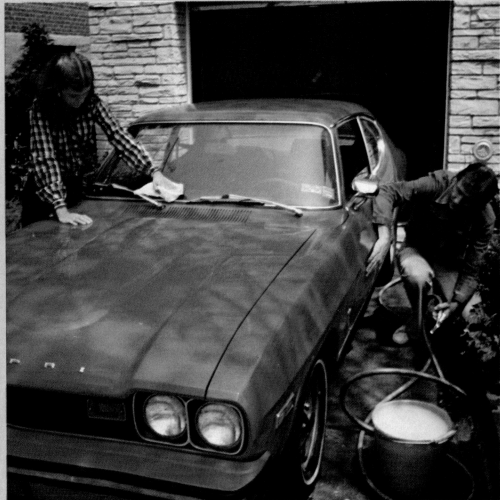

*Years of parking too close to the curb.*

*May 4. A post backed into me.*

*Ouch...the car was only ten days old!*

*January 11. Strange neighborhood, now a strange antenna.*

*August 26. I was in the supermarket!*

*November 24. Tailgated a gravel truck on Route 1.*

*Rust...I'm putting this car on a salt-free diet.*

*This sticking lock has been bugging me for months!*

1. Remove door and window handles, arm rest, and inside door panel. Inside the door, remove the vapor barrier to allow access to the interior of the door.

2. Insert a backing object directly behind the crease. This may be a pipe, dolly or other heavy metal object. Brace it so that it forces the crease out slightly. Maintain this outward pressure throughout the steps that follow.

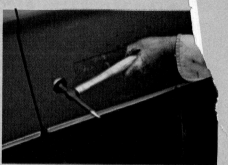

3. Hammer above and below the crease from the outside to flatten the area of the crease (see the hammering-off technique).

4. Use a large object such as a slapper file to distribute the force of the blows across the crease. By now the crease should be nearly flat. Continue working with the hammer until the crease is within ⅛-inch of the original surface contour to minimize the filler required.

5. Grind the area of the repair with #24 grit paper. Remove all paint and make sure that bare metal extends beyond the immediate area in which filler is to be placed. Featheredge with #100 grit paper to provide a smooth transition to the surrounding paint.

6. Mix the body filler according to directions, and smooth it on using firm pressure on the spreader. Work quickly and use only the amount of filler you need.

7. File when the filler has dried to a rubbery consistency. Use long strokes, keeping the surface of the file flat against the putty. Overlap each stroke into the adjacent area.

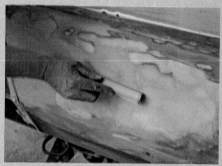

8. Smooth on body filler again to cover the low spots. Repeat steps 6 and 7 until the low spots have been filled and the surface is uniform in color. Then wait for the putty to dry completely.

9. Roll a piece of #100 grit paper into a tube and sand the repaired area. Sand from the center toward the edges of the repair to feather the filler with the surrounding metal.

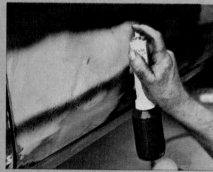

10. Continue sanding the area around the crease until it appears smooth and ready for final paint preparation. No glazing putty is necessary.

11. Wet-sand the primed area with #400 grit paper, using plenty of water. You can hold a wet rag or sponge above the area and squeeze a steady trickle of water onto the area you are sanding instead of dipping the paper into water every few minutes.

12. Mask adjacent trim and windows before final painting. Be careful to remove the masking tape and paper soon after painting and allow time for the paint to dry according to directions on the paint can.

## Looking for the lows

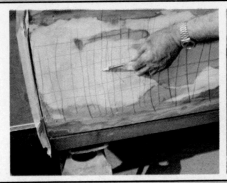

**Left:** To be sure you haven't missed any low spots, make a checkerboard with a grease pencil over the body filler.

**Right:** Sand with a large sanding board. Grease marks will remain in the low spots. Be sure that all grease has been removed before primer is applied.

 Fixing a front fender dent (using a dent puller)

**1.** Drill several evenly spaced holes in the recessed area. The hole should be just big enough to push the end of the dent puller through when the hook is attached.

**2.** Use a dent puller when there is no access to the rear of a dented panel. Insert the hooked end of the puller through a hole drilled in the dented area along one of the outer stress lines. While maintaining a steady outward pressure on the handle of the puller, slide the weight of the puller outward to create an impact. Many light strokes are better than a few heavy ones. Be sure the direction of pull is at right angle to the dent surface. Also, rotate the hook of the puller while pulling the dent so that the end of the hook bears on all sides of the drilled hole. Use the dent puller in several holes an inch apart to pull the entire dent evenly.

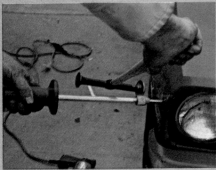

**3.** Hook the dent puller into a low spot. While maintaining a steady, outward pressure on the puller, gently tap the high spots around the hole with a body hammer.

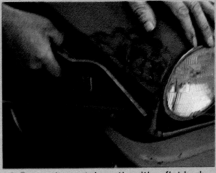

**4.** Bump the metal gently with a flat body tool such as a slapper file. This helps to restore the original contour line below the "iris" or ridge. Repeat steps 2, 3, and 4 until you have brought the metal to ⅛" or less from the original surface contour.

**5.** Mask any adjacent trim. Then grind away the old paint with #24 grit paper until you have gone down to the bare metal. Featheredge the area with #100 grit paper to blend the repair area with surrounding metal.    ⤳

6. Make a palette by wrapping a sheet of plastic around a rigid, flat board such as masonite. Squeeze out a small amount of body filler and two strips of hardener. Mix well, a little at a time, using a plastic spreader or spatula.

7. Smooth on a thin coat of body filler using one stroke and pressing fairly hard with the spreader. Then let it dry until it is just slightly sticky, ten to 30 minutes.

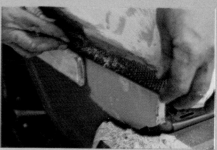

8. File down the high spots using a cheese grater file pulled toward you. Keep the tool flat and apply even pressure along the length of the tool. Go gently near the ridge.

9. Hand sand with #100 grit paper to smooth and level the filler. Repeat step 7 and sand again. Remember to feather the edges so that the putty will blend with the surrounding metal.

10. Roll the sandpaper into a tube and sand very gently under and above the ridge, keeping the surface of the sandpaper horizontal and the pressure even.

11. Apply prime using a long back-and-forth motion. If any low spots still show after priming, apply glazing putty, wet sand with #400 grit paper, and prime again.

12. Wet sand the glazing putty and primer with #400 grit paper. Then wipe the area with a clean cloth.

13. Prime again. Be sure the repaired area is now smooth and level with the original surface contour. Wet sand lightly with #400 grit paper before painting.

14. Spray several coats of paint. Allow each coat to dry and sand each lightly with #400 grit paper dipped in water. Remember to be careful when sanding near edges.

 ## Fixing the "barbed wire" fender scratch

1. Grind away the old paint and rust with #24 grit paper. Be sure to clear an area an inch or two on either side of the scratch.

2. Mix a small amount of body filler. Press fairly hard with the spread at a 45° angle as you smooth it on. Work quickly, using short strokes in an upward direction.

3. Use a cheese grater file to level the surface when the filler has reached a rubbery consistency. Sand with #100 grit paper held in a sanding block. Feather the edges of the repair to blend the filler into the surrounding metal.

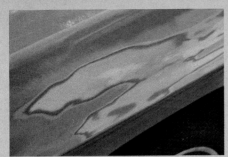

4. Repeat steps 2 and 3 until all the low spots have been filled and the surface is smooth. Dark areas such as these should be filled and sanded repeatedly until the surface is uniform in color.

5. Apply glazing putty in single, smooth strokes. Use thin coats and allow the putty to dry before sanding.

6. Roll a piece of #320 grit paper into a tube. Hold the tube perpendicular to the contour and follow the curve of the metal when sanding. This prevents you from making flat spots in a contour.

7. Using the technique described in step 6, wet sand with #400 grit paper rolled into a tube. Feather the edges carefully to eliminate sanding scratches.

8. Prime the area to protect bare metal from rust. Any remaining low spots will show after the primer has dried. If this happens, repeat steps 5, 6, and 7 and prime again.

9. Mask the surrounding trim and apply the proper paint for your car's year and model. Allow sufficient drying time before compounding and buffing.

 **Fixing stone chips**

1. Protect the surrounding areas of the car with masking tape and paper before starting. Then sand the scratches out to bare metal with #100 grit paper and featheredge them.

2. Apply glazing putty to the damaged areas in smooth strokes. Wet-sand the areas smooth with the surrounding surface, finishing with #400 grit paper. Several applications of putty may be necessary.

3. Prime the repaired areas to protect them until they are painted. Use a file folder or a piece of cardboard to limit overspray.

 **Replacing a taillight assembly**

1. Remove the bulb sockets from the taillight assembly and disconnect any wires. Mark each bulb and wire for easy identification when reinstalling.

2. Loosen all of the fasteners holding the assembly to the car.

3. Install the new taillight assembly by reversing the steps used to remove the old one. Test each light in the assembly to make sure that all of the electrical connections are correct.

**Inside the car—repairing and cleaning vinyl**

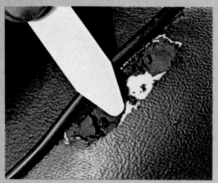

1. Carefully even up the edges of the hole with a sharp knife. If the original cloth backing for the vinyl is gone, fit a piece of cloth behind the tear as backing for the patch.

2. Spread the vinyl patching compound evenly in the hole to be filled. Make sure that there are no holes left and that the patching compound does not overlap onto the good vinyl.

3. Choose the texturing sheet which most resembles the texture of the existing vinyl. Then use a warm iron on top of the sheet to melt the patching compound and bind it to the rest of the vinyl. **CAUTION:** If the iron gets too hot, it may melt surrounding vinyl.

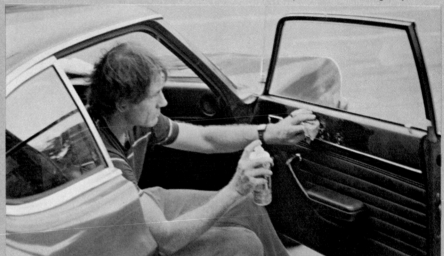

4. Check the patch over carefully to make sure that there are no holes or imperfections. If any flaws are found, add more patching compound and apply the iron again.

5. Clean the interior of the car to make the inside shine as brightly as the outside. Three types of materials are likely to be found in the interior of your car: vinyl (by far the most common), fabric, and genuine leather. All vinyl may be cleaned with a household cleaner and a cloth or sponge (avoid cleaners which contain ammonia).

Fabrics, including carpets, should be cleaned with mild soap on a rag, then wiped with a clean rag. Commercial car fabric cleaners are available; these are less likely to stain or fade fabric colors. Genuine leather should be cleaned with a commercial leather cleaning preparation which contains a leather conditioner.

 **Wheel cleanup**

1. Clean all of the road dirt and scale off the chrome wheels with soap and a steel wool pad. Wash off the soap with a hose and repeat the scrubbing on any dirty spots that remain.

2. Polish the wheels with a commercial chrome polish following the steel wool scrubbing. This will remove any tarnish and stains which remain on the wheels.

3. Buff the wheels thoroughly with a clean cloth to bring up the shine. Coat the tire with a silicone protectant.

## Those final touches

**1.** Lubricate the lock mechanism to free it from sticking. After using a solvent to remove all accumulated dirt, apply powdered graphite to keep the lock working smoothly.

**2.** Decals are easy to apply; just follow the manufacturer's instructions. Use a damp sponge to force trapped air bubbles from under the decal.

**3.** A broken antenna is also easy to replace. Feed the replacement antenna wire through the fender, behind the dashboard, and into the back of the radio. Install the new mast according to the instructions, then adjust the radio to the new antenna length.

 ## Compounding, waxing and buffing

**1.** Polishing compound is used to remove oxidized paint, overspray, ground-in dirt, and small scratches which dull the finish of a car. Go lightly with the lamb's wool attachment. Do *not* compound edges. These are very fragile and should be compounded by hand, if at all.

**2.** Wax the car with a good grade of car wax after cleaning off all of the polishing compound. Do a small area of the car at a time and try to work in the shade, no matter what the manufacturer's instructions say. **CAUTION:** *Never* put wax on paint that is not thoroughly dry. The paint job will be ruined.

**3.** Buff the wax with a buffing wheel to bring up the shine. Remember not to press down on the drill as you buff. The weight of the drill will put enough pressure to the buffer to do a good job.

*What a finish!*

# How to replace a door

**1.** Check the replacement part over carefully *before* you leave the salvage yard. Make sure that the part is exactly what you need and that there are no accessories missing.

**2.** Block the door up on something solid. This relieves the strain on the bolts being removed and frees your hands for the removal job. For safety's sake, make sure that nothing can give way and surprise you.

**3.** Loosen all of the bolts first before removing them. Penetrating oil sprayed on rusted bolts will loosen them and make them easier to remove. Have someone help you hold the door before you remove the last bolt.

**4.** Move all of the parts you need from the old door to the replacement door. Remove the lock cylinder by disconnecting it from the lock linkage and removing the lock retaining clip with pliers.

**5.** Lubricate all of the internal door mechanisms while the door is disassembled. Window and lock mechanisms should work smoothly before the door is reassembled.

**6.** Go carefully and slowly when reinstalling the door trim panel to the door. If there are any difficulties, don't hammer the clips in. First check to make sure that they are aligned properly.

**7.** Get someone to help hold the door while you install it. Put all of the bolts in before tightening any of them. Use a screwdriver or similar tool in an adjacent hole to help align the holes.

**8.** Position the door as closely as possible and tighten one bolt on each hinge. The gaps between the door and the body should be even. Adjust the striker plate if necessary, then tighten all bolts.

**9.** Sand the entire outside of the door and repair any surface damage with glazing putty. Wipe the door clean before priming.

**10.** Mask the door trim and the surrounding body with masking tape and masking paper. If masking paper is not available, grocery bags are a good substitute. Don't use newspaper since paint may bleed through it.

**11.** Spray the door with several coats of sandable primer. Wet-sand the primer between coats with #400 grit paper.

**12.** Any surface imperfections in the door will show up when the primer is applied. Fill these imperfections with glazing putty, then prime and sand again.

**CHAPTER** 1

# SIZING UP THE JOB

The first look at any body damage sustained by your car can be discouraging. You may think that even the simplest repair work will have to be done by a professional body shop. However, armed with a little knowledge, you can evaluate the damage yourself and decide which dents and scratches can be repaired, which ones mean replacing body parts, and which ones should be left in the hands of the experts.

Before you decide to repair a body part, knowing the full extent of the damage and knowing what to do at each step of the repair job will save you time and money.

Inspect the car carefully. Collision damage is repaired from the inside out, so investigate how far the damage extends in from the surface of the car. Check underneath to see if the frame is bent or if any part of it buckles. Drive the car to see if any damage has been done to mechanical parts.

Some damages on the body surface can be deceptive. A small rust spot on the outside of a body part may indicate a great deal of rust underneath. A simple dent may require only surface repair; a larger dent may mean that the part is easier to replace than to repair.

On the following pages, we photographically illustrate different types of body damage. The evaluation of the damage is accompanied by a description of how to proceed with the repair job. Some of these are do-it-yourself repair jobs, some require that you replace parts, and some jobs should be left to the experts. These evaluations will help you figure out what to look for. Remember that each case of auto body damage is unique and must be evaluated individually.

The repair process is a combination of the availability of tools, replacement parts, a place to work safely, and the amount of time and effort you want to put into it. Evaluate the damage to your car with these things in mind.

# To fix (YES) or not to fix (NO)

That is the question a Saturday mechanic must ask himself after looking over the damage. Some of the jobs described below and pictured on the opposite page may appear to be beyond your capacities and your equipment. But don't be put off by appearances alone.

Surprisingly, every one can be handled by the do-it-yourselfer. The YES and NO pictures on the following pages should also be very encouraging—you'll find so many more yesses than nos.

1    **Chips and scratches.** This is simple surface damage you incurred from flying stones and gravel. All the equipment you need is a hand sanding block.

2    **Broken window.** Sorry, you can't repair it. But your auto dealer or a glass specialist will be happy to sell you a new one. Replacement difficulty varies depending upon the make and model.

3    **Rusting out.** You must get rid of all the rust. Then, depending upon the extent of the damage, the job may be simply one of patching and filling. Or it may be as extensive as pop-riveting on a new piece of metal. Heavy rust damage on rear panels requires extensive treatment and it's not a job we recommend for the beginner.

4    **Dents.** The depth of the dent determines the procedure. Beyond ¼-inch you'll have to drill some holes and use a dent puller.

5    **White metal damage.** This is extremely brittle stuff. In case of injury, replace the part. The fender damage farther back will not be much of a problem.

6    **Front damage.** This example, the result of a head-on collision, looks worse than it really is. If there is no frame damage, you can replace everything yourself. This car took a pretty good whack, so you will also have to adjust the hood and latch.

7    **Front fender and bumper.** Accordion damage is impossible to repair. That fender will never look right again. But you can replace it. While you're at it, you may as well do the same with the bumper—it's very easy to remove—and the grille.

**To fix (YES) or not to fix (NO)**

# Yes

Replace it. The damage to this fender is too extensive to bother repairing. Too much time would be wasted and the result would not satisfy you. But the fender can be replaced. Devote some time to scouring a salvage yard for one that matches. When you find it, make sure it is complete with moldings and inner panels.

# Yes

This rust spot resembles a sad-looking dog's face, but that does not necessarily make the car a sad-looking dog. The damage can be repaired by a process of grinding, filling, and refinishing. You will also want to pull out the tiny dings and creases and tap down the high spots.

# No

A classic case of rust-out has attacked this car and, unfortunately, lingered there too long. Too expensive a repair job to tackle by yourself, the car should be taken to a professional bodywork shop where the panel will be cut off and a new one welded on. A little preventive medicine would have helped.

# Yes

Bumpers are easier to replace than to repair—the work goes faster and the end result is smoother. Bumper replacement is less expensive, too. A good place to look for a replacement bumper is at a salvage yard. Make sure you take not just the bumper but the entire assembly including all the back bars, supports, and hardware.

# Yes

Repair of this rust-out can be tricky but the result will be worth the challenge. Start the repair job by pop riveting a piece of new sheet metal over the wound. The difficult part is bending the patch around the edge and fitting it between the molding clips. When the sheet metal is attached, fill, sand, and prime it.

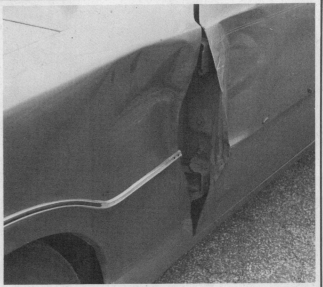

# No

You could handle the obvious damage. It simply means replacing the door and the left front fender. What you can't see is that the door post was knocked out of whack. Don't even think about trying to fix that one.

# Yes

The stretch marks and buckles in this fender are a sign that the damage is extensive. You can replace the fender faster and easier than you can repair it. When you purchase a matching fender from a salvage yard, be sure to get one that includes the inner panel and all hardware and moldings.

# Yes

Removing these dents is a do-it-yourself repair job that requires several separate steps. First, drill holes along the creases and pull them out with a dent puller. Then fill in any low spots and refinish the surface. You will also want to tap down any high spots.

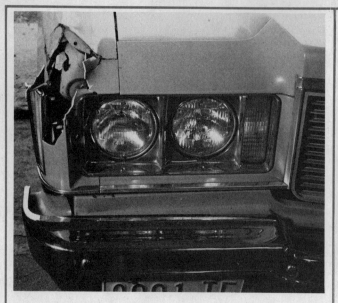

## Yes

Replace it. You would not be able to glue this one together even if you were clever enough to keep all the pieces. It's white metal and there's no way to repair it. As for the fender damage further back, that's no problem.

## Yes

This fender has had it. A recent impact caused extensive buckling and stretching and, as you can see, there was a previous patch job over the headlamp. You can't repair it but you can buy a new fender. You'll need a headlamp door, too.

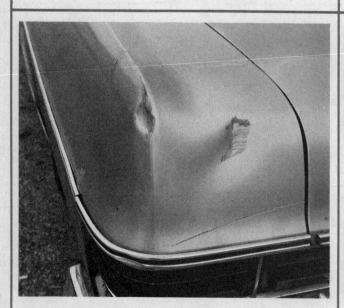

## Yes

Go to it. The dents and scratches on this quarter panel will be a breeze. A little straightening, a little filling, a little painting—that's all it takes.

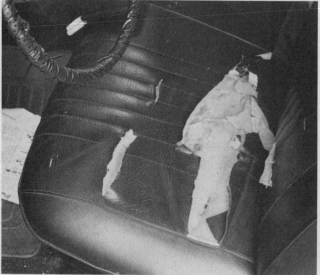

## Yes

Two bits of advice: 1) Buy a used seat; this one is hopeless. 2) Take the pointed tools out of your pocket before you get behind the wheel.

# Yes

First, remove the old glass. And watch your fingers. Next, carefully drive to the salvage yard and find a door just like yours. Now ask the man to sell the window to you. Finally, read and follow our instructions for replacing windows in Chapter 9. You can also deal with an auto glass supplier, which will be less troublesome but more expensive.

# Yes

You'll need a hammer, a couple of dollies, some filler, a can of paint, and a new piece of chrome trim. This one is called a wheel opening molding. But you can do it.

# Yes

This is a retouch job of some magnitude. Start by cleaning the area with a wax and grease remover. Sand out the scratches and apply a coat of primer. Don't paint until you've compounded the surrounding area. That way, you'll get a perfect color match.

# Yes

The top of your dash is splitting and you can see buckling close to the window. The only thing to do now is unbolt it and replace the whole thing.

# Yes

This is a multiple job but a do-it-yourselfer should be able to handle it all. Prepare the chipped areas and paint them. Align the door—which will be a lot less taxing if you can get somebody to help you. Then reglue the rubber strip with one of the new, fast-drying adhesives.

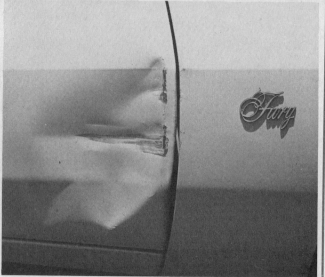

# Yes

Work this damage over with a dent puller and hammer while pulling out the low spots. Tap down the high spots with your body hammer and put a few layers of masking tape on the fender edge to avoid scratching it.

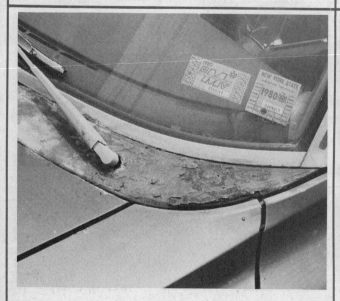

# No

This panel is too far gone to repair and it's factory welded, making replacement beyond you and your equipment. All you can do is take it to a pro to cut it away and weld in a new panel.

# Yes

Buy a new hubcap.

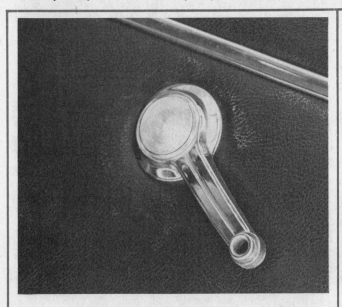

## Yes

You seem to have lost the knob to your window regulator handle. You won't be able to find a new one, so replace the whole handle. This kind can be removed with the help of a door handle removing tool.

## Yes

The lower part of this damage is shallow enough that you can push it out with your foot. Above that, you'll have to use a hammer and spoon to smooth out the dent before grinding and filling.

## Yes

You'll need a dent puller and a deft hand here. The dent should respond nicely. Start pulling in the area under the front molding while tapping down the high ridge. But that piece of trim over the headlight has got to go. Maybe the side trim too, because of the severe crimp up front.

## No

Forget it. You've got massive damage to a welded-on panel. Once you get the wheel back on, push the car to a body shop.

# What to look for in buying a used car

New cars cost too much, and so do used lemons. So the trick is to find a used car that's as good as new and a few thousand dollars less expensive. Impossible? Not if you can remove the gamble. And you can.

When you begin those treks down to used-car row, your best friend is patience. So often people are rushed into a used-car deal that they live to regret. Salesmen capitalize on buyer impatience. "Better hurry and decide now," the salesman might tell you, "because there's another customer itching to buy this car." Never let that sort of talk stampede you.

In addition to ascertaining that you're buying a mechanically trouble-free car, take enough time to make sure you're getting a sound body as well. This may take some time, especially if your suspicions are aroused by new welds or wrinkled fender panels. In such cases, have the frame checked by a pro. If the salesman is reluctant to let you do this, go elsewhere.

It may take you two weeks to find just the right car—even two months. That's OK—don't rush yourself.

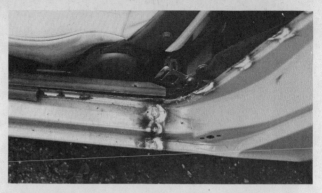

Check the center pillar post. It should be free of wrinkles. Then look at the joint between the post and the frame. Weld marks like this indicate that a new quarter panel was put on in a body shop. This is not necessarily a reason to turn the car down, but you should have the frame checked to find out whether there ever was major frame damage.

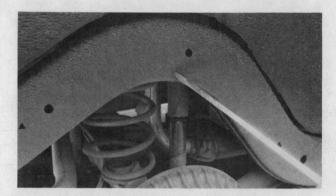

Take a rear wheel off if possible. Look at the curved part of the car's frame. It should look smooth and regular with the dirt evenly distributed as seen in this picture. If the dirt is irregular, scrape it away and check carefully for ripples in the metal. This is a sure sign of frame damage.

Open the trunk lid and look at the panel over the hinge. The factory has covered their weld with a body sealer, and a sharp body shop can do the same. Lift up and check the welds. Again, this is only a clue, but it may indicate severe damage.

## A few more clues

Here are four more symptoms that may indicate a skewed frame. The first two are observations you would make during a test drive. The others require a little snooping on the sales lot. If you see signs of any of these defects, be suspicious. Get a second opinion—preferably from a pro.

1 Is there evidence of dog-tracking? That is, when you drive through a puddle, do the front and rear tires make separate lines?

2 With only light steering control, does the car pull to one side?

3 Is the spacing around all the doors noticeably uneven?

4 Do you find buckles or bumps on the floor or the base of the trunk?

Open the hood and look at the cowl panel. It should be smooth and even. Wrinkles and lumps in the metal indicate that the panel was straightened. This also should not frighten you away, but be sure to have the frame checked by a professional before deciding whether to buy.

CHAPTER **2**

# SATURDAY'S TOOLS

When you think of bodywork tools, do you picture hammers and screwdrivers and maybe a set of socket wrenches? If so, you're right. Many of the jobs you'll find in this book call for nothing more than the range of basic mechanic's tools you probably already own.

Some people get the impression that to reshape a bashed-in fender, you need a box of bizarre-looking tools with strange-sounding names. They're right, too. Check out, for example, a few of the spoons you'll find illustrated on the following pages. The double-ended, heavy-duty driving spoon is quaint. Bet you don't have one of those. Even some of the hammers look weird. What it boils down to is this: some tools you have, some you'll have to get (not necessarily buy, mind you). For the infrequently used ones, keep in mind the possibility of renting or borrowing.

The tools you'll need fall into four categories: everyday, bodyworking, surfacing, and painting. This last group will be covered when we get into painting techniques in Chapter 13. The three remaining categories are dealt with in this chapter.

Everyday tools are those you may already have around the house, tools you use for home repair, engine tuneups, and other, non-bodywork jobs on your car. Most of these are inexpensive and extremely useful, so it's probably worth buying the ones you don't already have.

Bodyworking tools are surprising in number and variety. For the most part, they cost about the same as other do-it-yourself automotive tools, so the basic ones are worth buying even if you use them only two or three times. Try a tool-rental outfit before you buy the expensive, specialized ones.

Surfacing tools are used for cleaning and smoothing the surface just before you put on the paint. These are primarily hand and power tools for shaping and sanding, so you ought to have most of them in your home workshop anyway. You can even make some of them.

Use the following drawings and descriptions as a guide in determining the size of the tool collection you'll need.

# Everyday tools

A large portion of bodywork involves the use of tools most people already own. If you have ever done a complete tuneup on your car, you probably have a socket set and the assortment of screwdrivers and pliers you needed for the job. The everyday tools in this section are good ones to buy if you don't already have them. They will come in handy as you become increasingly involved in the maintenance of your car and are useful for myriad other jobs around the house. A suggestion: get a small tool box just for these tools. You will find very few tools in the box that will not be used every time you go out to work on your car.

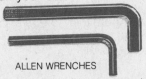

ALLEN WRENCHES

**Allen wrenches,** which are usually bent at a right angle, are useful bodyworking tools. They are inexpensive, and while you can purchase them individually, it is better to buy a set, which includes wrenches of different lengths and diameters.

COMBINATION WRENCH

**Combination wrenches** are a necessary part of the everyday tool kit because not every automobile fastener may be reached with a socket wrench. These wrenches combine the two most common wrenches, open-end and box. The open end grips the fastener with two flat sides. It is absolutely essential where a wrench cannot be slipped over the end of a bolt, but it tends to spread apart and slip when used with too much force. Box wrenches are much like sockets in their ability to hold without slipping; and you can use them in tight corners into which sockets won't fit. Combination wrenches come in graduated sets with the same sizes as sockets.

**The electric drill/sander** is a combination power tool which speeds the task of sanding for the home bodyworker. It has a sanding attachment, a rubber disc which is clamped in the chuck of the drill, to which sandpaper discs are then glued. This is a very versatile tool, since the drill may be used for so many jobs. If you don't already have one, a ⅜-inch chuck variable-speed drill is recommended. It has enough power to sand without burning itself out and the variable-speed capability is useful for sanding delicate areas at slow speeds. Try to get a 4- or 5-inch sanding attachment with a buffing pad which will come in handy when the job is nearing completion.

The orbital sander, so called because the sanding pad moves in an oval, does a fine, flat sanding job. This is the tool you will find in professional body shops, though the professional version is likely to be pneumatic. This is an excellent tool which will make your body surfacing go much faster.

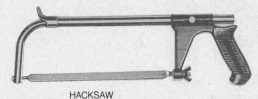

HACKSAW

**A hacksaw,** with its wide range of changeable blades, is one tool used for sawing smaller metal parts. A regular hacksaw grips the blade at both ends and works like any handsaw, that is, it usually requires lots of elbow grease. There are also hacksaw handles which grip only one end of the blade; these are useful for cutting in tight places into which a regular hacksaw cannot reach. Both variations should be in your tool kit.

**Jack stands** are included with the everyday tools because they are an essential part of safely doing any automotive job which requires getting the car off the ground. It may seem safe to crawl under a car supported by jacks. But remember, if the car slips off, you're in trouble. So use jack stands whenever you have to lift an auto. One inexpensive stand is made of bent sheet steel spotwelded together at the joints. Also available is a sturdier type, costing slightly more, which is made from forged iron and is less likely to buckle when used on uneven pavement.

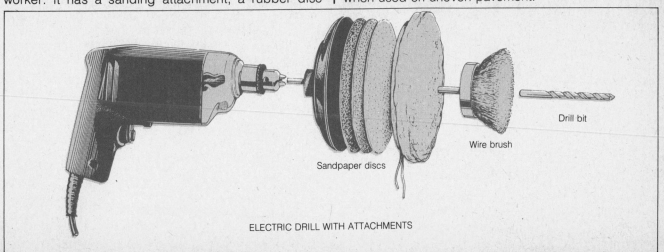

Sandpaper discs

Wire brush

Drill bit

ELECTRIC DRILL WITH ATTACHMENTS

ADJUSTABLE
JACK STANDS

**Pliers** are an all-around grabbing tool used for working with wires, clips, and pins. You should own several types: standard pliers for small parts and wires, needlenose for the really small parts, and large, adjustable pliers for heavy-duty work, including bending sheet metal. Pliers are another of those basic tools for the everyday kit; they have many uses around the house as well as around the car.

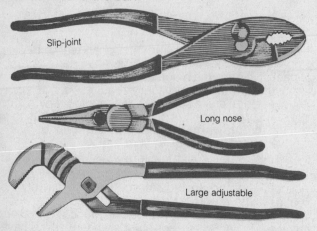

Slip-joint

Long nose

Large adjustable

PLIERS

**Locking pliers** are similar to the standard kind except that they lock closed with a very tight grip. They are extremely useful for holding parts together. For example, several pairs of locking pliers will come in handy when you try to hold a metal patch in place before pop riveting it. They are also useful for getting a firm grip on a badly rounded fastener on which wrenches and sockets are no longer effective. Locking pliers come in several sizes and jaw configurations for use in many auto body jobs. The ones illustrated, the "C" clamp, welding, and duckbill types, are among those frequently used.

**The sanding block** is the simplest, the cheapest, and yet one of the most essential tools for surface preparation. You should use one whenever you sand, except on corners and near molding. The block keeps the sandpaper flat and the pressure evenly spread across the surface, thus helping smooth off high spots and preventing scratches in the sanded surface caused by folds in the sandpaper. You can make your own simple sanding block from a piece of soft wood (pine is a good choice), around which the sandpaper is wrapped. Or buy blocks made of hard rubber or felt in the hardware store. These have grippers for holding the paper. The complete auto body tool kit has several sanding blocks of different sizes, from thin boards such as paint stirrers up to large plane-shaped tools for wide-area sanding.

RUBBER
SANDING BLOCK

**Screwdrivers** are necessary for the screws holding many of the smaller accessories to the body of the car. You will probably encounter both slotted and Phillips screws, so an assortment of screwdrivers is an essential part of the everyday tool kit. Be sure to have Phillips sizes 1, 2, 3, and 4.

**A socket wrench set** is the best tool system for removing and replacing the nuts and bolts which hold together your car. You are least likely to round off the corners of a nut or bolt with a socket, while ordinary wrenches have a tendency to slip and ruin both the fastener and your hand at the same time. A socket wrench also works faster, since the ratchet handle eliminates removing the tool from the fastener after each turn. Socket sets come in three common varieties: ¼-inch, ⅜-inch, and ½-inch drive. The term drive refers to the size of the hole in the back of the socket into which the ratchet handle fits. ⅜-inch is the most useful size. Sockets come in metric sizes as well, so if your car has metric fasteners, you will need a metric set.

There are 4-, 6-, 8-, and 12- point sockets. The number of points in a socket refers to the number of corners on the inside of the socket where it engages the fastener. 12 points are the most common, probably because they are easy to fit over fasteners. 6-point sockets fit six cornered fasteners exactly and are usually stronger than 12 points, although not quite so convenient to work with.

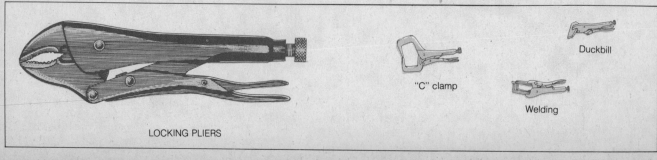

Duckbill

"C" clamp

Welding

LOCKING PLIERS

A socket wrench set usually includes a ratchet handle, ¼-inch to ¾-inch sockets, a breaker bar, and a 4-inch extension to help you reach into tight places. The breaker bar is a handle for turning sockets without a ratchet mechanism. It is used when a great deal of force is required to break loose a stubborn fastener (hence the name). To avoid damaging the mechanism, the ratchet handle should not be used when a lot of torque is required.

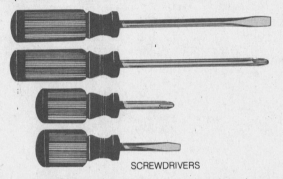
SCREWDRIVERS

½-inch drive sockets are an optional tool you may want to own as you take on larger auto body projects. You may discover that your ⅜-inch drive sockets and breaker bar aren't hefty enough to break loose those large, heavily corroded fasteners holding together parts like bumpers and frame extensions. Some of these parts really need a tool on which you can use your whole weight. ½-inch drive sockets are much stronger than ⅜-inch. With a heavy-duty ½-inch drive breaker bar

you can add a section of pipe to create a longer lever arm and really put some force on a stubborn fastener. And there is an adapter which allows the use of a ⅜-inch drive ratchet handle with ½-inch sockets so you don't have to change to a ⅜-inch socket after the fastener is loosened.

**The wire brush drill attachment** is an excellent cleaning tool with a variety of uses. You can grind out paint from low spots missed by the drill and grinding disc; knock off dirt, mud, and grease; and grind out rust around rocker panels, inside corners, and other hard-to-reach places. But if you're going to be working around chrome trim, be sure you mask it off. The abrasive action of the wire brush can ruin the finish. The hand wire brush is used on broader areas and is particularly good for cleaning behind wheels and larger parts of the underbody.

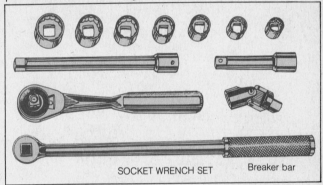
SOCKET WRENCH SET     Breaker bar

# Bodyworking tools

You will find most of the tools described here too specialized to be very useful for jobs other than auto body repair. They have strange names like "dolly" and "slapper file," and many of them have equally strange shapes. Fortunately for the home craftsman, they need not be expensive. You will find dollies, a body hammer, and a dent puller extremely useful and well worth the relatively small investment. And considering the cost of professional bodywork, plus the satisfaction you will derive from working with these tools (seeing a crumpled fender turn back into smooth sheet metal, for example), they are a bargain.

With the bodyworking tools pictured on these pages, you should be able to repair every type of damage illustrated in the following chapters. Of course, we can only offer a sampling of bodyworking tools here. As you be-

come more involved in bodywork, you may wish to add others to your collection, even some quite specialized tools for more complex jobs. But wait until you become familiar with bodywork techniques before you sink a lot of money into a complete tool set.

BALL PEEN HAMMER

**The ball peen hammer** is a useful, multi-purpose tool for all kinds of work with sheet metal. Heavier than the body hammer, it is used for straightening bent underpinnings, smoothing heavy-gauge parts, and roughly shaping body parts before work with a body hammer and dolly begins. A good ball peen hammer, which weighs between ten and 16 ounces (depending on how much you can swing comfortably), will see a lot of action in a bodywork job.

PICKING HAMMER

**Body hammers** are the basic tools for pounding sheet metal back into shape. They come in many different designs. Some have flat, square heads, some have rounded heads, some, called picking hammers, have points. Every style has a special use for which it is ideal, but the average bodyworker does not have time to change hammers for each change in the sheet metal contour. So most often he or she makes do with one or two body hammers, and you can too. The picking hammer will take care of most dents. The pointed end is used to hammer out small dents from the inside; a gentle tap in the center usually does it. The flat end is for hammer-and-dolly work to remove dents and ripples. When you are shopping for a body hammer, get one which feels good in your hand, but not one which is too heavy. A lot of the hammer work you do will require many light hammer blows, and a heavy hammer will only make your arm tired.

**A brazing torch,** used for joining two pieces of metal, is an optional tool for the bodyworker. Brazing is like welding, except that it requires less heat, and a bronze rod is substituted for a welding rod. The lower melting point of bronze allows brazing to be done with simpler, less expensive equipment than a gas welding rig. Brazing gas combines oxygen with another gas (acetylene or propane for example) to provide sufficient heat to braze large areas. Use a brazing torch to join sheet metal to its support members and to hold patches in place. Small and large tips are available, allowing you to make delicate joints or large repairs as necessary.

**The bumping and finishing hammer** is used right after the small sledge in metal shaping. You use it to pound sheet metal into final shape and to smooth out creases and ripples. This hammer has one flat and one curved end. Be sure not to buy one that's going to be too heavy for you to handle.

**A cold chisel** is a steel bar with a hardened cutting edge for shearing steel. These chisels come in various

sizes and a set can prove useful. You can use them for cutting off rusted-on bolt heads and wherever there is no chance of saving the fastener.

**The dent puller** is the essential tool in the bodyworker's collection for those dents which cannot be reached from the inside of the body. In such cases, you must drill one or more holes in the dent and gently pull it out with repeated blows of the slide. Several attachments come with the dent puller; the screw is used in most cases and the hooked end is useful for pulling the edges of panels. You will find more information about dent pulling techniques in chapter 5. The dent puller is also useful in other phases of auto work, particularly for pulling out bearings which are recessed inside their mounts.

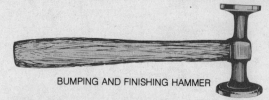

BUMPING AND FINISHING HAMMER

**A dolly** is used with the body hammer to smooth out dents in sheet metal. Like a blacksmith's anvil, the dolly is the smooth surface against which metal is pounded to take out irregularities. It is held against the back of the damaged area as the front of the metal is hammered, either directly against the dolly or slightly off to one side. Surprisingly, more of the actual smoothing ac-

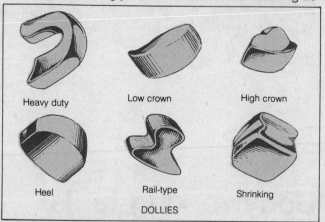

Heavy duty    Low crown    High crown

Heel    Rail-type    Shrinking

DOLLIES

tion results from the force of the dolly against the metal than from the blows of the hammer, so the dolly is indeed an important member of the team. You will find additional information on hammer and dolly techniques in chapter 5. Two of the dollies shown here, the low-crown, general-purpose dolly block and the rail-type dolly block, are the ones most commonly used in body

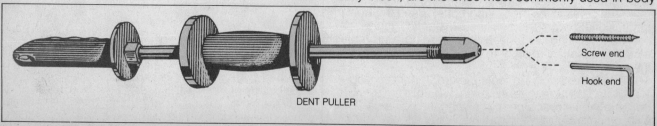

Screw end

Hook end

DENT PULLER

shops, and they should be sufficient for most situations. There are special dollies for some of the less common shapes found on today's cars. If you run into one of these problems, you can probably improvise a dolly from a section of heavy pipe or a piece of metal bar stock.

**A drift** is a round steel punch with a flat tip used for driving pins into or out of assemblies. A center punch has a point on the end and is used for marking metal before drilling a hole in it so the drill bit will not walk around the hole but will start off right. Drifts or large-size center punches can be useful for lining up sheet metal parts when bolting them together.

GRINDER/BUFFER

**A grinder/buffer,** an optional tool for the home bodyworker, is a power tool which either grinds or buffs depending upon the pad and speed you choose. As a grinder, these large, powerful tools make short work of removing old paint and corrosion in preparation for refinishing. Several varieties of grinding discs are available for every need. And as a buffer, this tool uses a coarse cloth pad to take the elbow grease out of compounding and a lambswool pad to buff the finished job. The drawback is the price. This tool, with all of the necessary attachments, is relatively expensive, and it is a tool you will use only for auto bodywork. But grinder/buffers may be rented by the day at quite a low cost. So plan your job properly and you should be able to realize a considerable saving in time and money by renting.

LIGHT SLEDGEHAMMER

**A light sledgehammer** is an essential tool for the first stages of reforming damaged sheet metal. It should weigh three to five pounds, depending upon the strength of your arm, and have a short handle so you can use it in tight places. It is just what you need to knock damaged metal roughly back into shape, and afterwards, it makes a nice dolly. Even when you're replacing the damaged part, the sledge comes in handy to clear away the damaged metal. But remember, it is

only for rough shaping. Smaller hammers and a lighter touch are better for the later stages of shaping metal.

**Metal shears** are a necessary bodyworking tool for the many cases in which damaged sheet metal must be cut away and replaced. These heavy-duty scissors require the same care as sewing scissors. Sharpen them occasionally, keep the pivot tight, avoid dropping them, and they should last forever. Be sure to wear gloves when you use metal shears since the cut edges of sheet metal are very sharp.

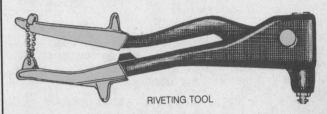

RIVETING TOOL

**Pop rivets** are one of the handiest inventions ever for auto bodywork. They may be inserted into a blind hole through two pieces of metal and then drawn up with the riveting tool, locking the pieces of metal together. There is no need to have access to the back of the rivets, and if enough rivets are used, the joint created is as strong as a weld. For any kind of sheet metal replacement such as rust hole repair, the pop rivet is by far the easiest and least expensive joining system available. In fact, most body shops use rivets extensively, either as a permanent repair or as temporary fasteners before the replacement sheet metal is welded into place. They have an advantage over welding in places where extreme heat would distort the metal or create a safety hazard (such as around the gas tank). A good riveting tool doesn't cost too much. The most commonly used rivets in bodywork are ⅛- and ³/₁₆-inch. You may need a few others of assorted sizes for special jobs.

**The pry bar** is used in situations where removal of damaged sheet metal requires prying a panel back into some semblance of its original form so that you can reach the fasteners. A pry bar is absolutely essential for this as well as for certain other bodyworking procedures. A short, hard piece of steel is ideal for prying, for hammering through holes in the underbody, even as a spoon, and it should be in every bodyworker's tool kit.

**The rubber mallet** gently bumps sheet metal without damaging the painted finish. Its most frequent use is with the suction cup on soft "cave in" type dents. Here is how you do it: while pulling upward on the cup, tap the mallet lightly all around the surrounding high spots. Listen for a popping sound as the high spots drop and the low spot springs back to its original contour.

RUBBER MALLET

**The saber saw** is an optional addition to your tool kit. It is a power tool which takes much of the effort out of cutting sheet metal and enables the bodyworker to negotiate tight corners when cutting away damaged metal. One of these may already be a part of your household tool collection. If so, make use of it in your bodywork projects.

SLAPPER FILE

**A slapper file** is shaped like a spoon, but used like a hammer. You can use it together with a dolly to bring up low spots and smooth curves. But resist the temptation to use it as a spoon. It may shatter if hit with a hammer.

**A spoon** is a type of dolly, and like the dolly it serves primarily as an anvil for the body hammer. Unlike the dolly, these tools have long handles which permit you to reach up behind sheet metal panels where obstructions prevent placing a dolly. Spoons may also be used for prying, and their edges are useful for reforming the sharp crowns on fenders and other body panels.

**The suction cup** is a simple tool which makes short work of shallow dents if they are not locked in by a crease in the metal. Simply attach the suction cup to the center of the dent and pull. If you are lucky, the dent may come right out with no damage to the paint and no refinishing required. It's an easy tool to use and may enable you to make a simple repair absolutely painlessly. Don't expect miracles, however, for once a dent is locked in, some hammer and dolly work will be necessary to smooth the metal. Even so, the suction cup method is worth a try.

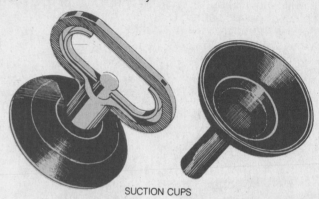

SUCTION CUPS

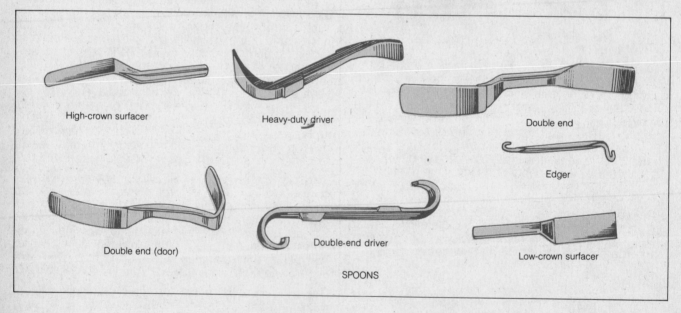

High-crown surfacer

Heavy-duty driver

Double end

Edger

Double end (door)

Double-end driver

Low-crown surfacer

SPOONS

# Body surfacing tools

Body surfacing tools are discussed separately from bodyworking tools because surface work, such as preparation for painting, is really a separate and final step in bodyworking. In some jobs, repair of surface damage for example, no bodyworking may be necessary. Surface-work tools are used for making the surface of the sheet metal as smooth and even as it was before it was damaged. These tools are surprisingly inexpensive and should present no budget problems. Having the right tools, though, is essential, since you will be doing a lot of work with them. In most cases, a poor tool is worse than no tool at all since it doesn't do the job right. Have a look at the complete selection of surface-working tools before you buy to ensure that the tools you get are of good quality.

**The flexible sander,** an optional tool, is made especially for auto bodywork. By twisting the ends of the flexible sander or file, its sanding surface can be made to conform to almost any body contour. This is a great boon to the auto bodyworker who wants to avoid flat spots. The flexible sander costs very little, so it makes a welcome addition to the bodyworker's tool kit.

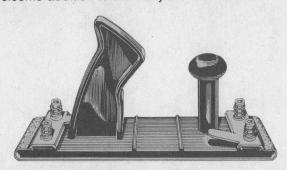

FLEXIBLE SANDER

**Grater or body files** are used to shape plastic body filler while it is still sticky but getting firm. These files look something like a kitchen cheese grater, hence the name. The Surform Company makes an entire line of these tools, which are very useful for woodworking as well as for body surfacing. Indeed, wood rasps may be used for this purpose, as may plastic body files sold in automotive parts stores.

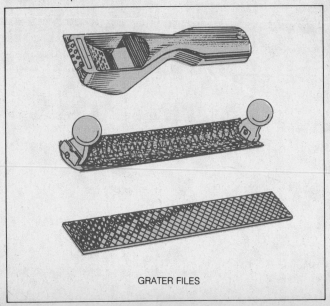

GRATER FILES

**A palette** of some sort is needed for mixing filler and holding it while it is being spread. You probably have something around the house which will serve the purpose, such as manila file folders, pieces of surfaced cardboard (with a shiny side) or a piece of sheet metal. Any firm, flat surface can be wrapped in plastic to produce a filler palette.

**The sandpaper sponge** is an optional tool, originally designed for sanding irregularly shaped wood like trim moldings, but great for bodywork. One side is coarse, the other side has finer paper. Dip the sponge with the sandpaper attached into water and use it for sanding rounded surfaces where a rubber sanding block would sand contours flat, on corners for example. A disadvantage of this tool is that the grit is usually no finer than #80. But you can easily make one to your own specifications just by wrapping whatever grit paper you need around a small, thin cellulose sponge.

**A short blocking file** is a sandpaper holder you might want to have for working on plastic body filler. It has a handle designed so you can sand all day without get-

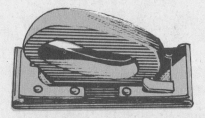

SHORT BLOCKING FILE

ting tired—something you cannot say about sandpaper wrapped around a block of wood. It has a 3-inch by 8-inch sanding surface, but longer files are available for large, flat surfaces. And if you're working on curved planes, there are contour files. In bodywork, you spend most of your time sanding, so you can make it easier on yourself with a blocking file.

**Spreaders and squeegees** are two important tools used in body resurfacing. The plastic spreader enables you to apply plastic filler and is available wherever the filler is sold. It comes in various shapes and sizes. You can buy just one or a set, but for all-around use we rec-

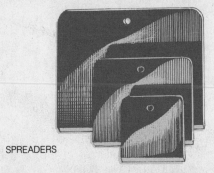

SPREADERS

ommend a medium-sized spreader such as the one shown here. Stay away from spreaders that have irregular surfaces, because once the filler has dried on such a surface, it is practically impossible to clean it up. The most important quality of a spreader is stiffness. This, along with hand pressure applied during spreading, forces out tiny air bubbles that get into the filler during

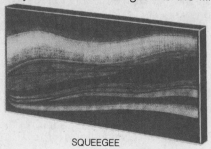

SQUEEGEE

mixing. Rubber squeegees are used almost exclusively for the application of glazing putty, which, containing no air bubbles, can be put on straight from the tube.

Both of these tools are inexpensive, so pick up one of each when you purchase filler and putty. However, if your tools get lost, broken or somehow disappear, a quick sprint to the kitchen drawer for a rubber cake spatula will save the day. Cake spatulas are firm enough to act as spreaders, yet flexible enough to double as a squeegee for putty. If you elect to use your cake spatula, break off the handle so the whole spatula fits easily into the palm of your hand.

The squeegee is also used when wet sanding to wipe the water away so you can check the surface for imperfections or smoothness.

## Keeping safe and healthy

Keep safety in mind at all times when you do bodywork. We recommend the following safety equipment for bodywork: a mask for filtering out dust and noxious chemical fumes (you must have a charcoal organic vapor mask for painting); goggles to protect the eyes, especially while grinding; hard-toed shoes; and a fire extinguisher. Safety also means keeping the area clean. A work area littered with old parts, dirt, and water puddles invites accidents. Clean up after each step; a shop vacuum is handy here. Dress properly to protect yourself. A pair of shop coveralls is a good idea. Wear gloves when the work involves chemicals or sharp metals. And if you put away your tools as you finish using them, you won't be tripping over something in the middle of a job.

CHAPTER **3**

# REPLACEMENT PARTS

Sometimes—and for the beginner almost always—it is easier and cheaper in the long run to replace a damaged part than to repair it.

In fact, Removal and Replacement (the pros call it "R and R") is usually the best way unless it is impossible to unbolt the damaged piece (welded quarter panels for example) or find a replacement for it (as in the restoration of antiques).

Here are some of the practical advantages of R and R:

R and R tools are more common and less specialized than bodywork tools, so they don't need to be rented. If a set of socket wrenches or screwdrivers cannot be borrowed and must be purchased, chances are they will be useful for other do-it-yourself jobs.

The amount of labor required to restore full strength to severely rusted sheet metal and to ensure that rust does not return is likely to exceed by far the cost of replacement, unless you value your time at zero and can borrow the tools.

If the damaged car is new or nearly new, the tremendous loss in resale value when a repair shows almost always is greater than the cost of replacement.

Cars are put together today with close tolerances between body parts. Ill-fitting repairs tend either to bind and squeak if they are too tight or rattle if they are too loose.

There are two sources for replacement parts: 1) dealers for new parts and 2) salvage yards for used ones. Giving the exact specifications of the part you want is simple if you use the information on the car's body number plate (see page 47). Dealers can give you exactly what you need, but they charge full list price for the item. Salvage yards now carefully sort and stock salvaged parts, making it relatively easy to find the exact part you need, at a price you can afford.

# Option 1: The new car dealer

When you need a part for your car, the first place to think of is your dealer's parts department. The dealer has or can get every part that might be needed to repair your car. Dealers can provide you with all of the trim pieces you are likely to replace, whether you or a pro does the bodywork job you have in mind. Dealers have the hard-to-find parts such as the little pieces of chrome that surround the windshield and the spring in the fuel filler cover. And they stock or can order any piece of body sheet metal, primed and ready for painting.

You can get sheet metal in two ways. Suppose you want to replace a door panel that is dented and torn. You may buy the whole door, into which you must transfer the window, the window mechanism, the lock, the door handle, and the trim. Or you may buy the sheet metal skin only, if the inner panel of the door is undamaged. The damaged door skin is removed and the new skin is welded into place. This is a job for a professional auto body shop which has the proper equipment for welding sheet metal.

The parts the dealer has are the same as the parts originally put on your car. Sometimes they may even be better. For instance, a design flaw often is corrected after the car is made and the replacement parts reflect this correction. This however applies more to mechanical parts than to body parts.

Also, you may want certain parts new even when purchasing a used replacement part. You may buy a used door to replace your damaged one, but you would be smart to get new hinges for it from your dealer. The same is true of certain other parts, like trim, for example.

Dealers usually stock parts for cars ranging from four to seven years old. Parts for older cars are available, but sometimes they must be ordered and there is generally a waiting period.

Dealers charge premium prices for the parts they sell in order to support the inventories they must maintain. So when checking the availability of a part with the dealer, ask the price. Getting a used replacement part may be a cheaper way to do the job. Also, the price you get from the dealer can put the used part price into perspective.

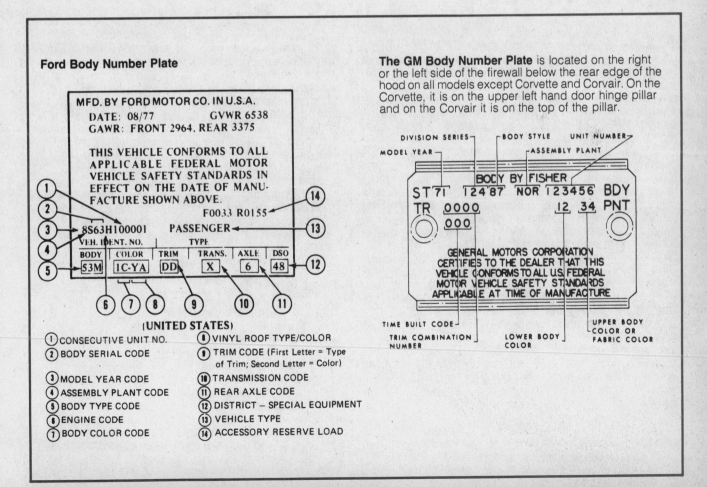

**Ford Body Number Plate**

MFD. BY FORD MOTOR CO. IN U.S.A.
DATE: 08/77          GVWR 6538
GAWR: FRONT 2964, REAR 3375

THIS VEHICLE CONFORMS TO ALL APPLICABLE FEDERAL MOTOR VEHICLE SAFETY STANDARDS IN EFFECT ON THE DATE OF MANUFACTURE SHOWN ABOVE.

F0033 R0155

8S63H100001     PASSENGER
VEH. IDENT. NO.        TYPE

| BODY | COLOR | TRIM | TRANS. | AXLE | DSO |
|------|-------|------|--------|------|-----|
| 53M | IC-YA | DD | X | 6 | 48 |

(UNITED STATES)

1. CONSECUTIVE UNIT NO.
2. BODY SERIAL CODE
3. MODEL YEAR CODE
4. ASSEMBLY PLANT CODE
5. BODY TYPE CODE
6. ENGINE CODE
7. BODY COLOR CODE
8. VINYL ROOF TYPE/COLOR
9. TRIM CODE (First Letter = Type of Trim; Second Letter = Color)
10. TRANSMISSION CODE
11. REAR AXLE CODE
12. DISTRICT — SPECIAL EQUIPMENT
13. VEHICLE TYPE
14. ACCESSORY RESERVE LOAD

**The GM Body Number Plate** is located on the right or the left side of the firewall below the rear edge of the hood on all models except Corvette and Corvair. On the Corvette, it is on the upper left hand door hinge pillar and on the Corvair it is on the top of the pillar.

DIVISION SERIES          BODY STYLE     UNIT NUMBER
MODEL YEAR                    ASSEMBLY PLANT

BODY BY FISHER
ST 71  124 87  NOR 123456  BDY
TR 0000              12  34  PNT
000

GENERAL MOTORS CORPORATION CERTIFIES TO THE DEALER THAT THIS VEHICLE CONFORMS TO ALL U.S. FEDERAL MOTOR VEHICLE SAFETY STANDARDS APPLICABLE AT TIME OF MANUFACTURE

TIME BUILT CODE
TRIM COMBINATION NUMBER          LOWER BODY COLOR          UPPER BODY COLOR OR FABRIC COLOR

**Modern salvage yards** no longer pile wrecked cars in heaps. They remove and inventory their salvaged parts. Here you see the front ends (noses) of salvaged cars neatly stacked in racks. A forklift is used to pick out the one you want easily and swiftly.

# Option 2: The auto salvage yard

The salvage yard is another place where you can buy a door for your car made by the same manufacturer that made the door you just bashed in. Not only is the replacement door worth about what your original door was worth before you smashed it, but it also comes with all of the parts—glass, lock, trim, and, if you're lucky, exactly the right color paint, so you'll have a really easy job of replacement.

The salvage yard is the final resting ground for cars that are no longer suitable for the roads. Despite their lack of value as operating vehicles, these cars have a large number of serviceable parts. The body parts of a car are not usually subjected to as much abuse as the mechanical parts, unless, of course, the car was involved in an accident. And even in this case, many of those spectacular, twisted wrecks seen along our highways contain a surprising number of body parts that can be reused. It is the value of these parts that makes the salvage yard a profitable business.

No longer a heap of abandoned, rusting metal, today's salvage yard is a prosperous business where parts are sorted and organized by groups and marked and stored for easy access. Gone are the days of crawling around under wrecks in the back lot, removing needed parts yourself. Now parts are removed and inventoried by the yard. There are still some yards where you may look at the wrecks and remove what you need, but you will save time and money by patronizing a modern salvage yard.

Changes in the auto salvage business are the result both of insurance regulations restricting customers from going into work areas and of the competition for the body shop dollar. Removing and storing the usable parts from wrecks saves not only retrieval time, but also space, an important consideration in metropolitan areas where land is at a premium. Some yards store their wares on racks and retrieve them with a forklift.

Once you've learned what a new part will cost you from a dealer, it's time to call some salvage yards in your area. The yellow pages will help you find the yards that deal in the parts you need. Yards specializing in one make automobile usually charge higher prices, but they are more likely to have the part, especially if you are having trouble finding what you need. Try several yards. One may not have quite what you want, while another may even have the part in the exact color.

Prices will probably vary. Keep a list of the yards you call in order to help you find the part you need in the best condition at the lowest price. Such a list is also useful for future reference.

## What is available?

There are different kinds of salvage yards. Some specialize in late-model cars, foreign cars, older cars or cars of a particular make. But no matter what their specialty might be, all yards have parts that will be useful to you in your auto bodywork.

Most doors, hoods, trunk lids, front fenders, noses, and a host of smaller parts unbolt easily from the frame of the car. Other parts of the body, such as the roof and rear quarter panels, may be cut from the body.

Depending on what is undamaged on the car being salvaged—and the needs of the customer—portions of the rear of the body may be sold. The complete rear section of a car body is called a "rear clip." It comprises that part of the body running from the back of one door all the way around the rear of the car to the back of the other door. This portion of the body is unbolted from the frame and cut away from the other body parts. But replacing the clip is really a job for the professional.

Front noses are also available and you can replace them yourself. They consist of both front fenders, the nose piece, the grille, bumper, headlights, and other assorted parts—a spoiler, for example. Some parts, like bumpers, are sold as part of a nose or by themselves.

In all cases, salvage yards try to include the accessory parts (such as the handle on a door) with the larger part when you buy it. Parts without these pieces bring less money, so you may have a hard time convincing them to sell you only the rearview mirror from a perfectly good door.

On the other hand, many accessory parts are removed from damaged body panels and saved for sale separately. This makes the salvage yard a perfect place to shop for parts you want to add those custom touches to your car. Parts like wheels are also an especially good buy at the salvage yard.

## The hotline

If you are having trouble locating a part, ask the salvage yard to put out a call for it on the "hotline." Most of the major yards are hooked into radiotelephone circuits that connect a group of yards together. A hotline works like an old telephone party line—the yards on the line stay tuned in, so by pressing a button, your salvage dealer can put out a call to every yard in the hookup.

If a part is found via the hotline, its price will be 15 to 25 percent higher because of shipping costs and the local yard's surcharge. However, if the hotline is the only way to get a part, you will appreciate the service. Incidentally, the hotline serves another function. By keeping every yard on the line informed of what the competition is charging, the prices for a given part will almost always be the same for all yards in a given area.

## Don't forget anything

When you have located what you want, make sure you get everything you need to do the job. For example, a complete door includes hinges, handle, hardware, and all interior parts. If you need these parts for the replacement job you are doing, make sure they are included in the deal. If you get into a job and have to go back to the salvage yard for something you overlooked, it will undoubtedly cost top dollar.

Salvage dealers don't like to haggle, but if you want to buy the whole nose of a wreck, he should be willing to give you a better price than if you bought each piece separately. A purchase of this magnitude could well be in excess of $500—more than the salvage dealer paid for the whole car.

## Look the used part over

Take your old part with you if possible when you go out to look at the parts you have located by phone. It is not easy to spot every variation in a part on the first inspection, so look the old and new parts over side by side. Try to work a deal whereby you can return the part and get a refund if it does not fit.

**A salvage yard** is a great place to look for parts for your car at a reasonable price.

You may choose one part over another because of variations in the trim. And if you are replacing an old part because it was damaged by rust, look at the same spots on the replacement part. Rust had the same opportunity to attack it so make sure you are not replacing bad with worse. Time spent now in getting exactly the right part will be made up when you are ready to do the replacement job. Also, check the Interchangeable Parts Book, which covers mechanical, body, and other car parts. A part from a different car may fit your needs.

**The hotline** provides a means of locating a hard-to-get part.

# How to replace a door

1 Check the replacement part over carefully before you leave the salvage yard. Make sure that the part is exactly what you need and that there is nothing missing.

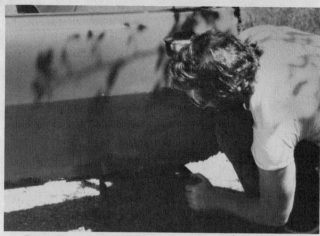

2 Block the door up on something solid. This relieves the strain on the bolts being removed and frees your hand for the removal job. For safety's sake, make sure you have someone help you when removing the door.

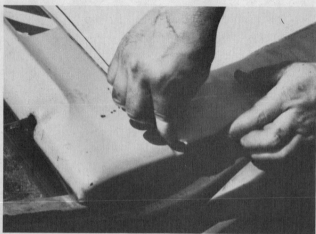

5 Go carefully and slowly when reinstalling the door trim panel to the door. If there are any difficulties, don't hammer the clips in. First check to make sure that they are properly aligned.

6 Get someone to help hold the door while you install it. Put all of the bolts in before tightening any of them. Use a screwdriver or similar tool in an adjacent hole to help align the holes.

9 Mask the door trim and the surrounding body with masking tape and masking paper. If masking paper is not available, grocery bags are a good substitute. Don't use newspaper since paint may bleed through it.

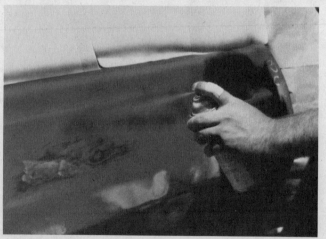

10 Spray the door with several coats of sandable primer. Wet-sand the primer between coats with #400 grit paper.

**3** Loosen all of the bolts first before removing them. Penetrating oil sprayed on rusted bolts will help loosen them and make them easier to remove. Have someone help you hold the door before you take out all the bolts or screws. Leave one bolt in the top hinge to do last.

**4** Lubricate all of the internal door mechanisms while the door is disassembled. Window and lock mechanisms should work smoothly before the door is reassembled.

**7** Position the door as closely as possible and put all the bolts in finger tight. Then tighten one bolt on each hinge. The gaps between the door and the body should be even. Adjust the striker plate if necessary, then tighten all bolts.

**8** Wash the door with wax-and-silicone remover, sand the entire outside of the door, and repair any surface damage with glazing putty. Wipe the door clean before priming.

**11** Any surface imperfections in the door will show up when the primer is sanded. Fill these imperfections with glazing putty, then prime and sand again.

## Body Shop

Whoa there! Be sure to transfer all of the parts you need from the old door to the replacement door. Remove the lock cylinder by disconnecting it from the lock linkage and removing the lock retaining clip with pliers.

## Unsticking tough nuts

What do you do when the nuts holding the part you want to remove are rusted or seized? First, liberally apply penetrating oil to the difficult nuts and any projecting threads. Tapping the head of the bolt with a hammer will help.

On really tough nuts, more leverage can be obtained by using a "cheater pipe." This is a length of pipe that fits snugly over the handle of a socket wrench and slides down to the head of the ratchet.

For nuts that simply can't be budged no matter what you do, try the hammer and chisel. A single blow of a sharp, cold chisel often will expand a nut enough to turn it when torque is not sufficient.

A hand screwdriver simply will not remove screws that were installed with power equipment at the factory. This is where the impact driver comes in. To use this tool, install the correct size bit, insert it, and rotate the tool in the direction you wish to turn the screw. Strike the impact driver sharply with a medium-weight ball peen hammer. The force of the hammer blow causes the handle of the driver to rotate and forces the bit into the slot.

For removing nuts with cutting tools, the old standby, the hacksaw, is indispensable. The nutcracker or nut splitter is another useful metal cutting tool. It fits over a rusted-on nut and can be tightened with a wrench, forcing a chisel blade into the nut.

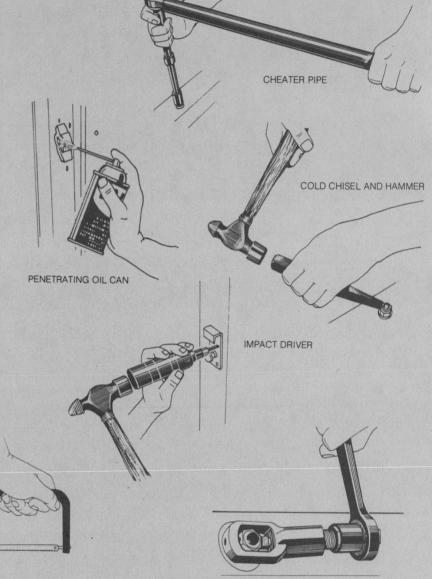

CHEATER PIPE

COLD CHISEL AND HAMMER

PENETRATING OIL CAN

IMPACT DRIVER

HACKSAW

NUT SPLITTER OR NUTCRACKER

## Plan ahead

When purchasing replacement parts, be sure you have the correct body code and other specific information. Even small model changes in body styles can mean that the part you purchase will not fit your car. Also, be prepared to transport your purchase. Don't be like the person pictured here, who has done everything right, but can't get it home.

CHAPTER

# SURFACE DAMAGE

If you have never done any bodywork on your car, minor surface damage would be a good place to start.

Three categories of damage are discussed on the following pages. First, and easiest to deal with, small chips or nicks in the paint caused by stones and gravel kicked up from the road. Second, depressions or dings no larger than a quarter and no deeper than ⅛-inch. Third, scratches, especially minor ones that you pick up in parking lots. Once you find damage of this sort on your car's body, and before you do anything else, make sure it is indeed minor. Then decide what type of repair is needed and round up the tools and materials you will need to do the job. Remember you will be working with some potentially harmful chemicals. Read the labels carefully before opening any containers. And when you've finished, store them safely.

Repairing surface damage requires several steps: cleaning the surface, sanding, applying plastic body filler, priming, putting on glazing putty, and compounding. The following pages detail the order to follow. Remember that the final coat of paint will not hide but rather magnify any surface blemishes or imperfections resulting from the refinishing process. So give each step the time and attention it deserves.

# Job steps Repairing surface damage

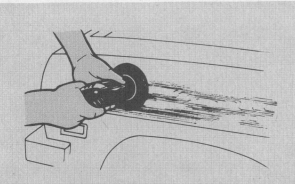

**1** Prepare the damaged area by grinding to remove all the paint. Use a #24 grit disc on a disc holder in a ¼-inch drill.

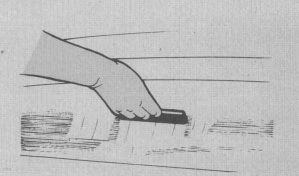

**2** Apply body filler with a plastic squeegee. Push firmly, moving upward, then across the scratch.

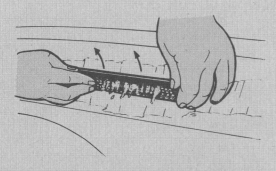

**3** When the filler is the consistency of cheese (about five minutes later), smooth with the grater. You may have to repeat steps 2 and 3.

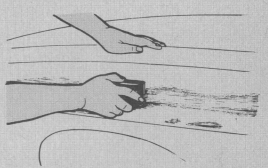

**4** Using sandpaper in a sanding block, featheredge or taper the area. Then apply primer.

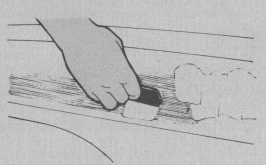

**5** Apply glazing putty in short strokes that overlap slightly. Make sure the putty is not too thick.

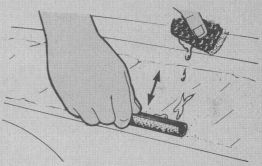

**6** Wet-sand the area with #220 grit paper rolled into a tube. Sand up and down and forward at the same time, with sponge dripping on area.

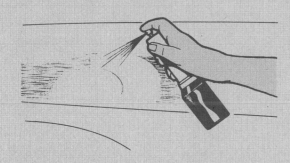

**7** Make sure the area is perfectly smooth to the touch, then apply primer.

**8** Compound around the primed area and clean with enamel reducer. Then sand with #400 grit paper and paint.

# Fixing chips and nicks

A chip or a nick is the most common kind of damage to an auto body surface and probably the easiest to repair. These small fractures are caused by flying stones and gravel which cut into the car's painted surface but do not make a dent in the metal. Chips and nicks should be repaired as soon as possible. Never allow the exposed metal to rust. The step-by-step process for repairing a chip consists of sanding the area down to the metal, priming it, applying glazing putty and several coats of primer, and painting the area. No plastic filler is necessary for tiny nicks and chips but the surface must be properly prepared to assure that the primer and the putty will adhere properly.

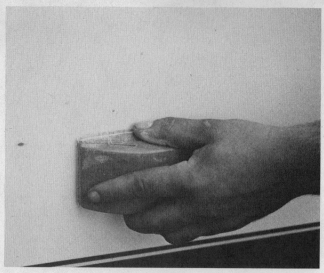

1 Clean the entire panel with a wax-and-silicone remover. Immediately wipe it dry with a clean, cotton cloth. Then sand the nicks with #80 or #100 grit paper in a sanding block.

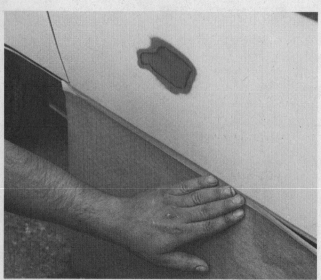

4 Before you begin to apply the primer, mask areas of the body, such as chrome trim, you want to protect.

5 Holding the can about eight inches from the surface, spray on the primer with light, even strokes. Remember to release the nozzle just before you reach the end of each stroke. Cover the damaged area with a single coat and allow it to dry thoroughly.

## Body Shop

Vinyl lacquer, used to restore vinyl tops, can also be used to create a vinyl-like, chip resistant surface for rocker panels. It comes in black or white, but the white can be tinted to match the color of your car. To prepare the surface, clean it with a wax-and-silicone remover. Featheredge any broken areas with sandpaper. Sand bare metal and rusted areas and prime them with epoxy primer. Then thoroughly sand the entire panel. If the finish is enamel, use a sealer. If the finish is lacquer, no sealer is needed. Vinyl lacquer should be applied in several coats following the directions on the can. The last coat should be thinned quite a bit. When this has dried thoroughly, apply a coat of clear acrylic lacquer to make the finish even harder.

### A quick fix for chips

If there are small chips in your car's body surface, you can repair them using this quick method and avoid a major repair job. It works with either enamel or lacquer. Always stir the paint well, and especially well if you are using metallics. First, clean the area with a wax-and-silicone remover. Then dip a toothpick or matchstick into the paint, dab on a little, and let it dry. Repeat this several times. Let it dry, then polish it if you are using enamel, or compound and polish if lacquer.

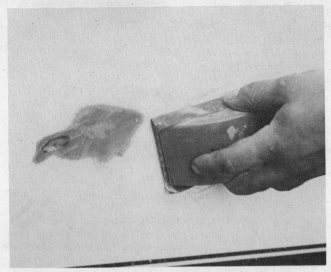

**2** Wet-sand with #320 grit paper in a sanding block to smooth the surface even further. Use a squeegee to remove the water as you sand, and check the area often for identations. You can spot these easily because water will remain in the depressions.

**3** Continue sanding until you can run your hand across the area in all directions and feel no indentations. Wipe the area dry with a clean cloth. Cotton is the most absorbent.

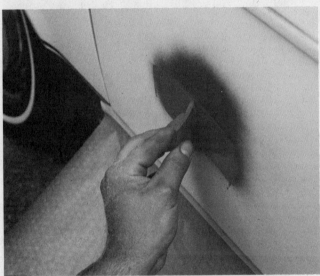

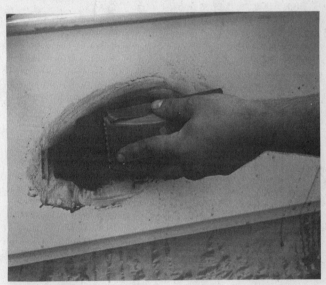

**6** Apply a thin layer of glazing putty to the surface, pressing firmly with a rubber squeegee. Allow the putty to dry thoroughly. This will take several hours and perhaps overnight, depending upon humidity and the thickness of the layer of putty.

**7** With #320 grit wet paper in a sanding block, wet-sand the glazing putty. Carefully feather the edges of the putty. When the surface is smooth, wash the area with water and dry with a clean cloth. Apply four coats of primer, following the instructions in this chapter.

**1** Clean the damaged area with a wax-and-silicone remover. Then dry it with a cloth.

**2** Stir the paint thoroughly. Then with a toothpick or matchstick, dab paint into the chip. Repeat this several times.

**3** When the paint has dried, polish the area if enamel. If the finish is lacquer, use compound and polish.

# All about sanding and grinding

Sanding and grinding are two ways to wear away a surface by using an abrasive. Sanding smooths any imperfections in the surface while grinding removes the entire finish. Sanding is important in preparing an auto body surface because minor flaws such as chips, scratches remaining from coarse sanding, and ridges left by removing only a portion of the old finish will be magnified when the final coat of paint is applied. Be sure you choose the right sandpaper and the right method of sanding for the job you are doing. The wrong choice can leave you with more problems than you started out with.

## Abrasive materials

Sandpaper, a term used to cover a range of abrasives, is made by bonding granular material to a paper backing. Several different minerals are used as abrasives, but only two of these—aluminum oxide and silicon carbide—play a role in bodywork. Aluminum oxide is used for dry paper and silicon carbide for wet or dry paper. Abrasives are commonly available in grit sizes from 16 to 600. The higher the number, the finer the grit. Sizes 16, 24, 36, and 50 are used on grinding discs; 40, 80, and 100 on dry sanding paper, and 220, 320, 400, 500, and 600 on wet-and-dry paper. Other sizes are available but their use is not as common.

## Open or closed

All abrasive papers, regardless of size and type of mineral used, fall into two categories: open- and closed-coat. These terms refer to the spacing of the abrasive particles. On open-coat paper, only 60 to 80 percent of the backing is covered with grit, while the backing of closed-coat paper is completely covered. Closed-coat discs are used after the metal finishing operation is completed. This is done to remove hammer or file marks and to smooth welds. Open-coat discs,

because they do not clog so easily, are better for removing paint.

## Hand or power

In hand sanding, the paper is held flat against the surface and moved back and forth. If sandpaper is used without backing, you will probably leave finger marks on the surface. To avoid this, use a block of wood or a sanding block. For curved surfaces, the sandpaper should be backed with a flexible pad or wrapped around a piece of hose or sponge.

When sanding by hand, move your hand back and forth in a straight line over an area no larger than 12 to 18 inches. Never use a circular motion. Too much pressure will not speed the sanding process and will probably clog the abrasive surface. Do not spend too much time on one area or you will get a depression in the surface or go through to the metal. If the repair job includes an application of primer and putty, you will probably want to use a power sander. There are various types: orbital or straight line, belt, and off-center orbital disc. There are also sanding attachments to use with your buffing machine and others to fit your electric drill.

The discs shown, left to right, are #16, #24, #36, #50.

A grinder is a high speed machine that takes a circular disc from seven to nine inches in diameter. To use it, tilt it slightly so that only about one inch of

The correct method of hand sanding is to put the paper in a sanding block. The backing creates even pressure on the surface of the body part.

The wrong way to hand sand, with no block to support the sandpaper, results in uneven pressure and grooves cut into the surface of the body.

the leading edge of the disc contacts the auto body surface. Never grind flat against the surface. This will leave sand scratches that are very difficult to get rid of. Also, due to torque, a grinder might jerk violently and you could lose control of it. But a grinder should not be held at too sharp an angle so that just the edge of the disc touches the surface. This will result in gouges. When the grinder is held properly, the sanding marks are nearly straight.

Sanders, on the other hand, should be held flat against the surface. Their motion is either orbital (that is, like

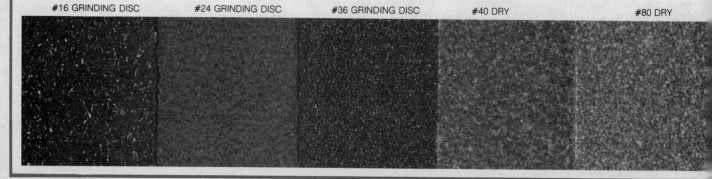

an off-center circle) or back and forth. Both belt and orbital sanders can be powered by either electric motors or compressed air. When using any sander, keep it moving to avoid scratching or going down to the metal. If you're using a heavy-duty grinder to remove paint, you will create lots of dust. So do it outdoors, if possible. If you can't, make sure the work area is well ventilated. Either way, it is absolutely necessary to wear safety goggles and a mask. Keep the grinder moving and do not press in too hard or the heat you generate will damage the panel.

## Wet or dry

You can dry-sand either by hand or by machine. The biggest problem is that the paper gets clogged from all the dust produced. One answer is zinc stearate abrasive papers which resist clogging. For wet sanding, you need waterproof materials—sandpaper and sanding block—and a bucket of water, a sponge, and a squeegee. Wet sanding solves the problem of clogged sandpaper and it's faster because both abrasive and surface are continually being washed by the water. Although wet sanding is more efficient than dry, it increases the cleanup time.

To wet-sand, dip the sandpaper and block into water and wet the body surface with the sponge. Then sand the same way you would dry-sand. When the paper begins to slide easily over the surface, it is probably clogged with paint sludge. Just dip the abrasive into water to clean off the residue. You can tell how well the sandpaper is working by the resistance you feel. As you wet-sand, use the squeegee to clean off the surface. This will help you see the progress you are making. Any low spots in the surface are readily visible because water will settle in the depressions.
CAUTION: Never wet-sand with an electric sander—you can get a shock. Wet-sand only by hand or with compressed air equipment.

A **burn spot** such as this can occur when a power grinder is held too long in one place. The correct way to sand with a power grinder is to keep it moving along the surface at an even pace.

## Featheredging

Featheredging means tapering the edges of a painted or body filler surface so there will be no detectable line or ridge when the final top coat is applied. Where there are several small chips or nicks close together you can treat them as one working area. The first step in featheredging may be done by machine with an orbital sander or by hand. Start with a #320 grit paper for hand sanding, a #220 grit for power. The second step is wet sanding by hand using a sanding block and finer paper, #320 for example. How professional the finish looks will depend on the care with which this step is done.

## Sanding terms

**Scuffing** is fine sanding to get rid of nibs, paint dust, specks, and dirt. You use a very fine grit paper to avoid cutting into the surface.
**Light sanding** is done before repainting an old finish that is in good condition. This improves the adhesion of the new coat. Use either the wet or dry process and work either by hand or with a power sander. But never use a disc grinder.

**Thorough sanding** is what you do when a finish to be repainted is in poor condition. This levels and smooths areas after they have been primed.
**Grinding** is deep sanding for the complete removal of a layer of paint. Use an electric or pneumatic disc grinder for this job.
**Bare metal grinding** is not necessary if the metal work has been done properly. But sometimes the metal is very rough from coarse grinding, and using a #50 grit disc will help to level out the burrs.

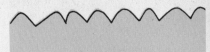

**A magnified section of metal** sanded with a coarse-grit paper shows that burrs still exist.

**This same section** has no burrs after scuffing with a fine-grit paper.

If you find that you are doing a lot of sanding and grinding, there is a way to economize in the use of discs. Save those that are worn out around the edges. You can trim off an inch or so around the edge and use them again with a smaller size backing pad. To cut the discs, you'll need an abrasive disc trimmer or a pair of heavyduty shears.

| #100 DRY | #220 WET OR DRY | #320 WET OR DRY | #400 WET OR DRY | #600 WET OR DRY |
|---|---|---|---|---|

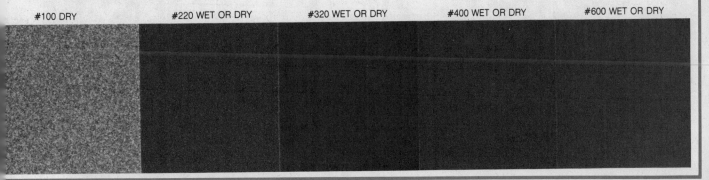

# Smoothing out dings

A ding is a depression no larger than a quarter and no deeper than ⅛-inch. It can easily be repaired with plastic filler. The metal does not have to be straightened with hammers and dollies. However, the car's surface must be carefully prepared to assure proper adhesion because filler does not stick to a painted surface. Repairing a ding involves cleaning with a wax-and-silicone remover, grinding the area so the metal is exposed and there is no paint on the surface, filling with plastic body filler, sanding the filler until it is smooth, spraying on primer, applying glazing putty and allowing it to dry, then sanding and finally painting.

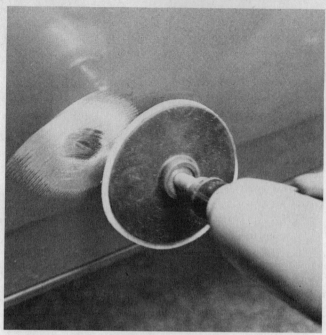

1 Apply a wax-and-silicone remover to the area and wipe it off with a clean, dry cloth. Then grind away the paint surrounding the ding with a #24 grit disc. Use your drill's wire brush attachment to remove paint from the center of the ding. You may have to scratch out the paint with a knife or screwdriver.

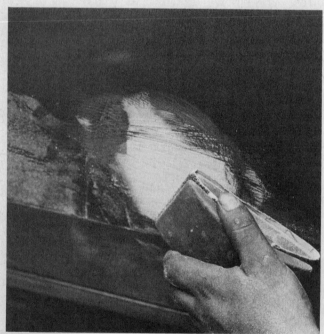

4 Use #40 grit paper in a rubber sanding block to sand the filler level with the surface. Do not press too hard. Keep feeling the area with your hand and when it feels level, stop sanding and change to a finer paper.

5 Using #80 or #100 grit paper, featheredge the painted area around the dent. Sand lightly until you can no longer detect the border between the filler and the paint.

2 Mix plastic body filler on a non-absorbent surface following the directions on the can. Mix thoroughly, not by stirring, but by stroking downward, in order to eliminate air bubbles.

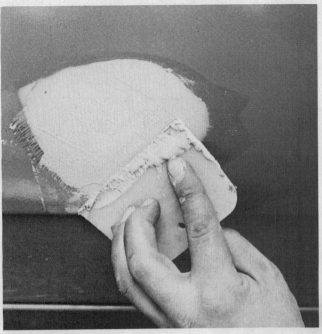

3 Apply the plastic filler, pressing it firmly into the dent. Then go over the filled area again using less pressure. Plastic body filler can be applied with a rubber squeegee, a putty knife or a plastic spreader. Make sure you wipe or scrape off any excess filler from the tool before it hardens.

6 When you have finished sanding the area and you are satisfied that it is absolutely smooth, it is ready to be primed. Use a spray primer and choose a color close to the color of the base coat. Spray primer on the damaged area only and use just enough to cover the filler and any bare metal.

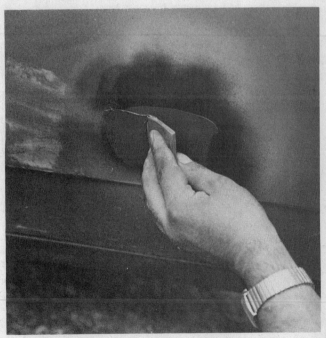

7 To apply glazing putty, dip the edge of a squeegee—about ¼-inch—into the putty. Pull it across the surface quickly but firmly. Make three passes from the left to the right, and then make three more passes from top to bottom, overlapping each time. Allow the putty to dry thoroughly before you wet-sand, re-prime, and paint.

# All about priming and sealing

Ideally, paint should adhere to the surface of your car's body through all kinds of weather and for the lifetime of your car. It's the undercoat—the primers, primer-surfacers, primer-sealers, and glazing putty, in lacquer or enamel—that provides this adhesion.

A primer makes possible complete adhesion of the top coat to the bare metal and helps prevent rust. This is the undercoat you would use over large areas of bare metal.

A primer-surfacer also provides adhesion but its most important property is the ability to fill in minor scratches and nicks and to bring the surface areas up to the level of adjacent painted surfaces.

A primer-sealer seals out the old finish and promotes adhesion between it and new paint. It provides "hold out," the ability to prevent the top coat from sinking in.

Glazing putty is similar in content to primer-surfacer but it is thicker. Squeegee it on to fill surface imperfections after a primer-surfacer has been applied.

**Before you start priming,** mask all chrome and glass. Be sure to wear a mask to prevent inhaling any of the particles. If you are doing the job indoors, work in a well-ventilated area.

## Primers

A primer is an undercoat that improves the adhesion and durability of the top coat. It is usually used over bare metal although it can be used over an old finish. Primers grip the metal surface and create a base for the new paint. Primer should be applied in thin coats. Don't expect it to fill scratches and nicks and never sand it. Use an enamel primer in place of a primer-surfacer before applying enamel on bare metal that is smooth and free of flaws.

Special primers are required for special surfaces: zinc chromate with aluminum; zinc dust with galvanized metal. Primers come in several colors, so try to choose one that matches the base color of your car.

## Primer-surfacers

Primer-surfacers provide adhesion for the metal and level featheredged areas and rough surfaces to provide a smooth base for the top coat.

Lacquer primer-surfacer can be used under either lacquer or enamel. It is the most frequently used type because of its fast-drying properties: it is ready to sand in about half an hour. In addition, a good lacquer primer-surfacer provides excellent adhesion for the top coat, creates a smooth surface by filling in the flaws, is easy to sand, and provides "hold out" which means it has a sealing quality to prevent the top coat from sinking into the primer-surfacer.

To apply a lacquer primer-surfacer, use two or three medium coats, allowing ten to 15 minutes flash-drying time between them. A thin coat can result in a loss of adhesion; a thick coat takes too long to dry. Also, it is difficult to tell when a thick coat is ready because the surface will appear to be dry while there is still thinner trapped below and shrinkage is still going on. Allow half an hour or more drying time after the final coat before you sand.

**A primer** bonds the original surface and the top coat.

**A primer-sealer** seals out the old finish and bonds to the new one.

**A primer-surfacer** is a primer that also fills in small flaws and scratches in the body surface.

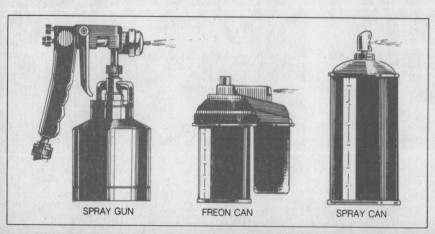

SPRAY GUN          FREON CAN          SPRAY CAN

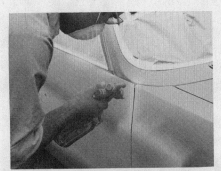
**Prime the edges of the door** where there may be small chips.

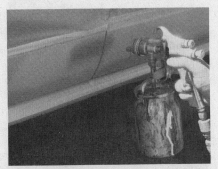
**When painting over an old finish** in reds or maroons, use a special sealer to prevent bleeding.

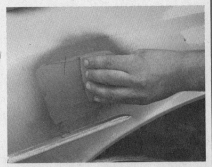
**To apply putty correctly,** make a firm pass with the squeegee. Do not go back over it.

Enamel primer-surfacer is used mostly on trucks, but you can also use it on cars where there are large areas of bare metal, such as panels where the old finish has been completely removed. An enamel primer-surfacer must be allowed to dry for several hours before it is dry sanded, overnight if it is wet sanded.

## Primer-sealers

Primer sealers are made from resins which, when dried, are not easily dissolved in common solvents. They act as a shield against the penetration of the top coat's solvents. Sealers also hide sand scratches and provide adhesion between the old and the new finishes. The type and condition of the old finish will tell you whether a sealer is needed. When working over original factory finishes, you can usually get along without. However, if sand scratches are noticeable, a sealer should be used.

## Bleeder-sealers

Bleeder-sealer is used over old paint containing dyes that "bleed" or dissolve in the solvents from the new paint. Reds and maroons are the colors likely to contain such pigments. You can spot-check for the presence of a bleeding color by painting a small area with white paint. If the red bleeds through, you should seal it. No other sealers should be used to seal bleeding colors, and bleeder-sealers should not be used for any other purpose than to prevent the bleeding of an old finish.

## Glazing putty

Glazing putty fills scratches and rough surfaces that are too large to be filled by the primer-surfacer but not large enough to require bodywork. A glazing putty has a higher solids content than primer-surfacer and, therefore, has greater filling properties. Glazing putty must be applied with a squeegee or a putty knife. Putty can be used to treat scratches and depressions up to 1/16 of an inch deep. Anything larger should be filled with plastic body filler. Some lacquer putties are applied over the primer-surfacer coat and others have good adhesion to bare metal. Like a primer-surfacer, a good putty should have these qualities: fast drying time, ease of sanding, good adhesion, and color hold out from the top coat.

## Thinners and reducers

Thinners and reducers dilute primers and top coats that are too thick to spray as they come out of the container. Thinners are used to dilute lacquer products, reducers with enamels. Never use a thinner with enamel or a reducer with lacquer or the paint will curdle.

The ingredients in thinners and reducers act to dilute the primer so it will not clog the spray gun. Once on the surface, a thinner or reducer should keep the primer in solution long enough for it to flow out and level but not so long that it sags or runs. It must evaporate completely and leave a smooth, durable finish.

If you are doing a spot job on enamel, ask for a thinner with a high percentage of slow solvents so the overspray will blend and flow into the surrounding enamel. When working on an acrylic lacquer finish, don't use a thinner with solvents that are too strong, because it will cause the old finish to swell and you will see the sand scratches.

When you are choosing a thinner or reducer, remember that two variables—temperature and humidity—affect the drying time. Hot, dry weather results in the fastest drying; followed by hot, humid weather; normal weather; cold, dry weather; and cold, humid weather. So when selecting a thinner or reducer, keep the weather conditions in mind. The more favorable the weather conditions, the slower drying the thinner or reducer should be. In cold, wet weather, on the other hand, a fast drying thinner or reducer is needed. For best results, painting should be done in temperatures of 60 degrees and over. Painting under colder conditions can result in a less than perfect finish.

## Some safety hints

In any spraying operation, proper ventilation and fire prevention are essential. Remove anything in the spraying area that could ignite the material you are spraying and cause it to explode. The danger is especially great during priming. Don't smoke in the work area and don't use heat-producing tools, such as welding irons or grinders, until priming is completed and the fumes are dispersed. Be careful when handling thinners and reducers. Their fumes are highly explosive. These materials must be properly stored and empty containers disposed of immediately. Place used cloths in a metal container with a cover and dispose of all empty containers immediately. And make sure you use a respirator whenever you spray.

# Fixing a simple scratch

For the new car owner, getting a scratch on the body paint is often the first initiation into the problems of owning a car. However disappointing it may be, a scratch can be easily and quickly repaired. The procedure for repairing a scratch consists of grinding away paint and rust, mixing and applying filler, sanding and priming, applying glazing putty, then final sanding and priming. Study the steps on these two pages and you'll discover how to quickly repair simple scratches.

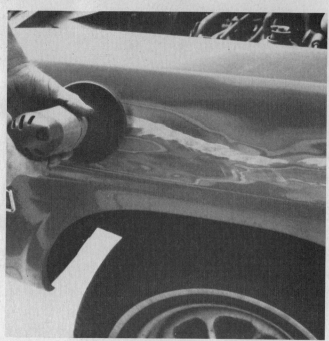

**1** Grind away the old paint and rust with a #24 grit disc attached to a ¼-inch drill. Be sure to remove the paint from an area extending several inches beyond the scratch.

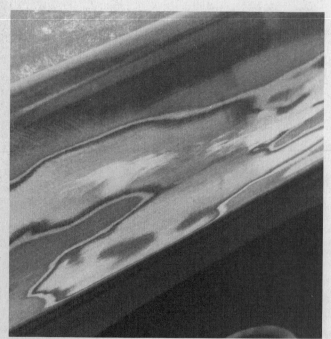

**4** Check to see if more filler is needed. If it is, repeat steps 2 and 3 until all the low spots have been filled and the surface is smooth.

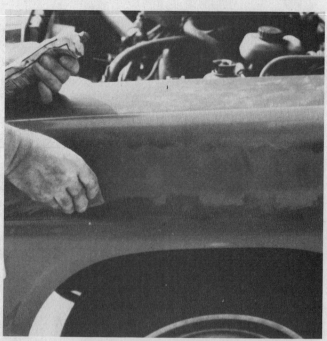

**5** Prime the area. Then apply glazing putty in single, overlapping strokes. Use thin coats and allow them to dry before sanding. You can speed the drying process with a heat lamp if you wish, but do not let it get too hot.

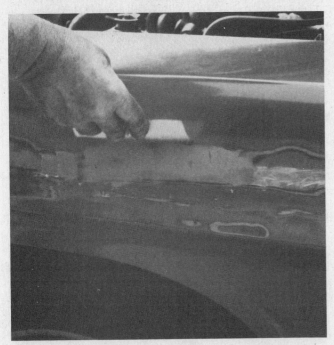

**2** Mix a small amount of body filler. Working quickly, hold the plastic spreader at a 45-degree angle and press the filler into the scratch using short, upward strokes. Then, using less pressure, press along the scratch from left to right.

**3** When the filler is completely hard (about ten minutes later), scratch it with your fingernail. Then sand with #80 grit paper in a sanding block, feathering the edges to blend with the surrounding metal.

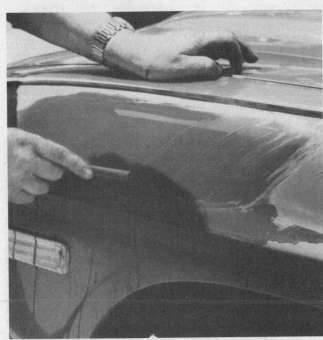

**6** Roll a piece of #320 grit paper into a tube and hold it parallel to the fender groove. Sand up and down as you are pushing forward. Reroll the paper for a clean edge. Then wet-sand using the same procedure, feathering the edges carefully to eliminate sanding scratches.

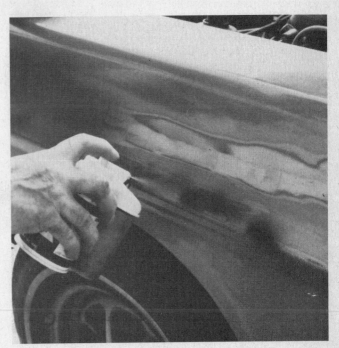

**7** Prime the area to protect the metal from rust. If you find any low spots, repeat step 5, then wet-sand as in step 6 and prime again.

## Types of moldings

Until several years ago, all molding strips were screwed on. But these had two drawbacks: it was expensive to manufacture and stock the large number and variety of screws required, and, water trapped in the strips, especially by the small screws, created rust problems. Clip-on moldings were an improvement because they were easier to remove and replace. But the rust problem remained. Now almost all new cars come with self-adhesive molding. These watertight strips are easy to attach and they have eliminated the problem of rust.

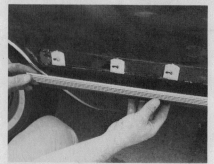

**Clip-on molding strips** are attached by snapping them onto clips that are screwed into the body. If you want to change from clip-on moldings to self-adhesive moldings, first remove the clips, then choose a self-adhesive molding that is wide enough to cover the holes.

**To attach a self-adhesive molding strip,** clean the area of wax or grease. Make a straight edge across the panel with masking tape, then peel off the protective backing and press the strip into place. To remove a strip, carefully insert a screwdriver under the leading edge and pull it off, being careful not to damage the paint. If the adhesive is too resistant for the screwdriver, try softening it with a hair dryer if you have one.

## Masking trim

Chrome is almost impossible to repair once it has been gouged by sandpaper or a ginding disc. So either remove it or mask it before sanding nearby. Not all molding strips are easy to remove. If your car is more than a couple of years old, the molding may be rusted on or you may not be able to buy new clips. If you have this problem, it is better not to try to take the molding off because it might break. Instead, mask as shown at the right. Moldings such as the lettering on the front of the car may be too intricate to mask, so you will have to remove these.

**Clean moldings** with a wax-and-silicone remover so the masking tape will adhere. Although gasoline will do the degreasing and dewaxing job, it tends to leave a film.

**Use cardboard to mask the center of large areas.** Lay on the tape and press down without stretching it. Be sure the edges are down and do not tape all the way to the paint. Allow a little chrome to show between the tape and the finish, about 1/32-inch or less.

## Repairing molding clips

If your clip-on molding is damaged or rusted, or before repainting, you should remove it. Here is what you do. Hit the trim sharply from below with the palm of your hand. This knocks the molding up from the clips holding it. The clips are fastened to the car body by small screws or rivets. To remove a clip, insert a screwdriver under it and gently pry it up. Occasionally, if a screw is rusted, it will break off. If this happens to you, simply drill another hole in the body a short distance from the original one. If your car is old and all the screws and clips are unusable, buy a new set and drill new holes.

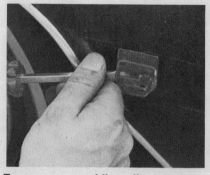

**To remove a molding clip,** insert a screwdriver behind it and gently pry it out from the screw.

**If the screw breaks,** drill a new hole in the metal about one inch from the old one and insert a new screw and clip. The top of the screw should be level with the clip so the molding will fit over it.

CHAPTER

# DENTS

Today's traffic combined with today's driving habits makes it very likely that at one time or another you will have some dents to repair. For small ones, you'll have to rework the damaged area until the normal contour of the metal has been generally restored, then apply some body filler to smooth out the low spots, and finally refinish the damaged area.

Methods vary and the one you choose will depend on the nature of the dent and, more importantly, its location. When you have easy access to the rear of the damaged area, bump it out with a body hammer and a dolly block. Where the damage is a high spot, try a body spoon and hammer. The spoon spreads out the force of the hammer blow. When you have access but it is too limited for the hammer and dolly, a spoon's handle lets you get up behind the dent where you can use it like a dolly. Spoons also come in handy as pry bars to bend metal back to its original shape.

Dents located where you don't have rear access can be handled with a dent puller, a device that is both ingenious and indispensable. Use a suction cup when the damage is shallow and broad—on the roof for example. After you have reworked the metal by one of these methods, all that remains is to apply plastic body filler to bring any low spots up to the level of the surrounding metal, and prepare the surface for finishing.

Skillful treatment of dents means restoration of your car's body surface so completely that only a professional can tell whether it has been repaired at all.

# Job steps Repairing dents

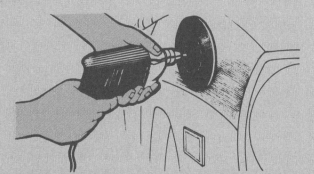

**1** Grind the paint away from the damaged area and a little beyond. Hold the drill firmly and press lightly.

**2** Survey the dent and drill ⅛-inch holes along the deepest parts of the dent or crease. Locate the holes about 1- to 1½-inches apart.

**3** With a dent puller, gently pull the depressed area up. As the metal is raised, you may tap down the high points with a body hammer.

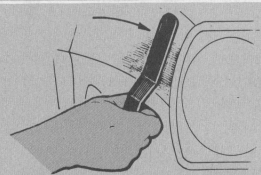

**4** On some dents, tapping with a body hammer may stretch the metal. In such cases, use a slapper file to tap down the high spots.

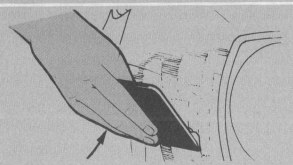

**5** When the metal is within ⅛-inch of its original contour, grind and sand. Then apply body filler to the low spots in the damaged area with a spreader.

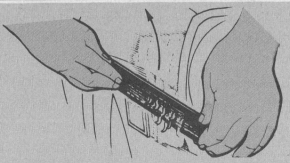

**6** Use a cheese grater file to knock down high spots on the filler. Steps 5 and 6 may have to be repeated several times.

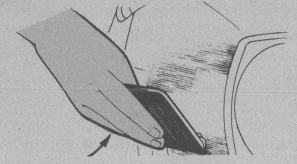

**7** Sand, featheredge, prime, and apply putty glaze with a squeegee to the damaged area. Then wet-sand, using #220 grit paper.

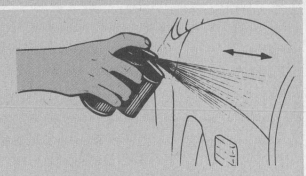

**8** Prime the surface again and wet-sand once more with #400 grit paper. Now apply the final paint.

# Dollying a small dent

The tools you'll grow most familiar with in bodywork are the hammer and the dolly. See page 72 for a full explanation of hammer-and-dolly techniques. The dent to be repaired is a common crunch caused by underestimating the distance between your moving car and a large immovable object.

It's a good idea to gather everything you'll need before starting this job. That includes, in this case, not only the hammer and dolly, but also a sledge, a cheese grater file, a hand drill and various sanding discs, body filler and spreader, some sandpaper and a block, a spray can or gun, primer, putty, and paint.

**1** It is relatively easy to fix this dent by dollying it out, filling, and refinishing. Go slowly and, as you work, check the contour of the repair by feeling with the palm of your hand. Learn to trust your hand. It often can pick up a slight unevenness that eludes the eye.

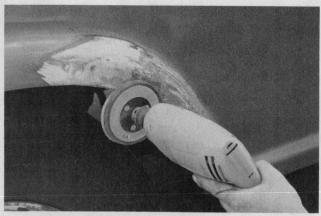

**4** After the metal has been brought to within ⅛-inch of the original contour, grind the surface down to bare metal with a #24 grit disc attached to a hand drill. Hold the drill firmly but don't lean on it or it may jump out of your hand.

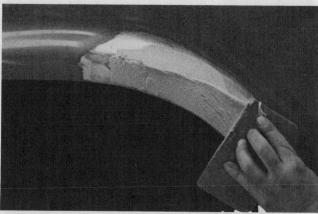

**5** Mix a small amount of plastic body filler and spread it on. For a more detailed discussion of fillers, see page 76. Press fairly hard with the spreader to get rid of small air bubbles which form during mixing.

**8** Put #80 grit paper in the sanding block and lightly sand the inside edges of the repair. Tap the block frequently to eliminate filler that may be clogging the paper.

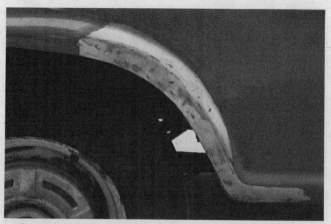

**9** After sanding, if the repair area looks like this, you will have to fill and file again. The dark spots are low areas. Apply several thin layers of filler and sand after each. Finish with #80 paper, featheredge all edges, prime, and paint.

**2** Begin by tapping the metal back toward its original shape with a sledgehammer. Although you may be tempted to really smack the metal to reshape it perfectly in one blow, you will find that a few controlled strikes with the hammer do a better job.

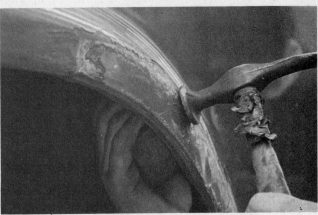

**3** Work on the contour with a rail-type dolly and a body hammer. Hold the dolly so the face matches the shape of the metal behind the surface. Then tap the metal with the body hammer, keeping the dolly directly behind the hammer. Moving slowly, work your way up and down the length of the repair area. You will have to experiment a little to determine just how hard to hit the metal.

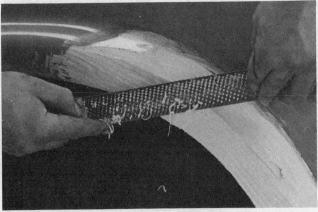

**6** With a half-round cheese grater file, knock down the high spots in the plastic. Always pull the grater toward you at a slight angle.

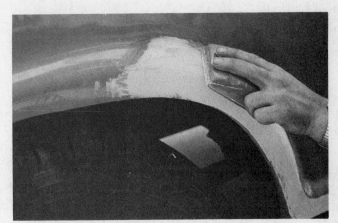

**7** Now sand the area with #40 grit paper on a block to remove some of the ridges and grooves left by the grater file.

**10** Prime the repair using short, light strokes with the spray can. If you are going to use a compressor gun for the paint job later on, use that for priming.

**11** Now paint, matching your car's original color, which you can learn by checking the body number plate (see page 47).

# All about hammer and dolly techniques

To dolly out dents successfully, you must be able to control the force and accuracy of your hammer blows. To gain proficiency in this, practice holding a high-crown dolly in your hand and hitting it squarely with the face of a body hammer, using the same amount of force for each blow. It's important to choose the correct hammer and dolly for the job. Use the flat-faced side of the hammer head on flat and convex metal surfaces and the curved-faced side for concave surfaces. Don't use a flat dolly to straighten a curved surface.

## Hammer-on-dolly

In the hammer-on-dolly technique, the blow of the hammer must fall on the metal directly above the spot where you are holding the dolly. By using the area on a dolly that closely matches the original contour of the metal, it is pushed back into shape. The area of metal in contact with the hammer is raised above the level of the surrounding metal. Take care not to use too much force when tapping down or you will stretch the metal.

Use light to medium blows. Heavy blows drive the dolly back away from the metal before the hammer blow stops. Accuracy is also important. If you strike off the center of the dolly, you will hit an unsupported area of the metal and displace it.

## Hammer-off-dolly

In the hammer-off-dolly technique, you place the dolly near but not directly under the point where the hammer blow will strike.

Hold the dolly at the low spot of the crease or dent and strike a series of light blows around the outside of it. Be sure to use a dolly whose contour matches the original contour of the metal.

Because the hammer blow falls on metal not supported by the dolly, the metal is struck *down*. This is just the opposite of the hammer-on-dolly technique where the metal surface is *raised*. In indirect hammering, the spot where the dolly is held is raised. Because you can't see the dolly, tap on the metal with the hammer until the ringing sound lets you know you've found it.

Strike only on areas raised above the original contour of the metal. Begin striking on the high metal farthest from the center of the dent or crease. Use light blows. Too heavy a blow will force the metal down, causing additional damage.

Remember: dollying out dents by either of these techniques requires coordination. Moving the dolly around under the dented area and striking directly over it or just near enough to it to be effective is a skill you can perfect only by practice. You can actually develop a feel which will permit you to control the hammer and position the dolly to make the best use of these techniques.

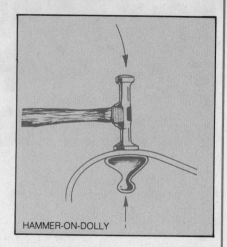

HAMMER-ON-DOLLY

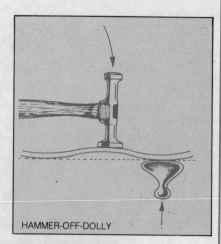

HAMMER-OFF-DOLLY

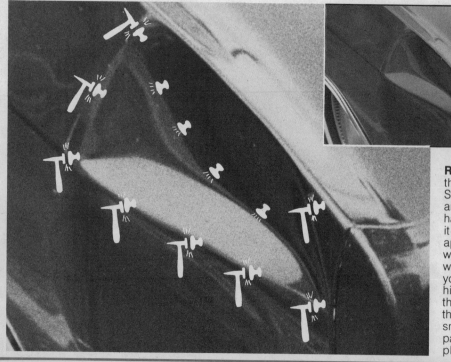

**Repairing a high-crown area** is just the right job for a hammer and dolly. Starting at the deepest part of the dent and using a general purpose dolly as a hammer, rough out the dent by hitting it from the inside until it returns to approximately its original shape. Now, working from the outside in, press up with the dolly on the low spots as you tap down with the hammer on the highs, and move toward the center of the dent. Hammer off the dolly for this job. When the repair area feels smooth and level, grind off the old paint and apply body filler to complete the job.

# Repairing a door-edge dent

This is what can happen when somebody leaves the car door open. An oncoming car hits it, pushing in the edge.

The repair involves removing the door, drilling and pulling the dent (see pages 78 and 79 for details), and hammer-and-dolly work with which you are already familiar. Use the hammer-off-dolly technique, in which you hold the dolly close to but not directly under the point where the hammer strikes the metal. The dolly pushes up on the depressed metal while the hammer taps down on the raised metal, returning the surface back almost to its original contour.

Be sure to tap lightly, going around and around the damaged area. Work from the outside in until the original contour of the metal is almost restored. Remember: heavy blows with the hammer can create secondary damage that may be harder to fix than the original damage.

**1** Drill along the stress lines in the deepest part of the crease. Then, drill the door frame, close to the panel (see the arrows). Begin by pulling the dent in the door frame. This has to be straightened first to relieve the pressure on the door panel. Then pull the crease on the outside panel.

**2** Because the edge of the door is accessible, you can bring the metal still closer to its original shape by using the hammer and dolly. Hold a rail-type dolly behind the edge of the panel for support and hammer-off-dolly. Begin tapping on the high spots farthest away from the center or the deepest part of the dent, while you push up on the dolly. Then work your way toward the center.

**3** Grind the metal with a #24 grit disc. Some of the screw-on discs come loose if you don't press fairly hard with the drill. If you have this problem, switch to the adhesive type. You can also run a screw through the center to get really good adhesion. Remove the paint from an area three or four inches beyond the damage.

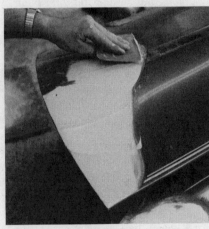

**4** Mix enough plastic filler to cover the repair area and smooth it on with a spreader. Large areas like this require a broad spreader. Never let the filler dry on the spreader or knife or you'll spend a lot of time trying to chip it off. The spreader must be clean and smooth to apply the filler.

**5** For rough filing, use a half-round cheese grater file. Always pull it towards you and be sure to maintain equal pressure on both ends to keep it flat.

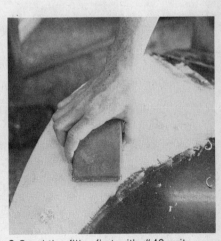

**6** Sand the filler first with #40 grit paper. Don't press too hard. If low spots remain, fill, file, and sand again. On a contour like this, use a sanding block. When you approach the painted area, lightly hand sand with #80 grit paper folded in half. Sand very carefully up to, not on, the edge of the metal. The filler is very vulnerable here and you risk sanding it all off. Finish by priming, glazing, and painting.

# All about body fillers

After bumping out the dents and creases, you will usually have to fill in the remaining low spots with plastic body filler. Fillers come in various size containers; select the quantity you need for your particular job. Be sure to keep the filler in a cool place until you are ready to mix it.

## Preparing the damaged area

Grind the area to be filled and a little beyond with a #24 grit disc. Remember, filler can only be applied on surfaces that are absolutely free of paint, rust or other contaminants.

## Mixing the filler

On a non-porous surface such as glass or metal, first mix the filler and then add the hardener. Cream hardener contains a coloring agent, and you can tell that the mixing is complete when the mixture has taken on a uniform color.

Add only about eight drops of liquid hardener or about ½- to ¾-inches ribbon of cream hardener from a tube to an amount of filler the size of a golf ball. With a wide putty knife, draw the filler out on the tray to about 1/16-inch thickness. Use a side-to-side, pressing-down motion in mixing. Push the filler into a pile, do not fold or air bubbles will be trapped in the mixture. Repeat this step five or six times until the filler and hardener are thoroughly mixed to a consistent color. Work quickly—the filler begins to harden as soon as it is mixed. Use the spreader to scrape the filler from the putty knife.

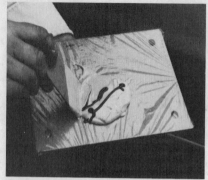

**Spread the filler** on the mixing tray, making sure it is well mixed. Then add a little bit of the hardener. Note that the tray is a piece of board covered with plastic wrap. When the filler hardens on the board, remove the wrap and the board is ready to use again.

## Applying filler to the surface

Apply filler to the damaged surface with the spreader in a very thin coat, pressing firmly as you go. This helps force out any remaining air bubbles. After two or three applications, the filler should build up above the paint surface evenly.

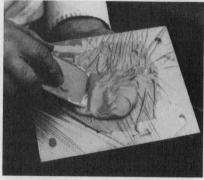

**Mix the filler and hardener** thoroughly. The hardener contains a coloring agent, so when the mixture is combined, it has a uniform color. Remember to work quickly. The mixture begins to harden almost immediately.

Normally, the filler will harden in five to 15 minutes at 70°F. Damp or chill weather will lengthen the hardening time; hot weather will speed it up.

If the surface to be filled is greater than about ⅛-inch deep, it is better to apply the filler in several thin coats, allowing time for each coat to harden and be filed down with the cheese grater file.

After the filler has been built up to the proper contour and filed, sand, prime, glaze, wet-sand, and paint the surface.

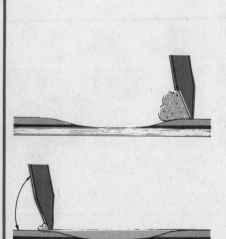

**Working out air bubbles** in filler with a spreader.

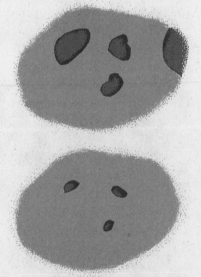

**After two successive applications** of filler to the surface, there are fewer low spots. Be sure to apply filler in a thin film and build it up through several applications until the lows are all filled in.

One of the most common problems in using plastic filler is pinholes caused by tiny air bubbles trapped in the filler during mixing and applying. Pinholes result from adding too much hardener to the filler mixture. If you are having trouble with pinholes, try using less hardener. Also, be sure to press down firmly when applying the filler. This will work out any bubbles in the mixture.

## Repairing a dent and tear with a fiberglass patch

**1** For this damage, you need a fiberglass patch to fill the hole in the door. Since water usually doesn't splash up inside the door high enough to reach this hole, we didn't use backing material such as undercoating.

**2** Begin by grinding the surface down with a #24 grit disc, removing the paint from an area two to three inches larger than the dent.

**3** Snap on the wire brush attachment and clean out the ragged edge of the hole. This attachment is handy for jobs where tiny specks of paint remain after grinding.

**4** Fiberglass patch kits come with a mixing tray and stir stick. After adding the hardener, be sure to stir the mixture thoroughly. Insufficient mixing is the most common error in making repairs with these kits. Make only as much as you need.

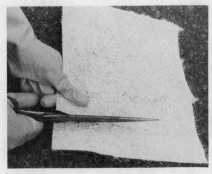

**5** Hold a piece of fiberglass cloth up to the dent to gauge how much you will need. Put gloves on before cutting. You will need two pieces of cloth. Dip them, one at a time, into the resin and soak for a minute.

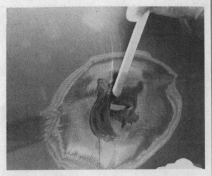

**6** Dip the stir stick into the resin and apply a fairly thick coat—but not so much that it begins to run—to the immediate area of the hole. This gives a little extra stickiness to the patch.

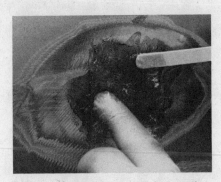

**7** Place the fiberglass patch over the hole and press it down on the metal right around the tear. Use heat to speed the hardening process. Place another piece of resin-soaked fiberglass cloth on the area and push out all the air bubbles. Allow it to dry overnight.

**8** Grind the patch lightly with a coarse #24 grit disc, then smooth down by hand with #40 grit paper and a sanding block. Keep feeling it with your hand. Stop sanding when the surface feels smooth and level. Be sure to use a dust mask when grinding or sanding fiberglass.

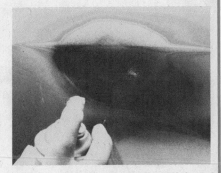

**9** Check the surface carefully. If there are any imperfections, fill with plastic filler, sand until smooth, and then featheredge with #80 grit paper, prime, and apply glazing putty.

# All about shaping and sanding body filler

Before the filler has hardened completely, you must shape it to the desired contour. Be sure to do this while the top surface is still soft. Later, it will become so hard it can only be worked with a grinder or extremely rough sandpaper.

Sandpaper files should not be used for the initial cutting of the filler surface when it is still soft. This cutting is done with a half-round cheese grater file or with a shaver.

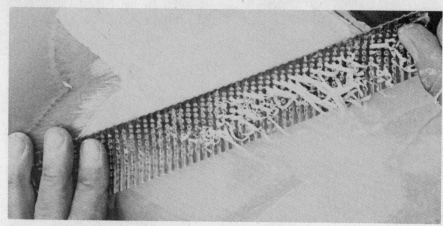

**Use a half-round cheese grater file** for knocking down high spots on the filler surface. As you can see, it is ideally suited for shaving away soft surfaces. Always make sure to draw the file towards you. Maintain firm pressure on both ends of it to keep it flat.

**The shaver** is a smaller version of the cheese grater file. Use it for cutting filler in areas too small to accommodate the larger grater file.

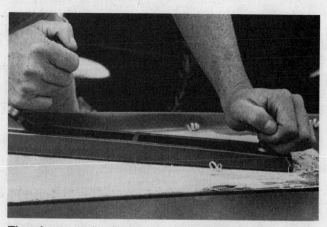

**The plane** will file filler to a smooth surface over relatively large, flat areas. It provides firm backing for sandpaper and is used after the filler has been filed with the cheese grater file.

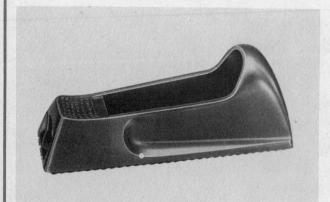

**The pocket plane** also provides firm backing for sandpaper when working filler surfaces after they have been filed with the grater file. While used very much like the plane, it is designed for smaller, flat surfaces where the plane will not fit.

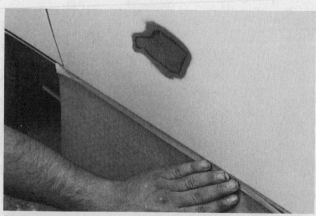

**This properly prepared body surface** is being masked for painting. The dent has been worked out, filled to the proper contour, and sanded, primed, glazed, and wet-sanded. It is now ready for final painting.

## Sanding blocks

To avoid oversanding the filler, you must learn to judge when the area being filled has reached the same contour as the surrounding metal surface. Filing or sanding after this point will destroy the correct contour of the filler area and result in an unsatisfactory job.

The most common problem encountered in sanding filler comes from pressing too hard. The metal surface bends under excessive pressure, then returns to its normal shape when the sanding is finished, leaving the filler area too low. Let the sandpaper do the work and don't press on it too heavily.

In hand sanding, use a block to obtain even pressure. For power sanding, it is important to hold the drill firmly and to press lightly at the proper angle.

**Use the sanding block** as backing for sandpaper. It allows you to maintain even pressure on a flat surface. Remember to tap it occasionally to knock off accumulated filler.

**"Seeing with the hands"** is a valuable skill in bodywork. Feeling the sanded area with your fingers often will reveal bumps and ridges that the eye cannot see.

## Electric drills

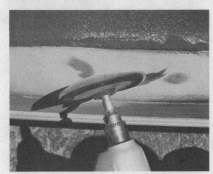

**The sander is touching the filler surface** at too great an angle. It will gouge and cut into the filler, leaving depressed areas.

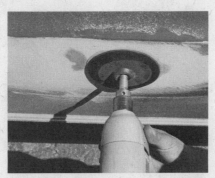

**This sander is positioned correctly—** not quite flat but touching the surface at approximately a five-degree angle. This puts as much grit surface as possible into contact with the filler.

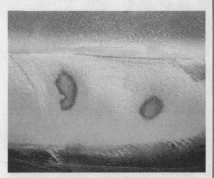

**An improperly held grinder** gouges depressions out of the filler because the grinder is at too steep an angle to the filler surface.

## Contour sanding

**Use the flexible sander** on curved surfaces where the sanding block will not do the job. This sander fits the paper to the contour of the work surface and allows for even sanding of the filler.

**Featheredging** means tapering the edges of the body filler surface so no line is visible between the worked area and the surrounding area. Do this by rolling the paper and going over the outer edges of the work area, especially in places where the sanding block would distort the surface.

Highs and lows are not always easy to spot. The flexible ruler makes an excellent tool for detecting peaks and valleys in filler. It conforms to the contour of the body surface, showing variations from this contour in the filler surface.

# Repairing a fender dent

The dent puller is used, often in combination with a hammer, to pull out the deepest portions of a dent or crease in areas where access to the back of the damaged area is limited. Be sure to work the dent puller carefully. You do not want to pull the metal too far out. Only far enough to return it to approximately its normal contour.

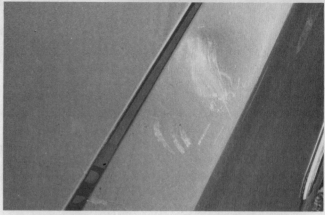

1 A heavy object landed on this fender and dented it. Where access to the back of the damage is limited, it's difficult to work with a hammer and dolly. In such cases, use a dent puller.

4 With the dent puller upright, slide the moving bar back until it hits the stop near the handle. Slowly pull up on the puller until you can see the metal barely move. Then tap lightly with a hammer all around the puller on the high spots surrounding the dent. Do this at least twice with each hole until the metal is within ⅛-inch of its original contour.

5 Now grind off the old paint using #80 grit paper or a #24 grit disc. Be sure to keep the paper flat against the surface of the repair area.

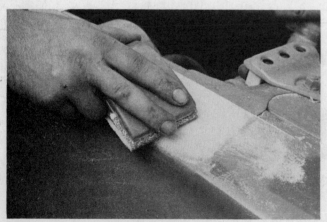

8 To knock down the remaining high spots, first sand with #40 grit paper and then with #80, feathering the edges as you go.

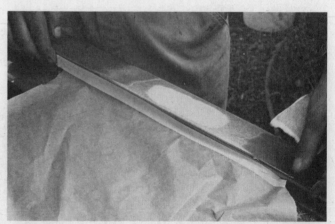

9 Open the hood. This prevents any overspray from getting on it. To avoid painting engine parts, mask them with tape and paper.

**2** Drill holes along the lowest points in the crease using a ⅛-inch bit. Before you make your first hole, be sure there's no electrical wiring on the underside of the fender.

**3** Push in and turn the dent puller clockwise until it bites into the metal. You will only need a couple of turns. The trick is to screw the puller in as little as possible while still making sure it will not slip out of the drill hole.

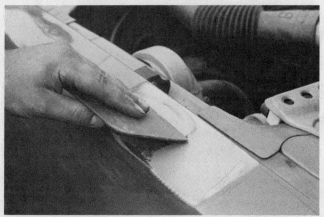

**6** Smooth plastic filler over the repair area. Press fairly hard with the spreader to get out any air bubbles that were produced during the mixing process.

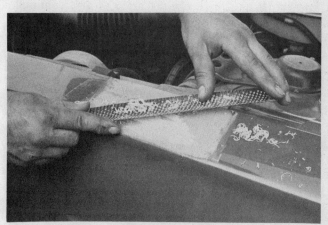

**7** Use a cheese grater file on the high spots in the filler. Again, pull the file toward you at a slight angle so it will cut the filler with maximum efficiency.

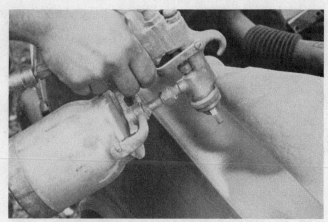

**10** Prime the filler. If you are using a compressor gun, it's a good idea to test the pressure and spray mix on a practice surface first.

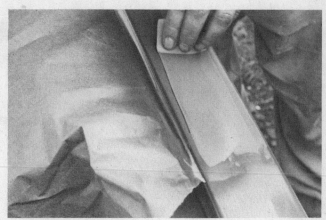

**11** When the primer has dried, dip a rubber squeegee lightly into glazing putty. Apply it in one smooth stroke. It dries very quickly, so if you have to make more than one pass, work as rapidly as you can. Cover all the primer area. Before priming again, wet-sand with #220 grit paper.

# All about dent pullers

The dent puller or slide hammer is a most useful tool for the auto body-worker. It has a long metal shaft on which a handle and a sliding weight are mounted. The weight moves up and down on the shaft, and there is a stop on the shaft near the handle. Either a screw or a hook attachment can be inserted in the tip.

When the puller has been inserted in the deepest portion of a dent or crease, slide the weight up to the stop, thereby exerting upward pressure on the metal. Avoid forcing the metal too far out. Begin pulling gently and gradually increase the force until you can just feel the metal move. Check the contour of the metal continuously to avoid damage caused by pulling too hard. Don't work the same hole too long. And don't point the handle directly at your face when pulling back on the weight. You can give yourself a nasty whack if the hook or screw comes loose.

**This dent puller** is attached to the front fender of the car by a self-tapping sheet metal screw. Note the sliding weight in the man's hand. This butts up against the stopper at the handle of the puller. The force of the blow pulls out the metal. Remember not to pull the metal out too far.

**The dent puller is often used** in combination with a body hammer. The metal is pulled out to approximately its correct contour and the surrounding high spots are tapped down.

**The dent puller has a screw attachment** which can be inserted in holes drilled along the deepest portions of a dent or crease. Screw it in only deeply enough so it will not slip out under pressure.

**The hook attachment** enables you to use the dent puller in holes larger than 1/8-inch or when the dent is right at the edge of a panel.

**When pulling dents,** the point of impact is generally the best place to start. The accident to this door caused stress lines in the door panel. Drill the holes about 1/2- to 3/4-inches apart or as needed along the deepest creases and begin pulling, following the direction of the impact (back to front in this case). Tap down the ridges as you pull. If you begin at the front edge, the metal will simply flop back and forth and not straighten itself correctly until the pressure causing the dent is relieved.

# Using spoons to repair dents

Body spoons are varied in shape and versatile in application. You can use certain ones as pry bars to force deformed or damaged metal back into place. Other spoons serve instead of dollies where you have limited space. Spoons can also be used in combination with a hammer or mallet. They have broad faces to distribute the force of the blow over a larger area than could be obtained by striking with the hammer directly.

Keep the surfaces of your spoons clean and highly polished. Any irregularities could be transferred to the surface of the metal you are working on, creating additional problems for you.

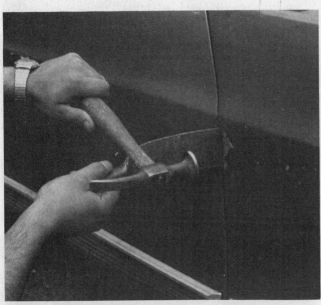

**Spoons can force damaged metal** back into place without disturbing or denting surrounding areas. Here a double-ended spoon is used with a body hammer to force back a dent in the front fender at the edge of the door panel.

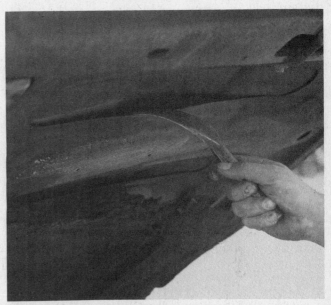

**Spoons are also used as pry bars** to eliminate irregularities in metal. Here a heavy-duty driving spoon is used to pry dented metal in the inside of a hood back into shape.

**Spoons may replace dolly blocks** as backup tools in areas where access is limited. This bodyworker is hammering out a dent with a spoon in place of a dolly and a mallet in the very limited area behind a door panel.

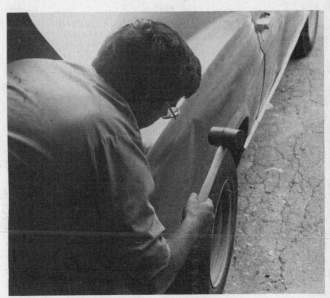

**Here is another example where a spoon** serves as a backup tool. A dent on the right rear fender is being hammered out with a mallet and spoon because it is too hard to place a dolly block behind the damage.

# Fixing a quarter panel dent

Professionals, with their years of experience and sophisticated tools, can handle jobs beyond the ability and equipment of the Saturday mechanic.

This '73 Buick had extensive left-side damage requiring a new quarter panel and fender skirt. This is not a job you could tackle on your own. Our pro first evaluated the repair job and arrived at the following steps:

1 Install a new panel.
2 Install a new fender skirt.
3 Straighten the door.
4 Replace the side molding.

The left-side rear door had suffered indirect damage which was repaired using the procedures outlined on page 73.

The pro got on the phone and ordered a new quarter panel. Then he removed the metal trim with a ratchet wrench. He also removed the left rear parking light, the rear bumper, and the rear quarter extensions.

The use of power cutting tools like the pneumatic chisel is one advantage the pro enjoys. This chisel makes it possible to cut panels away in far less time than it would take with metal shears. Welding, which this job required, is also a technique that should be undertaken only by a professional. It can be dangerous. It can also be done incorrectly.

## Some safety hints

When you are using portable power tools, common sense dictates certain safety precautions.

1 Check the tool for faulty wiring, broken switches, and improper grounding before you begin work.

2 Avoid using electric tools anywhere near flammable gases or vapors. It only takes one spark to set off an explosion.

3 When disconnecting an electric tool from the outlet, take hold of the plug, not the wire.

4 Always wear goggles when using power tools, and wear a face mask when grinding paint away.

5 Never operate electric tools with damp hands, and make sure the floor you're standing on is dry.

6 Be sure your extension cables are adequate to carry the load needed to operate the tool.

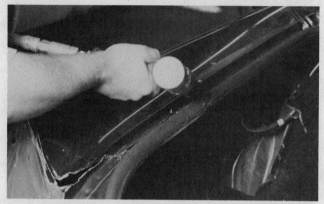

1 After completing the preliminary work, the pro used a pneumatic chisel to cut away the old quarter panel. He began near the vinyl and cut straight downward toward the fender skirt.

4 Fitting an oversized panel requires precise measurement and accurate and straight cutting. Our bodyworker held the panel up to the car once more to make sure the mark was correct. Then he used a pneumatic chisel to trim the panel.

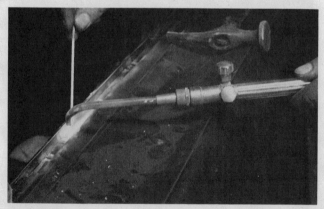

7 He tack brazed the new panel onto the body using an oxyacetylene torch and a flux-coated brazing rod.

2 Then our pro cut laterally above the fender skirt following the panel contour down the side of the panel and straight along the bottom. He pulled the carpet out of the inside of the trunk to avoid the possibility of fire when welding.

3 When the new panel arrived, the pro held it against the car to make sure it would fit perfectly. In this case, there was a slight overlap, and he had to trim the new panel before it could be welded into place.

5 Anchoring the new panel with double-jawed vise grips, the pro pop-riveted it in six places to hold it steady while he did the rest of the work. He first had to drill holes with a ⅛-inch drill bit.

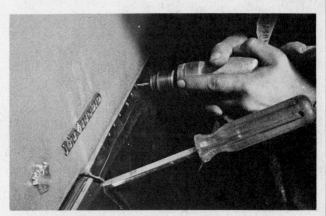

6 For stability, he popped in a rivet as soon as he had finished drilling each hole. The screwdriver wedged in the opening ensured that the panel was positioned to allow proper clearance for the rear door to open and close.

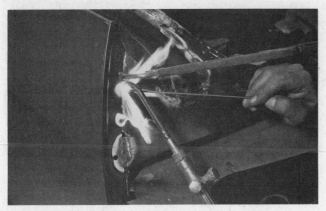

8 The pro continued to tack weld each of the joints shut. The bottom joint has just been welded together and tapped with the hammer to make the surface level.

9 Here is the finished job. The panel has been riveted and welded on and is ready to be wet-sanded and primed before painting. At this point, the trunk carpeting was replaced and the lid closed and checked for alignment with the panel.

# Pulling soft dents with a suction cup

Soft dents covering a wide area can be pulled out with suction cups. Damage of this type is often found on doors, roofs, and other wide, low-crowned panels.

To obtain maximum pulling force, wet the surface to be pulled before putting the suction cup in place. Tap high ridges and buckles with a mallet as you apply pulling force. This will relieve tension along the deepest part of the damaged area.

**1** Suction cups are perfect tools for dents covering large areas. This damage, believe it or not, is the result of someone sitting on the roof of the car.

**2** Some suction cups are fitted with a metal ring, allowing you to use a length of wood or pipe for greater leverage over a wider area.

**3** Dents remaining at the corners of the roof are repaired with a drill and a dent puller. Here the holes are drilled along the deepest points of the dents.

**4** A dent puller and body hammer are used to straighten out the dent. As upward pressure is maintained on the puller, surrounding high spots are tapped down with the hammer.

**5** Smaller dents without locking points can be pulled by using only a suction cup. While pulling, tap down the surrounding high spots with a mallet.

## Special tools: your feet

**1** This dent is accessible from the trunk, so you can use foot power to begin bringing the metal back to its original shape. This works only on straight-in damage and should not be tried on dents or creases resulting from impacts at either end.

**2** Look at the back of the panel and locate the highest spot on the inside. This is the lowest spot on the outside. Position your foot against the high spot and give it a good push. Then see how far the metal came out.

**3** The metal has recovered most of its original shape, although four dents remain. Drill along the deepest creases in each and use the dent puller. Then fill, file, sand, prime, and glaze before painting.

CHAPTER

# Rx FOR BODY RUST

If you are really serious about avoiding rust damage to your car, move to a pollution-free, rural area in the sunbelt. There, you will be able to avoid the two great causes of rust in automobiles—air pollutants and rock salt. Failing this, you will, very likely sooner than later, find rust spots on your car.

There are several approaches to the repair of rust damage. Generally, you will be able to make a decision on which to use only after grinding, for rust is usually more extensive than it looks. So grind it first, then repair.

For rusted-out areas up to the size of a 50-cent piece, use plastic filler, which is quick and easy to apply. Steel wool can be used as backing to give the repair extra strength. Grind an area four to five inches wide around the actual rust, for filler will adhere only to bare metal. Tap the center of the area to allow some depth for the filler.

For slightly larger areas of rust or cracks, use a small fiberglass repair kit. Follow the steps for surface preparation carefully. Otherwise the whole job might split and fall out.

When contours such as wheel housings are destroyed by rust, you can use fiberglass to reform the original line of the panel. Or, pop-rivet a piece of sheet metal over the damage if the contour is relatively straight.

Larger rusted areas are usually treated by welding or replacing the part. You can help prevent rust by applying undercoating.

The best time to take care of your car is when it is new. After just a few weeks you will find stone chips and nicks on a new paint job. There is a new urethane spray which can be put on by most pro shops. It not only gives a high gloss to your finish, but protects it against nicks, chips, water, and air pollutants.

# Job steps Repairing rust damage

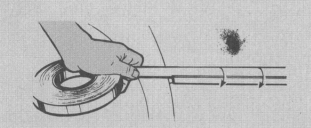

**1** Mask off nearby chrome and trim with a triple layer of tape so the grinder can't ruin it.

**2** Grind the paint down to bare metal, eliminating all rust around the hole. Smooth and featheredge with #40 grit paper.

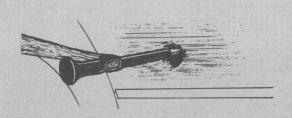

**3** Tap the perimeter of the hole with a pick to depress it no more than ⅛-inch below the contour.

**4** Fill small holes with plastic filler or stuff slightly larger ones with a wad of steel wool followed by filler.

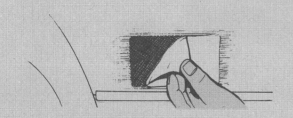

**or** Patch even larger areas with fiberglass.

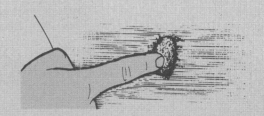

**or** Repair the panel with a pop-riveted metal patch. Fill around the edges and contour with plastic filler.

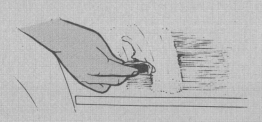

**5** Apply body filler firmly with a spreader.

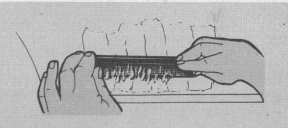

**6** Use a half-round cheese grater file before the filler hardens. You may have to repeat steps 5 and 6.

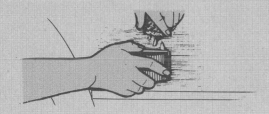

**7** Sand the plastic smooth after it has dried and featheredge with #220 grit paper.

**8** Spray four or five thin coats of primer on the front and back of the repair. Apply glazing putty and sand again with #320 paper.

# Patching a rusted-out hole with plastic filler

Rust can be tricky. Be careful when you examine what appears to be a superficial rust spot. The area of visible damage is almost certainly not the only place rusted. The rust often etches completely through the metal.

The proper procedure for dealing with this kind of problem is first to grind away the rusted surface. This means going beyond the area where the rust is visible. Remove the rusted metal and enlarge the hole by 50 percent or so to be sure you have good solid metal to work with. Also, grinding the area like this gives you a good idea of how extensive the rust is. You may have to change your repair method once you see how much damage actually exists.

After you grind the rusted area, fill the hole with steel wool for support, apply plastic body filler, and refinish.

1 Some rust that appears superficial at first glance may turn out to be more serious once you begin grinding. Here, what appeared to be a small rust spot turned out to be a hole.

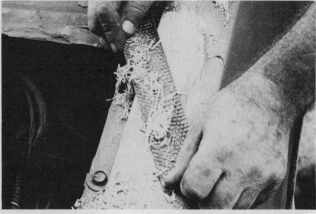

4 While the surface is still soft, knock down any high spots on the filler using a cheese grater file. Keep the file flat against the filler to avoid gouging and always pull the file toward you. Repeat steps 3 and 4 until there are no low spots in the filler after hardening.

5 Sand the filler with #40 grit paper in a sanding block. This smooths down any grooves left by the grater file. Replace the #40 grit paper with #80. Sand once more and then featheredge with #80 paper and finish with #220 grit.

## Preparing a rusted-hole surface for repair

1 Feel both sides of the rust spot to check the extent of the damage, but be careful. There may be sharp edges. Rust that works its way through the surface may spread out on the other side of the metal.

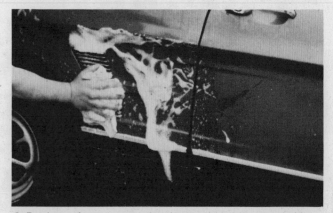

2 Begin surface preparation by washing the area with soap and water. Remove old grease and wax buildup with a chemical solvent, following the instructions on the container.

**2** Gently tap in and down any sharp pieces of ragged metal sticking up around the hole. Then tear off a small wad of plain steel wool and insert it snugly into the hole. Tuck in any strands of steel wool that may be hanging loose.

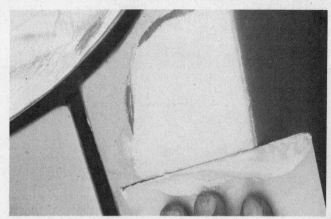

**3** Thoroughly mix the plastic body filler with the hardener. Then, working quickly, apply the filler to the repair area with a spreader. Press down firmly to work out any air bubbles.

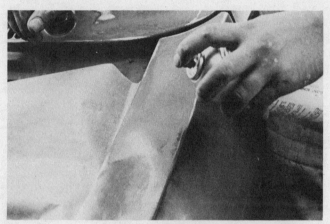

**6** To prevent any overspray from getting on the hood, open it and then lay down a sheet of masking paper to protect the engine. Prime the repair area using very short, light strokes, covering the filler a little at a time. Trying to get it on all at once only makes the primer thick and runny, and it takes a long time to dry.

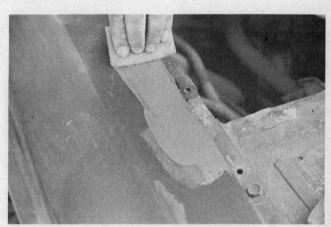

**7** Smooth on the glazing putty. Press fairly hard with the squeegee, making only one pass with each stroke and overlapping the previous one slightly.

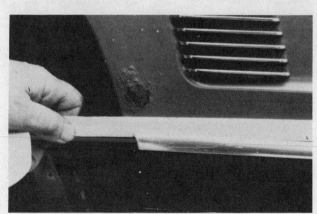

**3** Remove all trim near the rust spot or mask it. Slide tape between the trim and the car body with the sticky side facing you, then fold it over the trim.

**8** Using #320 grit paper in a sanding block, wet-sand the whole repair area until all the edges are smooth. If you dip a sponge in water and hold it above the block, you will have a constant supply of water. Keep checking for smoothness. Clean the area of putty sludge, dry thoroughly, prime, and prepare for painting.

# How to use lay-on fiberglass patches

When rust is advanced, a fiberglass lay-on patch may save you from having to replace the entire body part. Here's a case where a do-it-yourselfer tried to halt the rust with paint. It didn't work, because an enamel "hobby paint" was used without proper surface preparation. But even an acrylic paint, combined with the best preparation and finishing, won't stop a case of creeping rust, especially if it's moving into an area like this one. However, a lay-on patch, properly applied, could save this panel. Be sure to mask all trim, upholstery, and adjacent panels before doing the patch.

1 When rust creeps up to or very near the window track, remove it to give you access to all the rust.

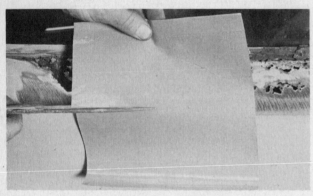

3 Cut a patch to the size of the repair area, allowing at least two inches of extra material.

4 Peel off the bottom blue paper liner from the patching material and place the patch on the repair area with the sticky side down.

6 The patch is cured when the material is stiff and the clear top sheet separates easily. Sand with a medium grit paper (#80). Mix and apply body filler according to directions. Spread it over the patch, especially on any low spots, and the surrounding area. Allow it to dry and file.

7 Sand and shape to the desired contour after the filler has hardened and has been filed. Use a medium grit and then a finer paper. Further coats of filler may be necessary.

2 Grind the rust down to the bare metal two to three inches around the repair area, using a #24 grit disc. Be sure to remove all the rust. Body patches will not adhere well to anything but clean, bare metal. Attach a wire brush to the drill for deep or problem edges, then gently tap in the edges of the entire repair area.

5 Press firmly to smooth any wrinkles. Moisten your fingers to shape the patch. Place the patches side-by-side. If necessary, remove the top clear liner to get a better fit. To cure, place outside in direct sunlight. If you must work indoors, use a heat lamp. Check page 149 for fiberglass curing times.

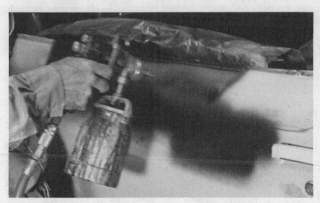

8 Prime with several very thin coats rather than one thick one. Let the primer dry, then sand it with #400 wet paper just prior to painting. Be sure to mask the trim and upholstery.

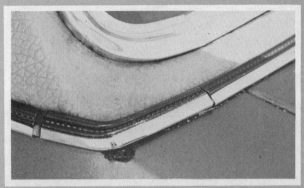

1 Chrome molding strips bordering vinyl roofs are perfect places for water to get trapped as it runs off the car's roof. This is one place you should watch diligently and treat at the very first signs of rust.

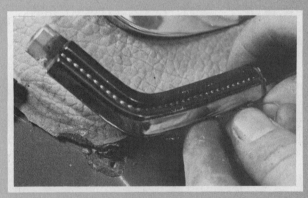

2 Remove the corner molding strip by prying it out, then peel back the vinyl. In most cases, you will find that the rust has spread under the vinyl.

3 Using the wire brush attachment on your drill, clean away the rust. Then fill, sand, prime, and glaze. Finish up by regluing the vinyl and replacing the molding strip. It is a good idea to wear goggles during a job like this because the drill can easily cause particles of rust to fly up and into your eyes.

# Pop riveting for stronger repairs

This Chevy Nova has extensive rust along the bottom of the quarter panel. With the metal weakened this much, you cannot use plastic filler. You have two options: either take it to a pro, who will remove the old panel and weld on a new one—or you can do a quick pop riveting job. You'll find aluminum easiest to work with if this is your first try at pop riveting, but remember that aluminum requires a zinc chromate primer.

1 Grind the top edge of the rusted section with a #24 grit disc. Grind away the rust area and up onto solid metal. Here the metal is firm and will give you a good surface to work with. Make sure this area is clean and free from paint and dirt so you will have a solid base for your filler (plastic) and paint to adhere to.

4 Hang the metal in the middle of the area you ground. Drill and rivet the panel at each of the top corners first. This will hold the piece in place while you bend it.

5 Pull the metal taut and bend it under the panel. Make sure it is just where you want it before bending. Wrap it well under the panel and press it against the back side.

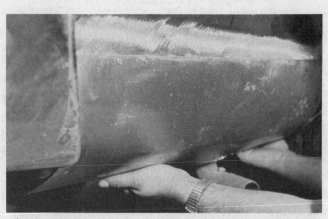

8 File the filler, by pulling a half-round cheese grater file toward you. You may want to change the angle of the grater once or twice as you go over the plastic so it knocks off all the high spots. Repeat steps 7 and 8 if necessary until the repaired area is level with the rest of the panel.

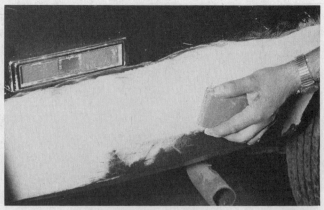

9 Sand the area with #40 grit paper in a sanding block. Finish with #80 grit, featheredging as you go.

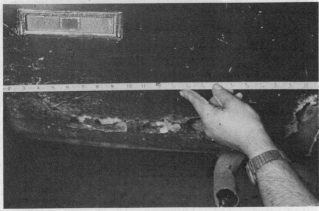

**2** Measure the length and width of the rusted area. Then get a sheet of ordinary aluminum siding such as you would use on a house.

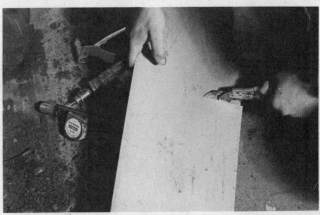

**3** Ordinary metal shears will cut aluminum easily. You could use regular sheet metal for this job, but it is less flexible. If you use aluminum, remember the special primer.

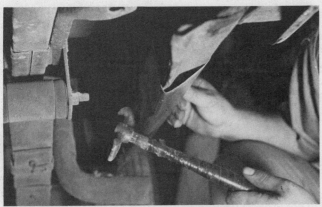

**6** Hammer each side of the metal so it conforms exactly to the shape of the quarter panel. Then, reaching behind the panel, drill and rivet these two corners as well. Jack the car up for this and be sure to use jack stands. Then rivet at ¾-inch intervals around the entire panel and tap down the rivet area where the filler is to be applied.

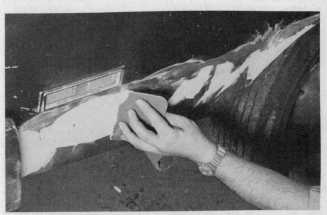

**7** Mix and apply plastic filler over the metal patch. Dab it along the top and sides where the patch meets the panel. Make several passes over the area to cover the entire repair.

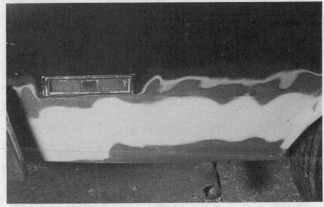

**10** The panel should look like this before you proceed. Notice there are no dark spots indicating lows in the filler, and the edges of the repair have been neatly featheredged. You can also spray undercoating on the back of the panel, but first use a wire brush to get all the dirt off. Inspect the panel carefully before applying the undercoating.

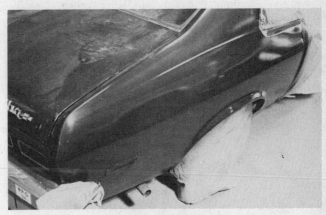

**11** Prime the area, glaze, wet-sand with #220 grit paper, prime again, then wet-sand with #400 grit paper. If painting involves a larger portion of the panel, prepare the metal with a degreaser and dewaxer. Then wet-sand, prime, and paint.

## Pop riveting step-by-step

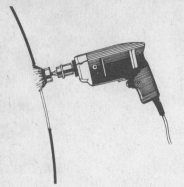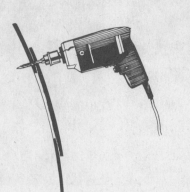

The pop riveting technique is useful not only for very large areas, but also for smaller holes where a repair stronger than the usual patch-and-putty is desired. Here are the procedures for repairing relatively minor body rot.

1. Put on your safety goggles. Then remove the rust with your electric drill and either a wire brush or a #24 grit grinding disc attachment. Continue grinding down to the bare metal on the solid surface surrounding the rust area. For good measure, clear an area four inches wide all around. 2. Cut the replacement sheet metal to size using metal shears. The patch should be large enough to cover the hole and extend over the solid area about one inch. Hold the patch in place over the hole with locking pliers if possible, or by hand if necessary. Begin drilling at the top of the patch, about ½-inch from the edge, using a drill bit of the same diameter as the rivets. 3. Place the rivet in the hole and fasten it. Repeat the drilling procedure at the bottom of the patch and rivet as before. Continue the drill-and-rivet sequence until the rivets are one-inch apart around the entire circumference of the patch. 4. Use a bumping hammer and carefully depress the edges of the patch about ⅛-inch below the body level. Fill and refinish the patched area as you would any surface damage (see Chapter 4).

# Fixing a grille with rivets

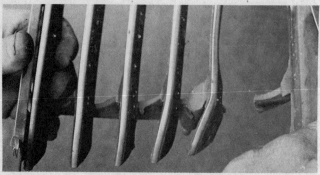

1 On older cars with white metal grills, corrosion can frequently cause breakage. Pop riveting is a method of rejoining metal that has corroded or has just plain snapped.

2 Measure a strip of metal like the one you want to replace. Then cut a piece of sheet metal or aluminum with metal shears to fit.

3 Brace the replacement strip against the old metal with a vise grip as close as possible to the area you plan to drill. You will probably have to move the grips around to get a satisfactory angle.

4 Once the vise grips are in place, drill a hole through the old and new metal with a drill bit of the same size as the rivet you plan to use. A relatively small rivet will do the job here and remain well hidden. To spruce up afterwards, you can wire brush the entire grille and spray on aluminum paint.

# Patching with a brazing torch

Brazing consists of joining two metals together with bronze, an alloy of copper. The base metal is not melted as it is in welding. The patch is held on by the adhesion of the brazing alloy. Brazing does not give the same strength as welding since it is actually a form of soldering. Pros never use brazing in situations calling for welded strength.

In this case, the muffler of an old van had rusted through. Rather than go to the cost of replacing it, the owner took it to a pro who brazed a patch over the damaged area. The patch was made on the tail pipe section of the muffler. If it had been on the engine pipe side, brazing would not have been advisable because the heat there is too high for a brazed patch to work.

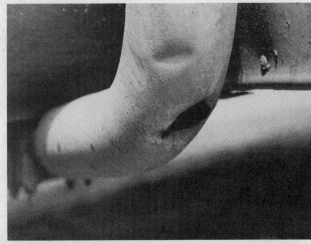

1 This muffler on an old van was rusted through. Our pro quickly and economically repairs it by brazing.

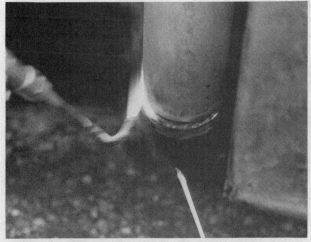

2 He cuts a piece of sheet metal to fit the hole. Before heating the area, he makes sure the engine is off and there is no gasoline nearby. Now he sets the controls about the same as for welding, according to the size of the tip. Our pro heats the area until it turns a dull red. Then he adds the bronze rod.

3 Holding the patch in place with a clamp, our pro continues brazing with the torch and rod until there is an even bead all around. In this case, it is not necessary to cool the metal off as he goes. He taps the edges of the repair with a body hammer to improve the seal.

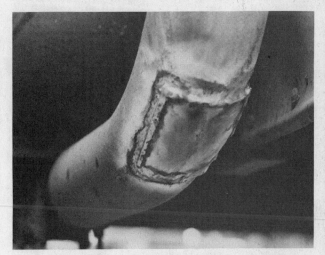

4 Here is the finished job. When choosing sheet metal for brazing, pros try to pick metal that will match the thickness of the metal they are patching.

# Welding a rusted-out quarter panel

Repairing a damaged area immediately is a good way to save yourself time and money. This panel suffered a dent and tear, but the owner neglected them. When he finally got around to having the repair done, rust had gotten into the exposed metal and etched out additional holes.

The professional method of making this repair involves grinding away the paint and all the rusted metal from the damaged area and welding the hole before refinishing. The welding is done with a filler rod that adds additional metal to fill up the hole, preventing any further cracking.

The pro must manipulate the torch and the filler rod at the same time. As the hole widens, he adds the filler rod more rapidly. He may have to add metal to the repair several times to fill all the spaces.

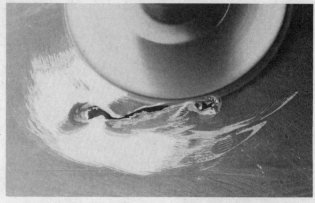

**1** The pro grinds away all the paint and metal where rust is visible, and a couple of inches beyond. This ensures that he is working on uncorroded metal.

**4** The oxygen ($O_2$) tank is larger and green. Its gauge is set according to the size of the tip. When welding, a bucket of water is always kept handy in case of fire.

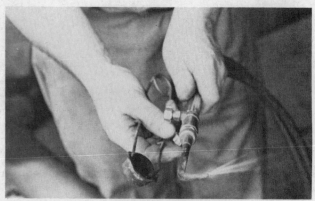

**5** Before lighting the torch, the pro puts on welding goggles to protect his eyes from the glare. Then he opens up the acetylene tank and lights the torch. The acetylene is adjusted until the flame loses its black soot and burns yellow. Gradually the $O_2$ is opened up and adjusted until the flame burns blue with about a 3/16-inch inner core.

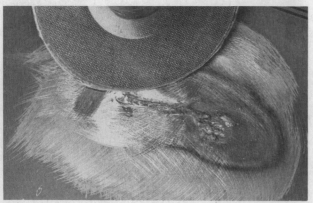

**8** The pro grinds and wire brushes the repair after welding. Failure to prepare the surface in this way will make it impossible to use plastic filler. It simply will not adhere.

**9** The pro mixes and applies plastic filler to the repair area with a spreader. Then he files the filler with a cheese grater file and sands it, first with #40 grit paper and then with #80 grit.

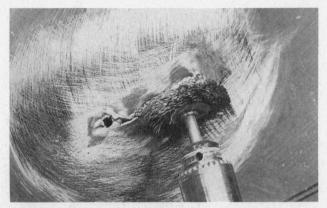

**2** The hole is wire brushed, making sure all the rusted metal in and around it has been removed. The wire brush removes paint and rust from areas like holes and tears which the grinder disc cannot reach.

**3** Our pro prepares the oxygen regulator for welding. The oxygen is always in the larger or green tank. The gauge should be set according to the size of the tip.

**6** The metal in the damaged area is heated until it flows. The pro holds the filler rod and the torch at approximately the same angle. As the rod reaches the melting point, he dips it into the puddle of molten metal, puddling the base metal and the filler rod together, filling in the section and welding the hole closed.

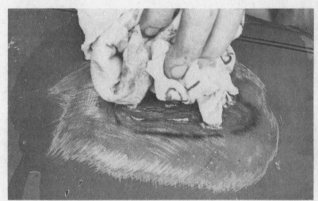

**7** Heating has caused the metal to expand and swell. The pro taps the metal down with a hammer and dolly, then cools it off by adding cold water to the area with a soaked rag.

## Safety tips from the pros

Tanks for oxyacetylene welding must be equipped with check valves. These are one-way valves allowing the gas to flow only away from the tanks. This prevents any fire that might occur in the hose from working its way back into the tank.

And pros never do oxyacetylene welding near flammable materials such as oily rags, paint or fuel. They always wear protective goggles when welding. Otherwise permanent eye damage could result. Finally, they always use the lighter provided to ignite the torch, never matches or other sources of flame.

**10** He primes the surface and glazes it with spot putty using a squeegee. After the glaze has dried, he wetsands the area with #200 grit paper, featheredging the repair before the final priming and painting.

# Rust prevention

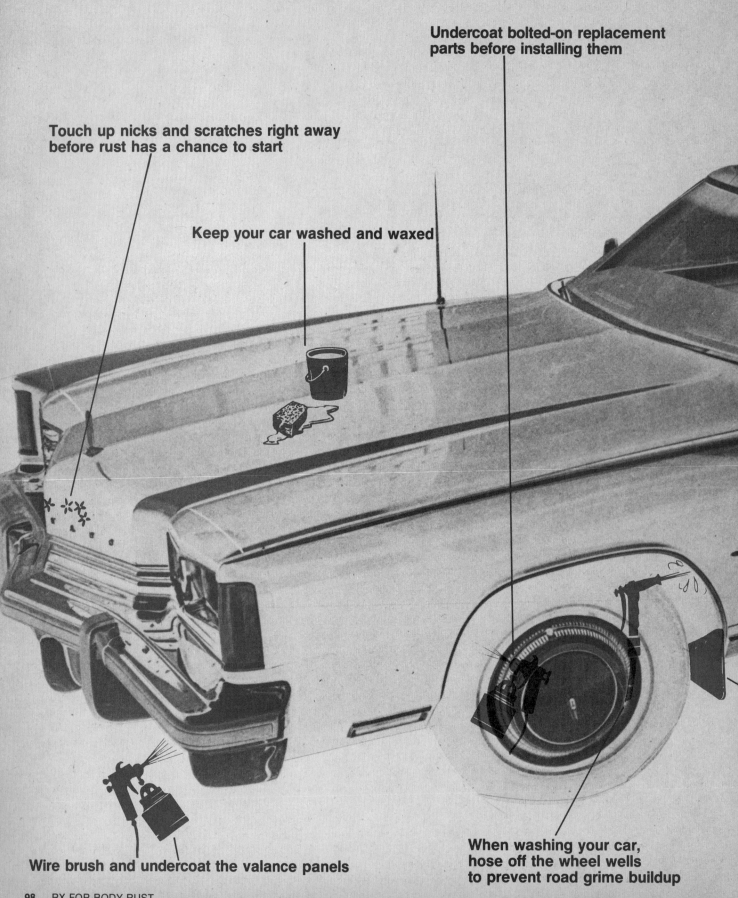

Touch up nicks and scratches right away before rust has a chance to start

Undercoat bolted-on replacement parts before installing them

Keep your car washed and waxed

Wire brush and undercoat the valance panels

When washing your car, hose off the wheel wells to prevent road grime buildup

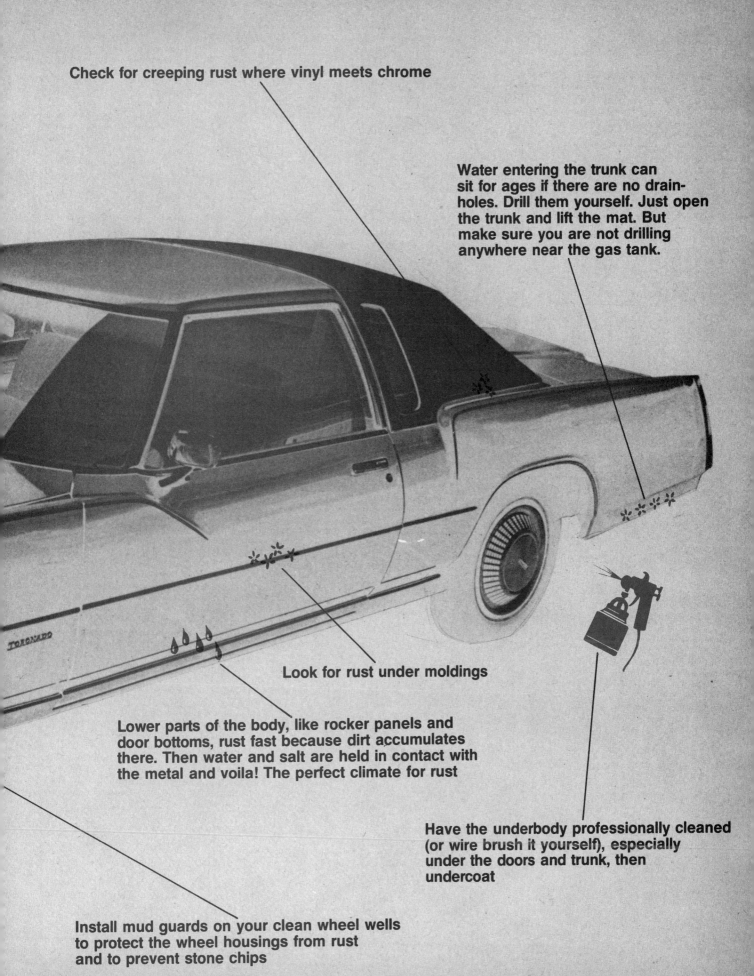

Check for creeping rust where vinyl meets chrome

Water entering the trunk can sit for ages if there are no drain-holes. Drill them yourself. Just open the trunk and lift the mat. But make sure you are not drilling anywhere near the gas tank.

Look for rust under moldings

Lower parts of the body, like rocker panels and door bottoms, rust fast because dirt accumulates there. Then water and salt are held in contact with the metal and voila! The perfect climate for rust

Have the underbody professionally cleaned (or wire brush it yourself), especially under the doors and trunk, then undercoat

Install mud guards on your clean wheel wells to protect the wheel housings from rust and to prevent stone chips

# Do-it-yourself undercoating

Undercoat prevents rust on fenders, quarter panels, deck lids, in fact any place where rust can get a start. Undercoat comes in spray cans and in buckets, for which you will need a brush. The spray is better because it gets into tiny cracks where rust is likely to begin.

The best time to undercoat is when the car is clean and new. The most important areas to cover are the lower rear of fenders; the front peak over the headlights; quarter panels behind the fender skirt (or quarter panel housing), especially behind the wheel; inside the door along the bottom of the panel; and the air scoops.

To spray inside the quarter panel, take out the carpet inside the trunk and the cardboard guard. Make sure the well and floor of the trunk next to the quarter panel are free of water. If water is found, drill two holes in the bottom and let it drain out. But don't drill near the gas tank. Most manufacturers do not provide drainage for water in the quarter panels, so it is a good idea to make drain holes if they do not exist.

On front fenders, the back of the wheel housing behind the tire is particularly susceptible to rust. Wire brush that area well and undercoat it.

**1** Apply undercoating behind the wheels at the back of the fender. Undercoating works best on clean, new cars. Never apply undercoating over dirt.

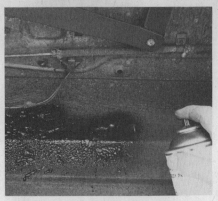

**2** Apply undercoating to the inside of a door along the bottom of the door panel. Undercoating also serves to deaden sound.

**3** Clean out all dirt and leaves under the front fenders. Straighten out a coat hanger and open the door to scrape out dirt or leaves from the inside and bottom of the fenders.

**4** Apply undercoating on and behind the fender. To reach the peak over the headlights, open the hood and squirt from there if you have access. If not, remove the headlight.

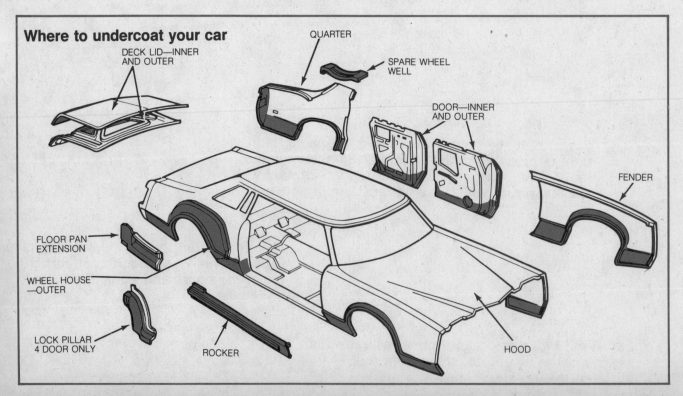

## Where to undercoat your car

DECK LID—INNER AND OUTER

QUARTER

SPARE WHEEL WELL

DOOR—INNER AND OUTER

FENDER

FLOOR PAN EXTENSION

WHEEL HOUSE —OUTER

LOCK PILLAR 4 DOOR ONLY

ROCKER

HOOD

CHAPTER 7

# FRONT END REPAIRS

Front end damage usually means major repair work. So the first thing for you to do is determine the extent of the work—and whether it will involve repair, replacement or a visit to a pro.

If your car has a unitized body and gets hit straight on at the bumper, grille or radiator support, you probably have frame damage. You should check for this first, since only a pro can repair such damage. On a conventional chassis, almost all the components can sustain damage without necessarily harming the frame.

A good preliminary check for frame damage is to look for buckled sheet metal away from the area of impact and wrinkles, shiny spots, and scrapes on the frame. Then see whether one side looks any different from the other. If the impact was above the bumper, chances are more parts were damaged than in an under-bumper bash, but frame straightening probably won't be needed. See the tips for evaluating frame damage in used cars in Chapter 1. Make your initial evaluation as complete as possible. Look beyond the obvious evidence of direct-impact damage for more remote, indirect damage.

Grilles, fender extensions, and header panels are particularly vulnerable to crunches. For economy's sake, visit a salvage yard to get these and any other parts you need. However, if the nearest yard is at a great distance, it might be less costly for you simply to buy a new part.

Confine repairs to the kind of damage you can handle—alignment, replacing parts, pulling dents, straightening buckles, fixing trim, and so on. The question of how far to go in repairing the front end often comes up. If there is extensive damage to the grille, fenders, bumper, lights, radiator, air conditioning condenser, and radiator support, for example, consider replacing the entire nose. The following two pages show you the anatomy of a front-end clip.

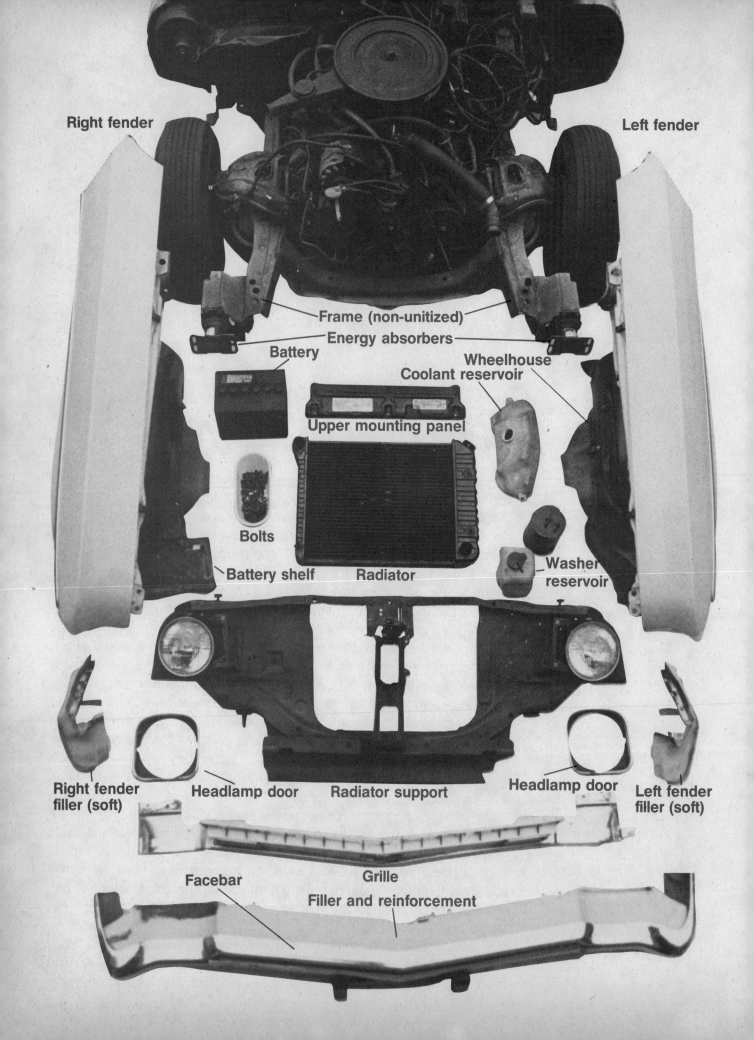

# Job steps Removing a front end piece-by-piece

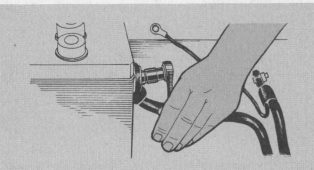

**1** Remove the battery. Disconnect the ground cable. Lift it out carefully to prevent spilling acid.

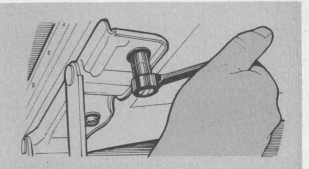

**2** Have someone support the hood. Then use a ⅜-inch-drive ratchet wrench to remove the bolts connecting the hinges to the hood.

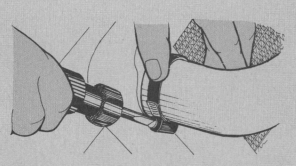

**3** Drain the radiator. Remove the hoses and the transmission cooler lines. Then remove the radiator and other retaining hardware.

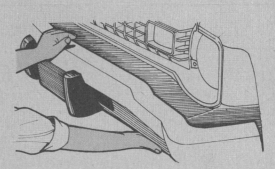

**4** Place a support under the front bumper. Then loosen the bolts to disconnect the bumper from the energy absorbers.

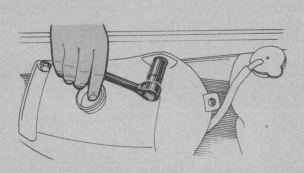

**5** Remove all wire connectors and liquid containers from the fender inner panels.

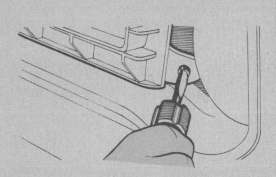

**6** Remove the grille, using a ¼-inch-drive ratchet wrench and a Phillips-head screwdriver.

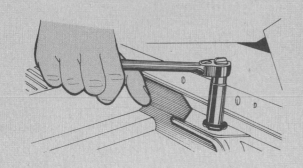

**7** Remove the bolts holding the front fenders to the cowl, inner panel, and radiator support.

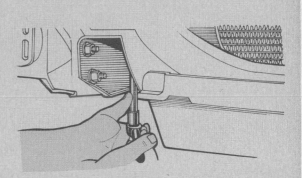

**8** Remove the radiator support by unbolting it from the frame on both sides.

# Bumpers: the first to be hit

First to be hit, the bumper is usually the last to be installed after other repairs are made. Since the bumper is attached to the frame and/or underbody rails, it's a good idea to check the frame for damage if the bumper is hit. If the frame is not in proper alignment, you will not be able to install the bumper properly. Have a pro fix the frame damage, if any. Then you can put on the new or used bumper.

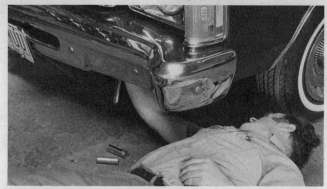

**1** To remove the bumper, locate the four nuts on either side holding it to the energy absorber. Of each set, remove three and loosen the fourth.

**4** To reinstall a bumper, get all the help you can to brace it in position while you tighten the bolts finger tight. Check the alignment before final tightening. If it is out of alignment, prop it up to the correct height and tighten again.

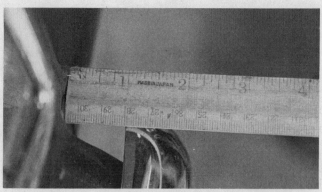

**5** Measure the distance between the bumper and the fender on both sides. If uneven, loosen the bolts and move the bumper left or right to make the distances the same. If no more adjustment is needed, bend the bumper back with a block of wood and a hammer, taking care not to mar the chrome.

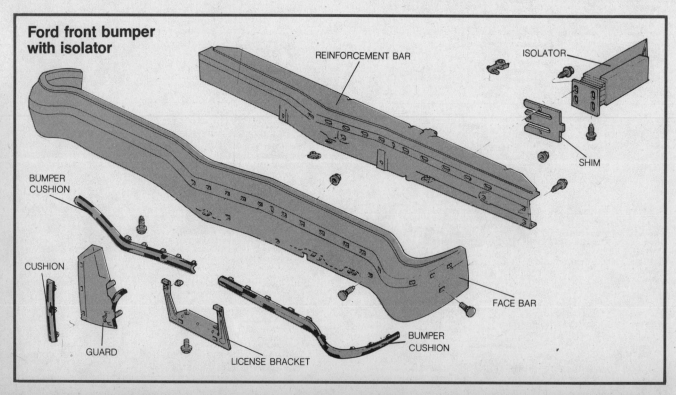

**Ford front bumper with isolator**

REINFORCEMENT BAR

ISOLATOR

SHIM

BUMPER CUSHION

CUSHION

GUARD

LICENSE BRACKET

FACE BAR

BUMPER CUSHION

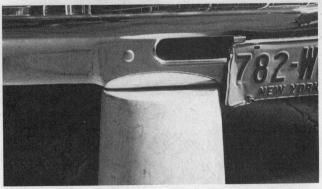

**2** Get somebody to help you remove the final two nuts and the bumper itself. Prop the bumper up with a large bucket or milk crate for extra protection.

**3** There are two methods for removing the bumper. The one illustrated here is recommended. The other calls for removing the entire energy absorber from the frame and involves an extremely heavy and bulky unit and tricky adjustments for reinstallation.

**6** Sometimes it is necessary to place shims between the energy absorber and the bumper to correct alignment.

## Spot welds: mostly for the pros

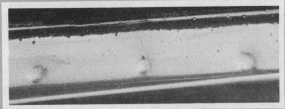

Although not common, a few European cars have fenders like this one. Don't try to replace them. They are welded onto the car. Unless you have the equipment and can weld, leave it to a pro. This method is a time-saver for the factory but makes it harder to replace individual front end components. If your spot-welded car has been damaged, the fender will have to be cut off before a new one can be put on. Leave it to a pro.

## GM front bumper with energy absorber

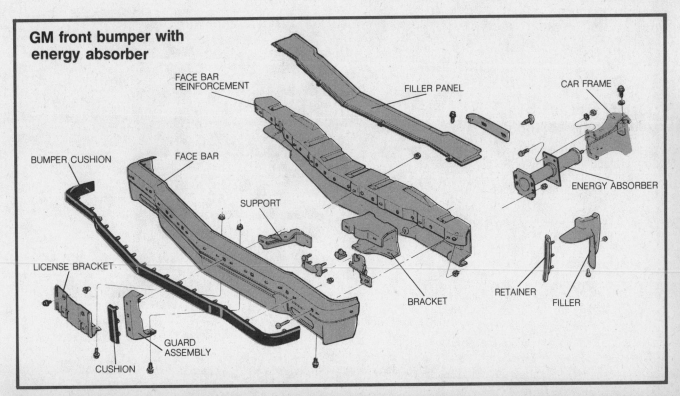

FACE BAR REINFORCEMENT

FILLER PANEL

CAR FRAME

BUMPER CUSHION

FACE BAR

SUPPORT

ENERGY ABSORBER

LICENSE BRACKET

BRACKET

RETAINER

FILLER

GUARD ASSEMBLY

CUSHION

# Know your energy absorbers

The most common type of energy absorber is designed on the principle of the shock absorber. There is another type called an isolator, which consists of rubber bonded to metal and which works much as a motor mount does to absorb impact. Both are located between the bumper and the frame.

The shock-type absorber should be treated with respect. It is, in effect, a miniature pressure vessel consisting of a piston tube and a cylinder tube. The piston tube assembly is filled with an inert gas under pressure. The cylinder tube assembly is filled with a hydraulic fluid. The gas pressure in the piston tube maintains the unit in an extended position. Upon impact, the hydraulic fluid in the cylinder tube is forced into the piston tube through an orifice. The controlled passage of the fluid provides the energy absorbing action. The hydraulic fluid forced from the cylinder tube into the piston tube displaces the floating piston, compressing the gas behind it. After impact, the pressure of the compressed gas behind the floating piston forces the fluid back into the cylinder tube assembly, extending the unit to its normal position.

The isolator, which you'll find on Ford cars, is a rubber-and-metal sandwich. When the bumper is struck, it moves away from the impact, stretching the rubber portion of the isolator. On the rebound, the rubber returns the bumper to its normal position, unless the blow was so severe that it ripped the rubber from its metal base. The safety tips below do not apply to this type of absorber.

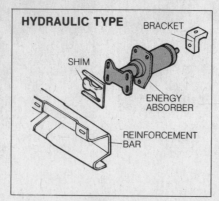

**HYDRAULIC TYPE**

**In the hydraulic-type energy absorber,** the pressure of inert gas in the piston tube keeps the unit extended. Upon impact, the hydraulic fluid in the cylinder tube is forced into the piston tube, absorbing the energy of the blow.

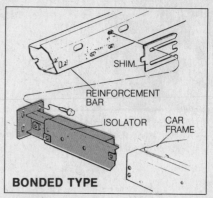

**BONDED TYPE**

**The isolator** works like a motor mount. When the bumper is hit, the metal recoils, stretching the rubber bonded to it and absorbing the impact. The rubber then returns to its original position on the rebound.

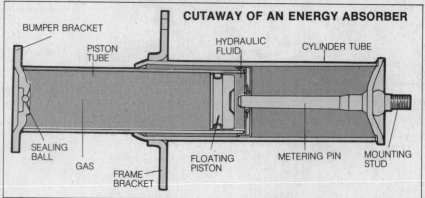

**CUTAWAY OF AN ENERGY ABSORBER**

## Safety precautions: shock-type absorbers

Warning: Heed the following rules when handling energy absorbing devices or personal injury may result.
1 Do not apply heat to such a unit.
2 Do not attempt to repair one. Always replace it with a new unit.
3 If an energy absorber is bound up as a result of a collision and will not extend, take precautions to avoid spring-back.
4 If the unit is to be scrapped, relieve the gas pressure prior to disposal. Make an indentation with a center punch in the small cylinder of the absorber. Then drill a hole in the cylinder wall.
Be safe! Protect your eyes and wear approved safety glasses when handling energy absorbers.

**Bumper shocks** perform on the principle of wheel shock absorbers—with a compression cylinder. The cylinder on the shock at the left has been pushed into its housing. It has to be replaced. Before throwing it away, drill a hole to let the pressure out. Under no circumstances should you leave it near heat or throw it into a fire.

# Removing a grille

You will find this one of the simplest bodywork jobs to tackle. Grills are made of molded plastic or metal held on by screws or speednuts. Screw-on grilles are accessible from the front. If held on by speednuts, they are accessible from the rear. You may find that the grille you are working on is held in place by a spring set-up, allowing it to move back under impact. Such a grille may remain back because the springs fail to work. Grilles come in many types and with many peculiarities, and removal and replacement steps vary. So examine your grille before you begin working on it.

**1** Remove the bolts and gently lift off the damaged grille. The bolts may be rusted on. If so, use one of the methods described on page 52 to get them off.

**2** A hacksaw is your best friend if a bolt breaks off as you're removing it. Saw straight across the top of the bolt, cutting a slot, then spray on some lubricating oil.

**3** Remove the bolt stub, using a screwdriver.

**4** The old emblem can be removed easily with a socket wrench once you've got the grille off. If you want to put your existing emblem on the replacement grille, this is the time to do it.

**5** Fit the replacement grille on, tilting it from the top so you can slide the bolts into the bottom holes first, then work your way up until the top bolt is in place.

# Removing a fender

After careful evaluation, you may find that the time and effort needed to repair various dents, dings, scratches or rust in your car's fender make replacement a sensible alternative. At first, removing a fender may seem a big, scary job. In fact, it's quite easy. The major problems you are likely to encounter have to do with bolts: 1) The bolts are too rusty to remove easily (see page 52), and 2) once you get them off, you lose them. If you can handle these problems, there are only two simple rules to follow. Remove the battery connections if the headlights are involved and unbolt from the bottom up.

**1** Use a ratchet wrench to take out the single bolt most cars have at the bottom in the cowl panel. Then remove the one or two bolts you may find on the cowl side panel when you open the door. Now unbolt the valance-panel and grille-panel bolts.

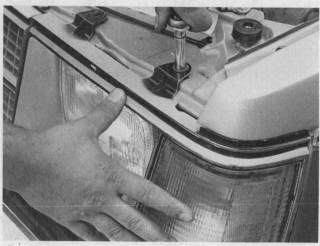

**2** Unbolt the light housing. CAUTION: Disconnect the battery and unplug the wires first.

**3** Remove the bolts along the bottom edge of the fender, which is now beginning to come loose.

**4** Now unbolt the fender across the top. If you don't wait to do this step last, the fender could shift, making removal of the lower bolts difficult. It might also fall on your foot.

**5** Remove the fender. This is a unitized body, so the substructure is welded together to form one piece. On some cars, you must remove the bumper.

# Aligning hoods

The hood panel is very likely to go out of alignment in a front end collision, so it is one of the first things to check. If misaligned, repairs should be made slowly and carefully. Repeat basic steps if necessary. Study this sequence with particular attention to the fine adjustment involved in each step. Remove the hood locking mechanism so it doesn't close when you put the hood down to check the alignment.

**1** This hood has moved out of alignment to the right. If the rest of the car is straight, you can assume the hinges are bent or the hood has buckled.

**2** Make vertical adjustments at the rear of the hood by loosening the bolts on the hinge and moving it up or down as necessary. Then tighten the bolts, closing the hood after each adjustment to see how close you are to proper adjustment. Scribe a line on the hinge and inner panel as a guide to see how much you are moving the hinge each time.

**3** Horizontal alignment is also a ratchet wrench job. Again, go slowly, adjusting a little at a time and closing the hood after each side-to-side adjustment.

**4** Insert a 2 x 4 and pry very gently toward the opposite side if earlier adjustment efforts have failed. Chances are your hinges are bent. Use wood to pry with; metal could dent the hood. Raise and lower the hood after each adjustment to check the alignment.

**5** Once the hood is aligned, adjust the lock and striker to their proper positions. Loosen the bolts and move the assembly slightly from side-to-side or back-and-forth until it is correctly aligned. Don't slam the hood down until it fits perfectly.

**6** If the hinge is still not straight, replace it. To change a hood hinge, remove the hood, install the new hinge, replace the hood, and start the alignment process again.

To loosen sticky hinges, apply any commonly available metal lubricating oil. Then push the hood up and down several times to distribute the oil.

# Removing the front end as a unit

Here's a job that isn't as tough as it looks. It requires no special tools. You can do it with wrenches and screwdrivers, a floor jack to get the car off the ground, a cautious approach to many of the procedures, and two good friends to help you lift the nose assembly off and replace it when your repair work is done. Keep the parts together (as shown on page 102), so you can easily reverse the job steps for re-assembly.

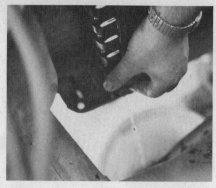

**1** Place a floor jack under the front cross member and chock the rear wheels. Jack up the car just enough to clear the wheels. Then, using jack stands for support, remove the wheels.

**2** Place a pail underneath the radiator drain cock and unscrew the radiator cap to allow air to enter. Then open the drain cock and drain the water or antifreeze out of the cooling system.

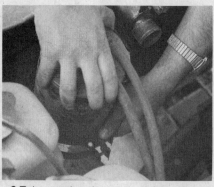

**6** Take out the charcoal canister if your car has one. To do this, remove the two clamps at the top. You can leave the top hoses connected to the canister.

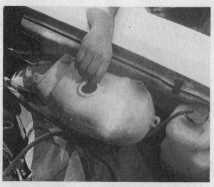

**7** Remove the antifreeze reservoir and the windshield washer reservoir. Disconnect the hoses running from the reservoir and the main electric connector at the firewall, if your car is so equipped. If not, all electrical equipment will have to be disconnected separately.

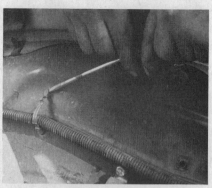

**8** Pry off the plastic clips on the wheel housing with a screwdriver. These clips hold all the hoses and wiring for the electrical circuits, so you are now ready to remove the headlight connectors.

**12** Hold the bumper firmly in the center. Have a friend unscrew the loosened bolts and pull the bumper forward.

**13** Unfasten the bolts connecting the radiator support to the frame. You'll find them on each frame side rail. You may find shims, spacers or washers between the support and the frame. As you remove them, make a note of their positions.

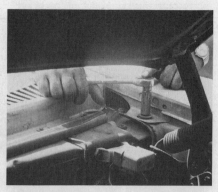

**14** Remove the fender-to-body bolts. There are usually two on each side at the rear of the hood as well as a connection to the body at the bottom of the fender. On some model cars, the hood will have to be removed from the hinges at this point.

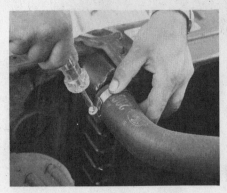  

**3** After all the fluid has drained, remove the radiator hoses by unscrewing the hose clamps. You'll find two— one on top, one on the bottom. You may have to twist and pull to remove the hoses. Also check the hoses for wear or drying out.

**4** Remove the coolant lines to the radiator. Plug the lines to prevent fluid loss. If your car has an air conditioning system, disconnect the condenser located in front of the radiator. CAUTION: Check an air conditioning manual for the proper way to empty the system of gas.

**5** Disconnect the negative and positive battery posts and the battery clamp on the shelf. Don't forget to remove the pigtail wire running from the ground cable to the body (see arrow). Then remove the battery carefully. Do not tip it or acid may spill.

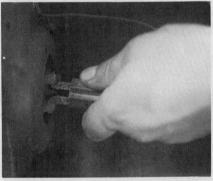  

**9** First pull off the plugs on both headlights, making sure you unfasten the thin ground wires next to the plugs. Also remove the side marker lamp plug and wire by twisting them 90 degrees to the left.

**10** Unclip the main headlight wire harness and feed it out behind the front grille. You'll find at least three plugs on each side, since the directional and side marker lights are also on this harness.

**11** Loosen the four bolts connecting the bumper to the energy absorbers with a ½-inch-drive ratchet and socket, if your car is so equipped. If not, loosen the bolts from the support bars. It's a good idea to remove three bolts on each side, leaving the last one in place.

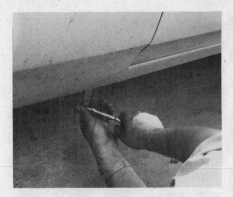

**15** The two bolts under each fender behind the wheel housing come off next. Disconnect anything joining the front end to the engine or frame. Removing the nose takes at least two people. Lift it up, then move it forward gently. This may require a bit of maneuvering.

## Reassembling the front end

With the assistance of your two helpers, pick up the nose section, place it over the frame, align the radiator support bolts with the holes in the frame, and put the nuts on loosely.

Replace all the bolts loosely, then align the fenders with the doors and cowl and tighten the rear fender bolts to the cowl panel.

Remove the hood lock, re-attach the hood to its hinges, align it to the cowl, tighten the hinge bolts, put the hood down, and align it. Move the nose in the slotted support holes to even the space between the hood and fenders. Tighten all bolts, and reinstall any other unattached parts.

# The soft nose repair

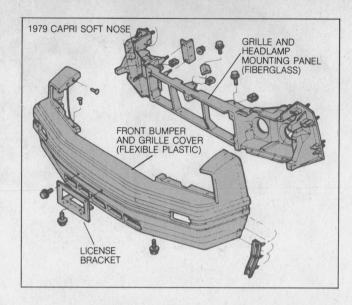

1979 CAPRI SOFT NOSE

GRILLE AND HEADLAMP MOUNTING PANEL (FIBERGLASS)

FRONT BUMPER AND GRILLE COVER (FLEXIBLE PLASTIC)

LICENSE BRACKET

Here we show you how to repair a flexible plastic front end. In general, the work steps are the same as in filler work (see page 74). But there are three important exceptions: 1) The filler material is quite toxic. 2) It requires 24 hours to dry. 3) You'll need a special paint for touching up. Ordinary paint will crack and fall off when the plastic flexes.

Soft noses are fairly easy to remove from the car. So make it easy on yourself—take it off and set it on saw horses. This eliminates a lot of masking as well as problems gaining access to the underside.

**1** Here is a typical gash in a flexible plastic front end. It is easily repairable.

**2** Start by sanding with a #80 grit disc. Remove the old paint from about three inches on all sides of the hole. Now turn the nose over and do the same on the underside.

**3** Use a vise grip to hold the broken pieces together. In this case, a double-jawed vise grip works best, but don't squeeze too hard.

**4** A patching kit for urethane bumpers will work on soft noses too. Wear gloves, work in an airy space, and mix only as much filler as you need. This type of filler does not dry as quickly as body plastic, so you can take your time. Make sure the filler is well mixed.

**5** Dab the filler around the hole. Then push a small amount into the hole, smoothing the surface with a paint stick. Use the same method for the underside.

**6** Spread the filler over the entire repair area. Smooth it out before leaving it to dry. Wait 24 hours before sanding and priming. You'll need a can of matching paint to complete the job.

**CHAPTER**

# REAR END REPAIRS

Repairing major rear end damage is usually a job for a pro, because the rear section, in contrast to the front with its many bolt-on sections, consists mainly of welded sheet metal. The first step, as in checking the front end, is to look for damage to the frame. Frame damage can only be handled by a professional. Your check should also include indirect as well as direct damage. This examination will uncover the repairs you can handle yourself—dents, dings, buckles, and damage to bolted-on parts.

The most common rear end damage is relatively easy to handle by repair or replacement. Rear quarter extensions, taillights, possibly the deck lid and the bumper are candidates for replacement. Repair jobs may include tiny cracks in the plastic around a taillight (easily patched with one of the new super adhesives), realigning the trunk lid, and pulling dents or dings out of quarter panels and the rear body panel (see Chapter 5, Dents). This chapter will show you how to make these minor repairs and replacements.

Dents and dings are one thing, but replacing a welded panel is strictly a pro job because it requires more sophisticated tools than you may have access to: a pneumatic chisel to peel off the panel and an acetylene torch to weld on a new one, for example. See "How the pros do it" on page 82. Thorough evaluation of the nature of the damage is important. It might be a good idea to review the points on evaluating damage in Chapter 1 to map your plan for tackling rear end repairs.

# Job steps Replacing rear end elements

**To remove the taillight housing,** take off the lens or frame screws, then remove the lens and unbolt the housing. Some units may have to be removed from inside the trunk.

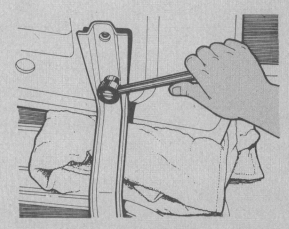

**To remove the trunk lid,** unfasten the bolts connecting it to the hinges. Be sure to use a towel or pad to protect the panel finish.

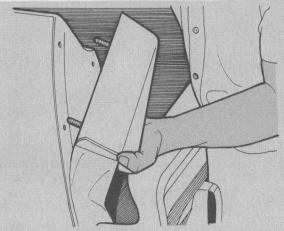

**To replace the rear quarter extension,** open the deck lid. Reach inside the trunk and remove the nuts holding the extension in place. With a slight motion downward and to the rear, it can be removed. On some cars, you will have to take the bumper off first.

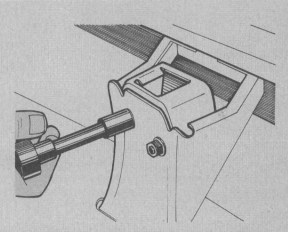

**To tighten the trunk lid,** loosen the striker bolts just enough to move it. Re-tighten the bolts and close the trunk to test the fit. If the adjustment is proper, you will not have to slam the trunk lid to close it.

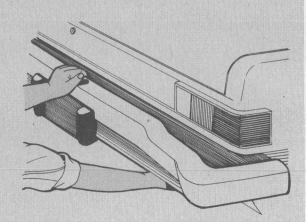

**To remove the bumper** from the energy absorber, unfasten three bolts and loosen the fourth on each side of the bumper. Get somebody to help you remove the final bolts and support the bumper.

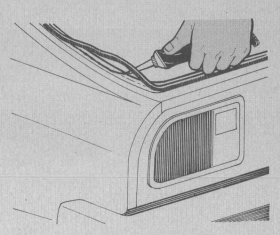

**To weatherproof the trunk,** remove the old rubber weatherstripping and clean the gutter. Apply a liberal amount of sealer cement and press the weatherstripping onto it.

# Aligning a trunk lid

Don't be surprised if you find the lid of your luggage compartment out of alignment after even a mild rear end collision. Any jolt to the rear of your car could disturb the alignment of the trunk lid, the lock or the hinges. These misalignments are usually easy to fix, however, because most deck lids can be shifted fore and aft—and many from side-to-side—by simply loosening the bolts attaching the lid to the hinges. The procedure is similar in many ways to hood alignment (see page 109). A block of wood, for example, will assist you in straightening a twisted or bent hinge. Raising and lowering the lid as you make adjustments helps you judge how close you're coming to correct alignment.

1 This trunk lid is obviously out of alignment, as you can see from the overlap of the rear quarter panel.

4 Align the lid by bringing it down into the opening and moving it back and forth or to the right and left. After each movement, tighten the bolts and check the position again. Repeat these steps until the lid is aligned.

5 Once the lid is properly seated in the trunk opening, you must match the lock to its striker (shown here). Keep the striker attaching bolts snug so it can be easily moved either up and down or side-to-side.

8 When the lid is aligned, tighten the bolts securely so the lid and lock will not move.

If the lid is out of alignment after an accident and you can't get it to fit, the hinges are probably bent. Get replacement hinges. Installing them is usually a nut-and-bolt job, but some are welded on and this is a job for a pro. **Caution:** Spring-loaded hinges, the ones that keep the lid raised without your effort, can pack quite a wallop. Don't try to remove these.

**2** Holding the lid with one hand, loosen all the bolts and make sure they are just snug, leaving one a little tighter than the others so you can move the lid with a little pressure.

**3** Don't lock yourself out. Remove the lock or striker if you suspect they are misaligned, because if the lid accidently closes, your key will not help you and you may have to pull out the back seat to open the trunk.

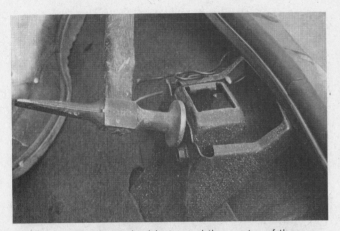

**6** If the striker is pushed in toward the center of the car a little (which could mean the rear body panel has been damaged), a few taps with a hammer will in most cases return it to its proper position. Then continue jockeying it around as in step 5.

**7** If the lock and striker still do not mate, loosen the lock and position it by moving it right or left until it lines up with the striker.

## The rear end

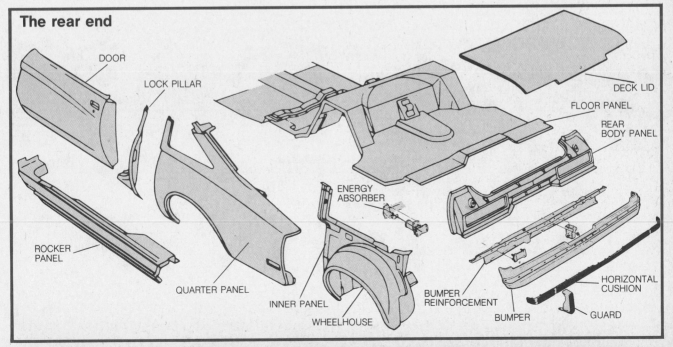

DOOR

LOCK PILLAR

DECK LID

FLOOR PANEL

REAR BODY PANEL

ENERGY ABSORBER

ROCKER PANEL

QUARTER PANEL

INNER PANEL

WHEELHOUSE

BUMPER REINFORCEMENT

BUMPER

HORIZONTAL CUSHION

GUARD

# Removing and replacing a trunk lid

If your trunk lid has been hit in an accident, it is more economical in terms of time for you to replace it rather than attempting to fix anything greater than surface damage, dings or small dents. This sequence shows the usual steps for removal and replacement. If the lid has been straightened but fails to line up with the opening, it's a safe bet that the hinges are bent. Most hinges can take some straightening. However, they can also be replaced. Some are welded in (a pro job) and some are a nut-and-bolt job.

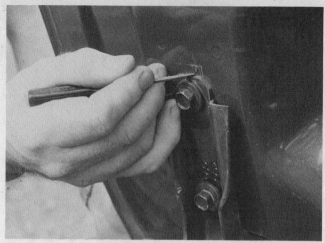

**1** Scribe marks around the hinges if the alignment is reasonably close. This will help you to replace the lid and save time in realigning it.

**2** Place a towel or pad on the upper panel. This prevents scratching it if the lid should slip.

**3** Remove the bolts holding the hinges to the lid, starting with the top two, then taking out the bottom two. Since the lid is awkward to handle, a helper here will be necessary.

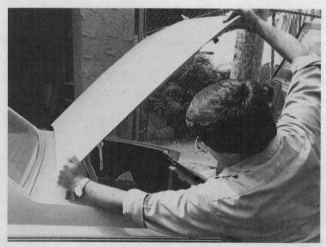

**4** To put on a new lid or re-install your old one, with the help of a friend rest it on the upper panel (where you put the towel or pad). Then place the lid against the hinges and put in the bolts, starting with the upper ones. Draw them up snug. Then close the lid to test the fit.

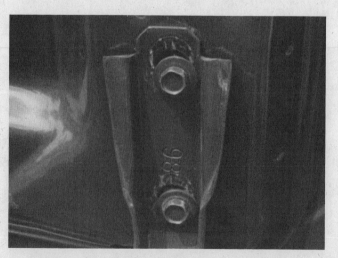

**5** To align, loosen the bolts and move the lid a little bit at a time. Loosen one side and slide the lid on the hinges. This moves it sideways as well as back and forth. From this point on, see pages 116–117 on aligning trunk lids.

# Repairing and replacing a taillight assembly

The procedures for repairing taillights vary depending on your car's make and model. This Buick taillight repair is quite typical, however. Some hints: If the screws for the taillight assembly are not visible from the outside, open the trunk and check behind the carpet. And be sure you save all the screws or speednuts you remove.

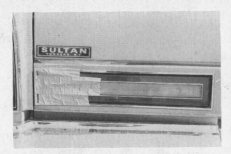

**1** This left rear taillight and a small portion of its plastic housing are broken. Order a new light or buy one of the new super adhesives to fix the plastic.

**2** First disconnect the battery, then unplug the wires connecting the light. Make sure you mark the wires so you can easily replace them. And tape them down so they don't fall behind the bumper.

**3** Remove the taillight from its housing by unscrewing the fasteners with a ratchet wrench.

**4** Squeeze a small amount of glue along the cut edge of the taillight housing.

**5** Press the edges together firmly for several minutes until they adhere. Allow the glue to dry thoroughly before reassembling the taillight.

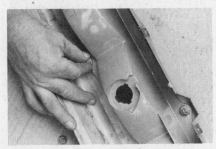

**6** After placing the new light in its housing, put the nuts on by hand all the way around the assembly.

**7** Reconnect the wires. On this particular job, you will also have to reconnect part of the rubber panel to the edge of the taillight housing.

**8** Close the trunk to make sure everything is properly spaced and aligned, then tighten the nuts on the housing. Now reattach any adjacent trim.

---

## Butyful!

You can replace a broken lens quickly and inexpensively with one having a butyl seal. Just get rid of the pieces of old lens remaining in the lamp body, press a strip of butyl onto the bezel, and stick the lens on the seal. No muss, no fuss, no hardware. Here's how you do it.
1 Go through the trunk to remove the bulbs and sockets. This will prevent damage while you're hammering away at the old lens.
2 Break out the major chunks of lens with a small hammer and chip out the rest with a screwdriver.
3 Reinstall the bulbs and sockets and test them.

4 Press a strip of butyl seal—it comes with the replacement lens—onto the edge of the lamp body. There are two drainage notches on the underside of the lens. Cut away a ½-inch gap in the butyl strip at locations corresponding to those on the lamp edge so water won't get trapped inside.
5 Position the new lens and press it firmly onto the seal. Maintain pressure for at least ten seconds. CAUTION: Press toward the edge of the lens rather than at the center or it might crack. For peace of mind, tape it in place and leave it overnight.

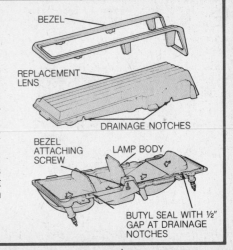

BEZEL

REPLACEMENT LENS

DRAINAGE NOTCHES

BEZEL ATTACHING SCREW

LAMP BODY

BUTYL SEAL WITH ½" GAP AT DRAINAGE NOTCHES

# TROUBLE SHOOTING

## FOR THE BODYWORKER AND PAINTER

There is no special magic involved in achieving good results in bodywork and painting. As with all do-it-yourself repair, professional results come from following directions, practicing using unfamiliar tools and materials, avoiding shortcuts, and, above all, not hurrying through any part of the process. On these pages, we've assembled a group of photos illustrating common bodywork and painting problems as well as how to correct them.

### Frozen locks

If your lock freezes on a cold day, there are de-icing sprays you can use to help thaw it. But you can prevent the problem by using a lubricant spray. Most locks freeze because water gets into the lock cylinder through the spring-loaded door on the outside of the lock or because condensation forms on the inside. Use a lubricant spray on the locks frequently during cold weather. If the lock is frozen, heat the key before inserting it. Then, as soon as you get the lock open, spray lubricant on it. If the lock freezes often, check the weatherstripping at the bottom of the window. Water can get in if the stripping is not properly installed.

### Adjusting the hood cable

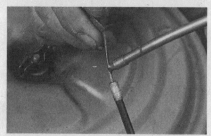

If your hood release cable is sticking or if it is so loose the hood pops open when you go over a bump, the cable is probably rusty or out of adjustment. To tighten or to oil it, you will need a helper. Have your assistant disconnect the hood latch control cable from the inside of the car and hold the end while you open the hood and remove the cable retainer plate and cable clip. Pull the cable back and forth through its casing. You should be able to see if it is rusty. Squirt small amounts of oil into the cable casing as you and your helper pull the cable back and forth to distribute the oil. Then reconnect the cable, checking for proper tightness before attaching the cable clip.

### An extra cleanup

Don't create extra work for yourself by having to clean the interior of the car after sanding, priming, and painting. Always close the windows before beginning any bodywork job.

### Getting into the trunk

If you lock the trunk and do not have the key, you can still get into it. Remove the rear seat, then whittle down one end of an old broom handle so you can fit a 7/16-inch socket over it. Holding the end of the broom in one hand and a flashlight in the other, loosen the bolts holding the lock-assembly to the floor of the trunk. Another way to get into the trunk is to jimmy the lock open. Tape a screwdriver to a broom handle and spring the lock.

RIGHT  WRONG

### Using vise-grip pliers

You will prolong the life of a tool if you learn to use it properly. One of the most common mistakes with vise-grip pliers is to pull on the locking lever when tightening nuts and bolts. The correct way to hold the vise-grips (far left) is to pull against the main shaft. The incorrect way (near left), pulling on the locking lever, strains the hinge linkage and can break the tool.

## Rough edges

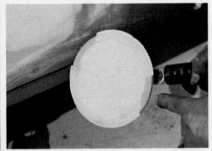

Trim sanding discs to fit the backing. Since sanding discs are held at an angle to the work surface, it is necessary to trim and secure the paper well.

## Blushing

Blushing is caused by painting or priming on a damp day. Water in the atmosphere gets into the primer or paint before it can dry, leaving a permanent, whitish halo. You can control this if you use a gun and compressor for the job. When the primer begins to blush, add a little retarder to it, mix well, and spray over the surface of the repaired area. If you are using a spray can, the best solution is to sand the area lightly when it has dried and apply the primer again when the humidity level has gone down.

## Leaving metal unprimed

Make sure that whenever you grind down to bare metal, you prime the surface right away. This repair spot formed surface rust in an hour on a particularly damp day.

## Sanding the wrong way

Sanding with the fingers alone produces an uneven job both in sanding and feath-eredging. Your finger marks will show on primed areas. Generally, it is better to use a sanding block so that pressure is evenly applied. Sandpaper wrapped around a damp sponge achieves the same effect and allows the paper to conform to the surface contour of the car.

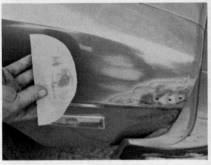

## Mixing it up right

Improper or careless mixing of paint causes most failures in do-it-yourself paint jobs. At best, the finish turns out dull. As soon as the can has been opened, scrape the paint from the inside of the lid into the can with a stirring stick. Stir the paint well for several minutes, then pour it into another container and add a small amount of thinner to the bottom of the can. Swish it around, using the stick to push paint from the sides of the can down to the bottom where it can mix. When the sides of the can are nearly clean, swirl the paint once or twice and pour it into the other container. Mix again with the stick and continue stirring for several minutes. Strain the paint into the spray gun through a paint filter. No matter how good the paint nor how carefully it has been mixed, some small particles will remain. Straining removes these before they have a chance to clog the gun or dull your car's finish. Read the directions to make sure that your paint and thinner are compatible.

2. Pour the paint back and forth into another container once or twice to be sure that none of the darker pigments remain at the bottom of either can.

1. Pigment settles to the bottom of the can when stored on the shelf. Add enough thinner to cover the bottom and swirl until it has mixed well with the paint on the bottom and sides.

3. Always strain the paint through a filter before spraying it on the car. It's a good idea to test your color match by first spraying a hidden surface, such as the inside of the trunk lid. If you ordered the original factory paint according to your car's ID plate, it should match perfectly.

## BLEEDING

**Bleeding:** Surface discoloration after repainting.
**Cause:** Solvent penetration from fresh paint dissolves old finish, usually reds and maroons, releasing a dye that comes to the surface.
**Remedy:** Remove all color coats and apply bleeder sealer over reds and maroons, then repaint.

## BLUSHING

**Blushing:** Finish turns milky looking.
**Cause:** Fast thinners in high humidity.
**Remedy:** Add retarder to thin the spray. Use a retarder or reflow solvent when spraying on humid days.

## BLISTERING

**Blistering:** Broken edged craters; lack of gloss if blisters are minute.
**Cause:** Painting over oil or grease, moisture in spray lines or prolonged exposure to high humidity.
**Remedy:** Sand and refinish, allowing proper drying time between coats. Drain the air line of water frequently.

## CHALKING

**Chalking:** Powdery surface and lack of gloss.
**Cause:** Insufficient agitation of paint and natural weathering of paint films.
**Remedy:** Sand to remove soft surface material, then clean and refinish.

## PITTING OR CRATERING

**Pitting or Cratering:** Tiny holes throughout the surface.
**Cause:** Same as blisters except that blisters have not broken.
**Remedy:** Same as for blistering.

## CHECKING, CRAZING, & CRACKING

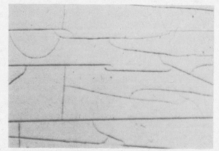

**Checking, Crazing, & Cracking:** Appears as an irregular, crowfoot separation.
**Cause:** Insufficient drying time between coats, coats too thick, ingredients not thoroughly mixed or mixing of incompatible brands of thinner and paint.
**Remedy:** Remove finish down through checked paint film and refinish.

## DULLED FINISH

**Dulled Finish:** This is probably the most common paint problem for the do-it-yourselfer.
**Cause:** Compounding before the thinner in the paint has evaporated, using poorly balanced thinner or reducer, poorly cleaned surface, top coats put on wet subcoats, washing with caustic cleaners.
**Remedy:** Allow the finish to dry hard and rub with a mild rubbing compound. When applying the final coat, be sure that the surface has been cleaned thoroughly and that you use compatible products, follow the directions for mixing, and allow all coatings sufficient drying time.

## ORANGE PEEL

**Orange Peel:** Texture resembles the skin of an orange.
**Cause:** Improper thinning solvent, lack of proper flow, surface drying too fast or improper air pressure.
**Remedy:** (Enamel) Rub surface with a mild polishing compound.
(Lacquer) Sand with #600 grit paper or use rubbing compound. Then sand and refinish.

## FISHEYES & POOR WETTING

**Fisheyes and Poor Wetting:** Raising and swelling of wet film or peeling when dry.
**Cause:** Improper drying of previous coat, sandwiching enamel between coats of lacquer or acrylic paint.
**Remedy:** Remove lifted surface and refinish.

## RUNS AND SAGS

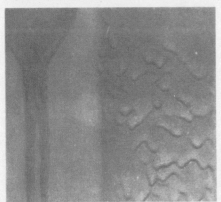

**Runs and Sags:** Mass slipping of total film or partial slipping of paint in curtains.
**Cause:** Paint film too heavy to support itself. Usually due to holding the gun too close or improper adjustment of the gun.
**Remedy:** Sand or wash off and refinish.

## PLASTIC BLEED-THRU

**Plastic Bleed-thru:** Discoloration (usually yellowing) of the top coat color.
**Cause:** Using too much hardener or applying top coat before plastic is cured.
**Remedy:** Remove patch. Or cure, sand, and refinish top coat.

## UNDERCOAT SHOW THRU

**Undercoat Show-thru:** Variations in surface color.
**Cause:** Insufficient color coats, repeated compounding.
**Remedy:** Apply good coverage of color and avoid excessive compounding, especially on new paint.

## WRINKLING

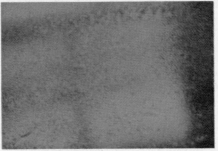

**Wrinkling:** Enamel puckers like a prune skin. Finish will show lack of gloss as it dries due to minute wrinkling not visible to the naked eye.
**Cause:** Too little thinner or air pressure too low causing excessive film thickness, fast reducers creating overloading.
**Remedy:** Break open the top surface by sanding and allow it to dry thoroughly. Check the paint can to be sure the directions for application have been followed.

## RUST UNDER FINISH

**Rust Under Finish:** Raised surface spots, peeling or blistering.
**Cause:** Improper metal prep results in broken paint film, allowing moisture to get in under surrounding finish.
**Remedy:** Seal off point where moisture enters. Sand down to bare metal and refinish.

## LIFTING

**Lifting:** Paint raises and swells while setting. May also peel when surface is dry.
**Cause:** Improper drying of previous coat, sandwiching enamel between coats of lacquer or acrylic paint, recoating improperly cured enamel or spraying over uncleaned surfaces.
**Remedy:** Sand off and thoroughly clean the lifted surfaces. When refinishing, allow all subcoats to dry fully, then seal.

## WATERSPOTTING

**Waterspotting:** Dulling of gloss in spots or a mass of spots appearing as a distortion of the film.
**Cause:** Spots of water drying on finish or washing finish in bright sunlight.
**Remedy:** Sand and refinish. Do not allow water to dry on new finish.

## PEELING

**Peeling:** Paint separation from the sub-surface.
**Cause:** Improper surface prep or incompatible paint products.
**Remedy:** Remove peeling paint completely and prepare metal properly. Refinish with compatible materials.

## STONE BRUISES

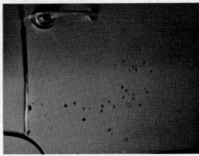

**Stone Bruises:** Small chips of paint missing from an otherwise firm finish.
**Cause:** Flying stones from other vehicles; impact of other car doors.
**Remedy:** Thoroughly sand the remaining paint film back several inches from the damage point. Follow the steps for surface prep found in "Weekend Shapeup" and refinish.

## Filler flaws

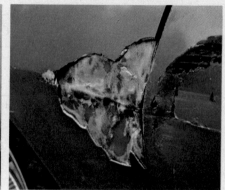

This filler job was only a month old and already starting to fall away. The owner filled the dent with putty without bringing the dent out first.

The body filler was not filed or sanded smooth, and the owner did not mask adjacent areas. The resulting repair was already beginning to fall away only a few weeks later.

Lack of proper surface preparation—the original paint was not removed—caused this filler to fall away from the repaired area.

## Stick with it

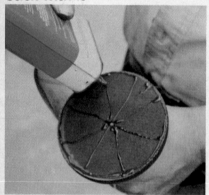

Apply adhesive in a star pattern. Then press the sanding disc firmly onto the backing, peel off gently, then restick, applying pressure to insure a good seal.

## Respect those tender edges

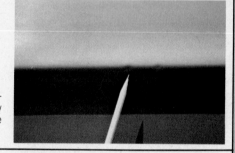

Sanding directly on sharp edges will expose the metal in no time at all (see photo at right). It's better to sand both sides of the edge rather than the edge itself. If direct sanding is needed, it should be done delicately with very fine sandpaper.

A primed surface will show any small irregularities in the original contour. Low spots that appear after priming should be covered once again with glazing putty.

## Mismatch

Test for color match by spraying a non-absorbent surface and checking it against the surface to be painted. If it does not match, recheck the ID plate on your car to be sure you got the right color.

## Drain hole hygiene

Rust along the bottom edge of door panels is usually caused by clogged drain holes.

A regular part of auto maintenance should be to clean the drain holes out with a pointed object such as a coat hanger. Never spray water to clean it out.

CHAPTER

# WINDOWS, DOORS, LOCKS

At one time or another, you are bound to have a door that won't open, windows that won't close, locks that won't turn, and leaks that won't stop. The causes of many of these problems are well-known, so you can be prepared when they crop up. For instance, proper alignment is the most important adjustment for car doors. This will save you a lot of annoying problems like water leaks, wind whistles, and lock damage.

Most door maintenance involves the door lock and window operating mechanisms. Periodic lubrication of the latter helps prevent problems with movable windows. Also, bolts can work loose, causing the window to malfunction. Check the regulator if you are having window trouble.

Broken or cracked windows should be fixed as soon as possible. Replacing door glass is a fairly straightforward procedure, but replacing a windshield may be beyond the scope of the do-it-yourselfer. In this case, you'd be better off buying a replacement from a salvage yard and having a pro install it. Movable glass can be adjusted from the inner door panel in several different ways to eliminate rattles and leaks.

Door locks are subject to periodic failures, but many of them can be prevented or fixed by lubricating the lock assembly, the inner door lock, and the inner door pull handle mechanism. When a lock is damaged, it is generally easier and less time-consuming to replace the lock cylinder than to attempt to fix or replace individual parts.

Be careful not to turn a simple problem into a major one by forcing window glass up or down or by using force on sticking locks. Undue stress on these systems can cause damage.

On the next page, we show a photo of a car door with the outer skin cut away so you can get a good view of the basic door mechanisms and their relationship to one another.

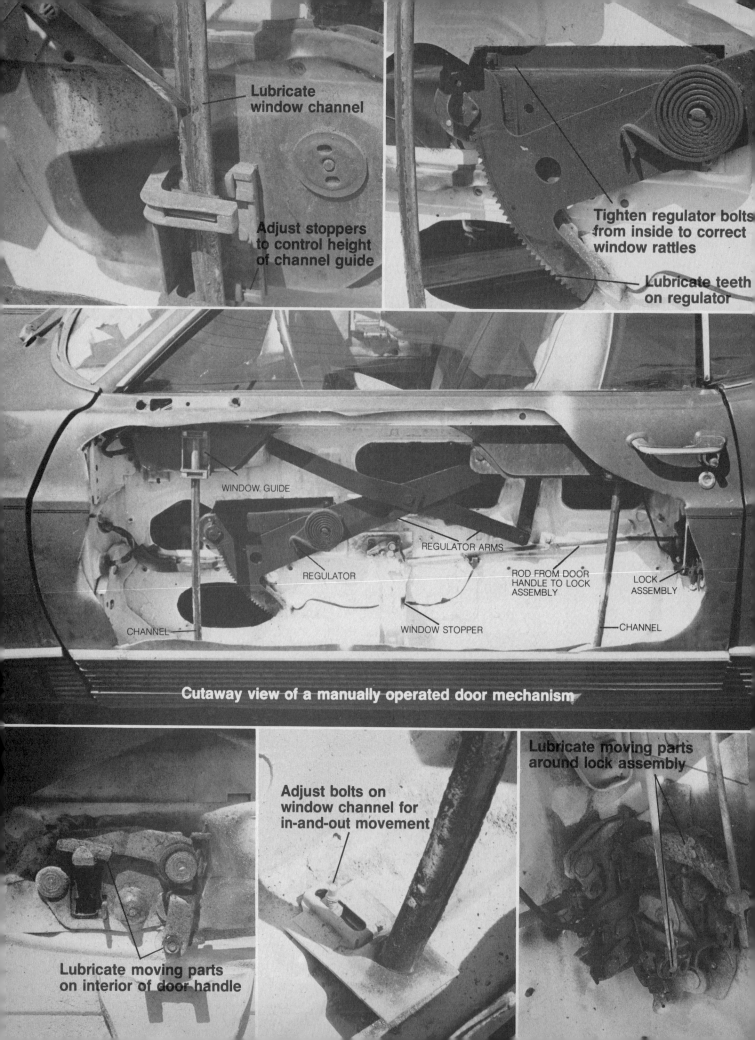

Lubricate
window channel

Adjust stoppers
to control height
of channel guide

Tighten regulator bolts
from inside to correct
window rattles

Lubricate teeth
on regulator

WINDOW GUIDE

REGULATOR ARMS

REGULATOR

ROD FROM DOOR
HANDLE TO LOCK
ASSEMBLY

LOCK
ASSEMBLY

CHANNEL

WINDOW STOPPER

CHANNEL

Cutaway view of a manually operated door mechanism

Lubricate moving parts
on interior of door handle

Adjust bolts on
window channel for
in-and-out movement

Lubricate moving parts
around lock assembly

# Job steps Fixing windows, doors, locks

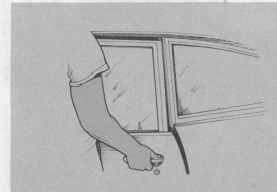

**1** First check the door alignment and correct any misalignment. Then adjust the striker plate, if necessary.

**2** Remove all the inner door upholstery panels and the vapor barrier.

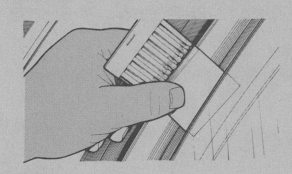

**3** Check the window position, window glass supports, and rattle and whistle adjustments.

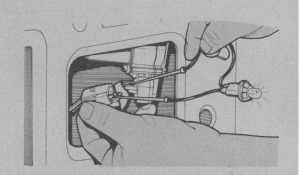

**4** Check the fuse in the electrical system for shorts. Check for broken cables or bad connections.

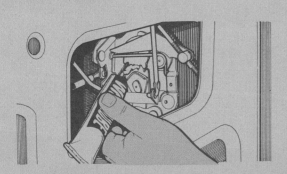

**5** Lubricate the window operating systems and lock mechanisms, using both grease and liquid lubricant.

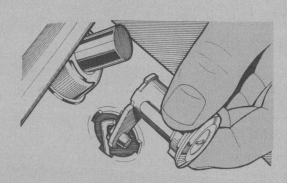

**6** Remove the lock cylinder if the lock is damaged and replace it.

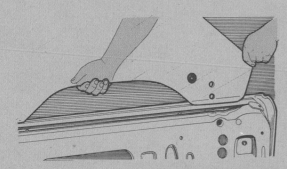

**7** Replace any damaged glass, movable or fixed, both bolted-in and glued-in types.

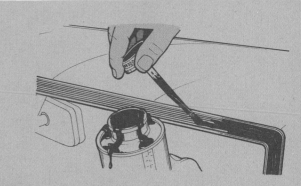

**8** Apply sealant directly to leaks around weatherstripping and in body seams.

# Getting at the mechanisms

**1** First remove all the screws from the inner upholstery panel, then pry out any remaining clips attaching the panel to the door frame. Remove the inner pull handle, if there is one, and then remove the panel itself. This door has a double panel. Other doors have panels that come out in one piece.

**2** After removing the upper panel, store it out of the way while working. This car has a remote control mirror and you do not have to disconnect it. When installing this panel, make sure the remote control cable is not touching the glass.

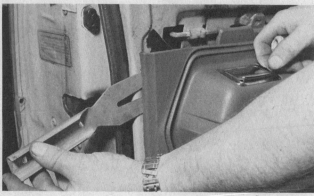

**3** Remove the screws from the lower section of the upholstery panel and use the upholstery tool to remove the clip holding the window handle to the regulator. Pry out the lower section of paneling.

**4** Peel off the vapor barrier or moisture retarder. This gives you access to the door mechanisms and allows you to make window adjustments or apply lubrication to window and lock mechanisms.

## The upholstery tool

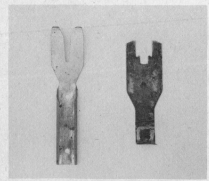

**1** There are two types of upholstery tools. The one on the left is used on all cars for removing plastic fasteners and door upholstery panels. The one on the right is strictly for removing window and door handles.

**2** The upholstery tool can perform a variety of jobs. In this case, it is being used to pry off the door handle. Insert the tool behind the edges and push inward. Use the upholstery tool instead of sharp instruments like screwdrivers that can bend metal parts or tear vinyl.

**3** Here the upholstery tool is used to move the small ring clip holding the handle to the panel. When the handle is off, insert the clip back into its position. Then, when it's time to replace the handle, select the position you need and press it on.

# Fixing those annoying window rattles

1 After removing the inner door upholstery, check these double adjustments, which both hold the upholstery (metal clip) and press against the window glass (felt-covered section). Note: The adjustments in steps 1 to 6 are all for hardtop cars.

2 Using a screwdriver and wrench, move the adjustment screw to tighten the felt part against the window. Do the same with the rear adjustment. Avoid forcing the glass too much or it will move stiffly and put undue pressure on the regulator.

3 With the height-adjuster screws you can control the height to which the glass can be raised. You will be able to judge by eye whether the glass rises too high or not high enough for a snug fit. This is the front height-adjuster.

4 On this car, the rear height-adjuster is located by looking through a hole in the metal panel. It's the one to the right. Beside it you find the front-to-back adjustment. Use this to correct unevenness between back and front as the window rises.

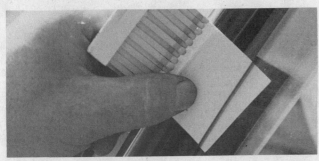

5 Use the matchbook test to see if the window is fitting snugly against the roof rubber. You should barely be able to insert a matchbook cover between the glass and the rubber. Too much in-out play in the window will allow wind and rain to come in along the edge.

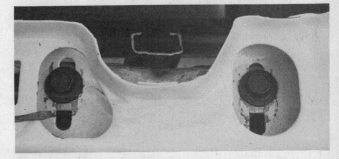

6 Eliminate excessive movement of the window glass with these two in-out adjusters.

## Fixing wind whistles

Wind whistles are caused either by air leaking out of the car or by air turbulence. To pinpoint the cause, drive the car at cruising speed on the highway, opening and closing the ventilation ducts. If the noise lessens when the ventilators are closed, the air is finding a way out of the car, probably around one of the windows.

If the ventilators have no effect on the noise, the problem is probably one of air turbulence caused by loose moldings, gaps between seals or protruding parts.

Air leaks around windows can be fixed by some of the same adjustments you used for fixing window rattles.

# All about fixing locks

It is important to lubricate the moving parts of the door lock mechanism to keep them from sticking. Also check the rods connecting the lock mechanism to the inner door lock, the key lock, the front door latch, and the inner door pull handle. If the rods are disconnected, the lock will not work.

In wintertime, water often gets into the key opening and freezes. Heat your key and then try it in the lock. Do not use hot water to unfreeze the lock because it will collect and freeze later when it cools.

When a lock is damaged, it is often necessary to remove the lock cylinder completely and replace it. And when replacing a door on your car, remove your old lock and install it on the replacement door. Otherwise your key won't work.

A word of caution when working on doors—the metal behind the panels is not finished so be careful or you will cut your fingers or hands.

1 Inspect the rods leading from the lock assembly to the other parts of the lock mechanism. The slanting rod at the left goes up to the inside door lock, the center rod goes up to the key lock, and the right rod goes up to the outer door handle button. The horizontal rod going off at the left goes to the inner door pull handle latch. Make sure all these rods are attached and lubricated.

2 When the lock mechanism on a door is not functioning properly, it is often because this large spring at the bottom of the lock assembly has either broken or come loose. Replace the spring or tighten it.

3 Shown here is another spring in the lock assembly that is liable to break, causing the door lock mechanism to malfunction. Again, replace the spring.

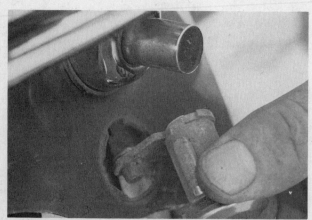

4 Often when a door is damaged the entire lock cylinder must be removed and replaced. First, the clip holding the cylinder is pried out and the cylinder is removed.

5 Now put the clip back on the cylinder so you don't lose it. Follow the same procedure to reinstall a new cylinder.

## Troubleshooting electric locks

**1** Check your fuses. If they look burned out, replace them. If the fuse is all right, check the current at the switch.

**2** Disconnect the wire from the rear of the switch and, using a small, single contact bulb with two wire leads, put one wire into the red (current) wire and use the other as a ground. If the bulb lights, you have current. If not, check to see whether the current wire is loose or disconnected. If it is OK, take the problem to a pro.

**3** To check whether the problem is the switch, insert a U-shaped wire into the hole corresponding to the red current wire. If this method activates the lock, you need a new switch, since the lock is obviously operating properly.

**4** Trace the wires to the solenoid. If the wires are OK, your solenoid is bad. Attach a test light to the wire on the solenoid and check with the light after grounding. If the light goes on but the solenoid does not operate, the problem is in the solenoid, which should be replaced.

**5** The top dome-shaped portion of the solenoid is pulled inward which in turn pulls the connecting rod downward, locking the door. If there appears to be a problem with the depressing action of the cap, replace the solenoid. This solenoid differs from the one in step 4, but both are checked the same way.

If your electric lock stops working after an accident, you can safely assume that part of the lock is jammed because one or more of the parts has been pushed out of position. If you are pulling or spooning out the dents from the accident, check all your electrical mechanisms before replacing the inner door trim panel.

## Removing the lock cylinder

If the door lock cylinder is damaged, it is easier and cheaper to replace it than to try to repair it. To remove the cylinder, first raise the window and take off the inner door upholstery and the vapor barrier. Then use a screwdriver to slide the lock-cylinder retaining clip (on the door's outer panel) out of engagement. Now remove the cylinder.

To install a new cylinder, just reverse this procedure. Place the re-taining-clip pawl over the new cylinder, insert the cylinder in the door, and slide the outer-door retaining clip into engagement, again using a screwdriver. Replace the vapor barrier and the inner door upholstery panel.

When you replace a door lock cylinder, you may want to replace the ignition lock cylinder as well. This will save you the trouble of carrying an extra key that will open only one lock.

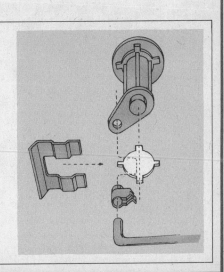

# Repairing a mechanical window

1 To fix a window that won't go up or down, work from inside the door. Usually, loose bolts attaching the regulator to the door frame and to the mounting panels are causing the trouble.

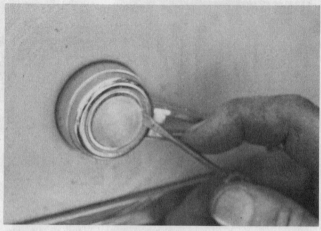

2 Examine the window handle. Some have a protective covering over the bolt or screw which must be removed. Then unbolt and remove the window handle.

3 Remove the upholstery panels and then the vapor barrier or soundproofing materials to gain access to the regulator mechanism.

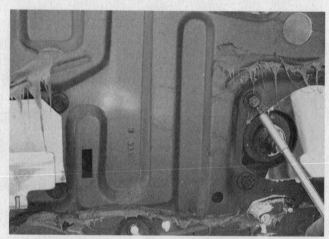

4 Check all four bolts attaching the regulator to the door frame for tightness. If they have worked loose, they could be causing the malfunction.

5 Check the bolt securing one of the regulator arms to the front mounting panel. This bolt also holds the glass to the mounting panel, to the window guide, and to the up-and-down channel.

6 Check the bolt attaching the other regulator arm's running channel to the rear mounting panel. All bolts must be in place and tight or the window will not work properly.

# Troubleshooting electric doors

**1** Remove the arm rest control panel, disconnect all the wires, then remove the upholstery panel.

**2** The regulator is mounted slightly below where it would be on a manual door. If one or two bolts on the regulator work loose, the window will not line up or close properly.

**3** If a loose regulator is neglected, constant use of the electrical motor to move the misaligned window will cause undue stress on the metal, making it crack.

**4** Check the connection to the motor to make sure it is snug. Also check the up-and-down channels, window guides, stoppers, and regulator. If all the mechanisms are secure and working, lubricate the moving parts.

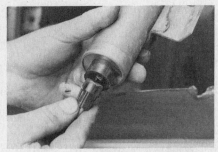

**5** Check the current to the solenoid. If current is flowing and the solenoid is grounded yet it still does not work, the solenoid must be replaced.

**6** Using a screwdriver, remove the wire from the solenoid, the two 7/16-inch bolts, and the connecting rod. Then install a new solenoid. Check a few times to make sure it is working properly. Be sure the wire is secured and out of the way of moving glass.

## Where to lubricate

Periodic lubrication of window and door mechanisms is one of the most important steps you can take to prevent problems in these areas. Whenever you have reason to remove the panel from your car door, be sure to inspect for rust on the rear of the lock cylinder and on other mechanisms.

You should lubricate everything shown here. You may need a new vapor barrier if you find moisture getting into the inner door or if you have torn the old barrier while removing it. Also, squirting some graphite into the lock from the outside where your key fits helps to prevent frozen locks in the wintertime.

**1** Apply white lubrication, a paste, to the window guides and to the channels the guides run along.

**2** Apply white lubrication to the teeth of the regulator. This will help correct stickiness or stiffness when raising or lowering the window.

**3** Apply a liquid lubricant to other parts of the regulator, especially the arm joints and the spring.

**4** Apply paste lubricant to the lock gears (indicated by arrow). Use liquid lubricant on other moving parts. It penetrates tight places better than paste.

# All about aligning doors

90 percent of all wind and water leaks around door windows are caused by faulty alignment of the door rather than by worn or torn weatherstripping. Also, a door out of alignment is likely to cause an annoying rattle. A misaligned door either does not fit exactly to the contour of the car's body or is not centered in the door opening.

To center a door, move it up or down and forward or backward. Open and close the door, observing the up-and-down movement of the edge at the lock pillar. If you see an up-or-down movement as the door latches, your door is out of alignment. Also look at the door sill or scuff plate for signs of scraping—a sure indication of door sag. When the door is closed and latched, look all around it to see if the spacing between it and the car body is uniform at the front, top, and rear.

Occasionally, problems of door alignment may be the result of a mispositioned front fender or quarter panel. If your car has suffered damage to either of these areas, be sure it is corrected before trying to check door alignment. Also, the car body or the door may be distorted so no amount of adjustment will make the door fit. In a case like this, a pro must diagnose the problem by cross checking the area and if it is not correct only a pro can fix it.

Here are four common types of door misalignment, ways to detect them by visual inspection, and the steps to take to remedy them.

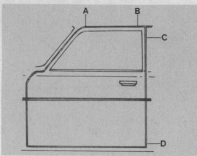

**Door sag.** If the gap between the door and the body of the car is wider at B than at A, or if the gap is wider at D than at C, you have door sag. This is generally due to a fault in the upper hinge which can be corrected by adjusting it.

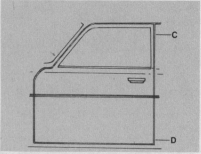

**Faulty hinge position.** If the gap between the door and the body of the car is more at C than at D, the problem generally is in the placement of the hinges. Adjust the hinges up or down to correct the misalignment.

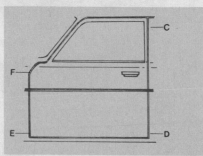

**Bent hinges.** When the gap between the car's body and the door is greater at C and D than at E and F—or the reverse, greater at E and F than at C and D—the problem is very likely a case of bent hinges. Most hinges can be straightened. Spread tight hinge leaves by putting a wooden block between the leaves and shutting the door. If the leaves must be closed, remove the hinge, squeeze the leaves in a vise and then reinstall. The best solution is to replace the old hinge with a new or used one.

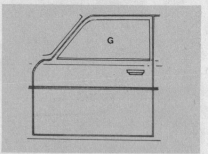

**Window misalignment.** If the window glass, G, does not fit the opening, it may be that the glass is not mounted properly. Check for this by raising the glass to see if it makes the proper contact with the weatherstripping (on a hardtop) or the upper frame channel (on a sedan). You can correct window alignment by adjusting the window regulator and the guide tracks. For example, you can adjust the in-out movement and the forward-backward movement of the window for a better fit. You can also set the maximum height the window rises.

## Removing hinge pins

**1** To remove hinge pins, you must first remove the two burred edges with a chisel. Then file off the remaining portion of the burrs with a file.

**2** Tap down the pin with a hammer and then use a punch if necessary to tap it all the way out.

**3** Here, the pin is nearly out. If you are working with a spring-fitted hinge, hold the door open and remove the spring with a heavy screwdriver. Use caution.

## Striker plates

Striker plates, located in the body lock pillar, hold the door closed. Some have a separate guide block which limits the up-and-down movement of the door when it is closed. Others have no guide block but act themselves as the guide for the door.

If you need to make a striker plate adjustment, first check to see if it is worn enough to warrant replacement. This is especially important where there has been damage to that area of the car.

If a door is not closing properly, adjustments can be made in the striker plate by loosening the screws holding the plate and tapping it gently into the desired position, then tightening the screws again. After adjusting it, don't slam the door shut. If the adjustment is not correct, you may damage the latch and lock mechanism.

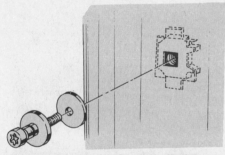

**The door-lock striker installation** consists of a single metal bolt-and-washer assembly, threaded into a tapped, floating cage plate located in the body-lock pillar. The device secures the door in the closed position when the door-lock fork bolt snaps over and engages the striker bolt.

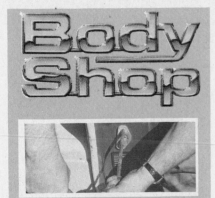

If you cannot loosen the striker plate screws, tap straight in with a hammer and screwdriver. This will often loosen the rust on the screws so you can make the adjustment.

**1** The striker plate can become misaligned by repeated bumping or jarring. When a door is closed and locked yet still shows a considerable amount of play or does not close tightly or rattles, you probably have a misaligned striker plate.

**2** Check door alignment by looking at the space between the fender and the leading edge of the door. If it is very large, adjust the hinges. Always align the door before adjusting the striker plate.

**3** Loosen the screws on the striker plate and tap inward if the door is not tight enough, or, if there is no guide block, tap the striker plate up or down to adjust the vertical play in the door.

**4** After adjusting the striker plate, push hard on the door to make sure there is no play in it when it is closed.

**5** In the event of a misaligned rear door, it is easier to adjust the hinges because they are more accessible. The inner bolts on the rear door are for vertical and backward-and-forward adjustment. The bolts on the door itself allow side-to-side alignment.

**6** This type of striker is slightly more complex. Within these bolt holes, the screws are adjustable 360°.

# Replacing movable glass

When replacing movable glass, first roll the glass up to its maximum height. When the glass is bolted in, as in this case, carefully remove the bolts holding the glass to the mounting panels and to the front and rear window guides.

Now remove the old glass from the door, making sure it is free of all guide screws. When bolting in the new glass, be sure you never touch metal to glass. Insert the plastic buffer or washer into the screw hole before putting in the metal bolt.

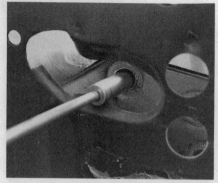

**1** This window is bolted in, so first remove the bolts holding the glass to the front and back mounting panels.

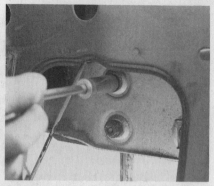

**2** Remove the two bolts or nuts holding the glass to the front window guide.

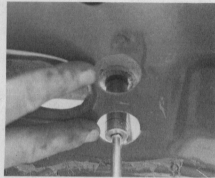

**3** Remove the two bolts or nuts holding the glass to the rear window guide. Have a helper hold the glass so it won't drop when you pull out the bolts.

**4** The glass is now free. Remove it from the door, making sure it is clear of all guide screws, the guides, and the front and rear channels.

**5** Position the new piece of glass in the door, making sure the holes line up with those in the guides and channels. Screw in the bolts on the front and rear channels and on the mounting panels. Insert plastic washers in the holes before screwing in the metal bolts.

## Bolted-in vs. glued-in glass

All door windows are either bolted in or glued in, depending on the make and model of the car. The bolted-in type is usually easier for the do-it-yourselfer to work on.

Bolted-in glass has holes along the bottom into which bolts are inserted and the whole assembly is then secured to the mounting panels and the window guides.

Glued-in glass has no holes along the bottom. It is inserted in a channel which in turn is attached to the regulator arms.

Be sure to keep in mind which type of glass you need when you go to a salvage yard or buy used replacement glass.

**Bolted-in glass** has holes along the bottom into which bolts are inserted attaching the whole assembly to the mounting panels and the window guides.

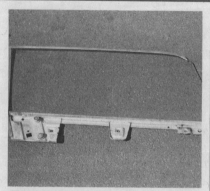

**Glued-in glass** has no holes along the bottom. It fits into a channel attached to the regulator arms.

# Removing and installing movable vent glass

Procedures for removing vent windows vary according to the make of the car. You can save time by evaluating carefully what must be done before going ahead with removal and re-installation.

In particular, check to see whether the door window must be removed before the vent assembly can be moved. Also, find out if the door window must be supported while you remove the vent assembly. (In this case, it is not necessary to do either.)

To speed up reinstallation, remember to keep all the bolts and screws together as you remove them.

If the vent glass was pried open, you may find the window brackets bent. If so, you will have to replace them along with the weatherstripping.

**1** Remove the screws or adjusting studs attaching the vent assembly to the door. Here, the top pins were drilled out with a hand drill. The bottom pins were held by a clip.

**2** Lift the glass out gently. On car bodies with upper door frame (sedan-type windows), the vent assembly must be lifted backward and upward and then rotated 90° before you can remove it.

**3** To install a replacement vent window assembly, fit the bottom screw into its place along the bottom of the window channel.

**4** Push the vent lock all the way back so the window will snap into place easily.

**5** Finally, insert the small screw holding the top portion of the window in place.

## Hardtop vs. sedan windows

Hardtop and sedan cars have different types of windows. The hardtop window has no door post or door frame. It must fit snugly against the roof rubber so it doesn't rattle or let in wind whistles.

When checking a hardtop window for alignment, check the door for alignment first. A window out of line may mean a door out of line.

The sedan window has a door post and is surrounded by a door frame. The sedan window can work perfectly even if the door is out of line because the window fits completely inside the door frame.

**Hardtop windows** have no door post or door frame. When a hardtop window is not aligned, the problem may be door misalignment.

**Sedan windows** have a door post and a door frame. The sedan window is always easier to align because it fits into the door frame.

# Replacing bolted-in glass

**1** This type of window is common on foreign cars. In some cases, it is a pop-out type with hinges creating a vent. If yours is broken, clean out all the glass chips from the window channel. A screwdriver is handy for this.

**2** Remove the hardware holding the window in place. It's a good idea to run a vacuum over the rear seat and floor to pick up any remaining pieces of glass.

**3** Clean all the chips out of the window hardware using a small screwdriver. Check for broken glass pieces in the inner door and vacuum, if necessary.

**4** Install rubber grommets in the new glass. Grommets are more common on foreign cars. On American cars, the glass is usually held in position by a rubber channel.

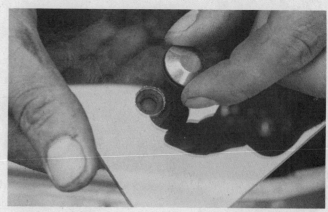

**5** Install the new glass in position. Check to make sure the holes all line up. Then hold the glass while you tighten all the bolts. In some cases, the windows are glued in (see page 136).

**6** The window should now be tight. If you discover a water or air leak, very likely one of the mounting brackets or the rubber is not in the proper position. Continue adjusting until the leak is corrected.

# Replacing fixed window glass

If the glass to be removed is still intact, you can often use the adhesive caulking remaining in the pinch-weld flange of the window frame as the base for the new glass. This is possible because the amount of adhesive left in the window opening can be controlled if you are removing intact glass. This procedure is known as the short method of replacement, in contrast to the long method, in which all the old caulking is removed.

If your car has a vinyl roof, be sure to mask off the vinyl next to the window opening. This will save time in clean up and also prevent damage to the roof fabric.

Test for leaks after you have replaced the window by pouring a moderate flow of water over the roof and vent window assembly. Apply sealant directly to those areas where you see a leak. Continue to do this until there are no more leaks.

**1** Using a screwdriver, remove the inner door trim panel.

**2** Place the screwdriver under the rubber molding and insert a piece of cord under the rubber along with it.

**3** Wrap the cord over the inner lip of the rubber and pull all the way around until the glass is loose. Gently lift out the loosened glass.

**4** Wrap a cord around the outside of the replacement glass rubber. Position the glass as accurately as possible in the door frame. Pull the cord toward you as you apply pressure on the window along the side and top. This will help set the window perfectly in the frame.

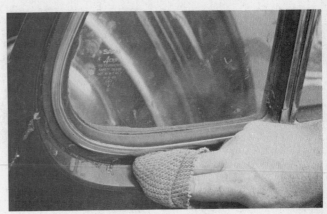

**5** Clean all around the replaced window using gasoline or metal degreaser to remove all the remaining grease and sealer.

# Replacing a windshield

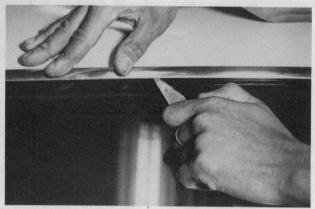

**1** First, our pro removes the trim around the windshield using a special tool called a trim remover. When the windshield is to be used again, he is careful not to scratch or break the glass.

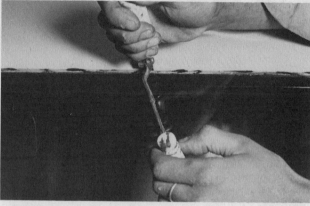

**2** With another special tool, a windshield knife, he cuts away the rubber holding the windshield in, exercising care again if the windshield glass is to be reused.

**5** Our bodyworker cleans the inside of the glass thoroughly and applies primer all around the inside edge of the windshield. Note that the glass is resting on a protective plastic wrapping.

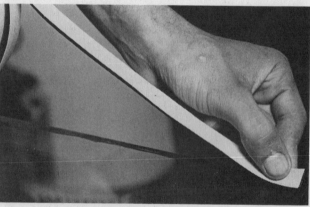

**6** He now applies self-adhering butyl tape around the edge of the windshield, using his index finger as a guide and pressing with the thumb. The tape comes in three sizes—5/16- and 3/8-inch for American cars and 1/4-inch for foreign cars.

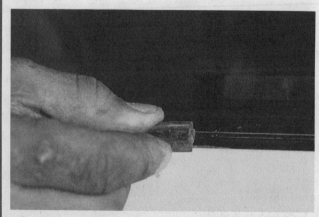

**9** When dealing with foreign cars, our pro installs a stop on the bottom of the windshield after the glass has been put in place. American cars have built-in stops and do not require this step.

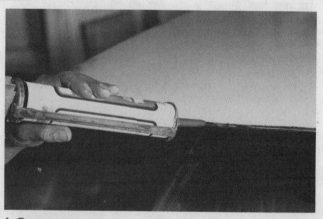

**10** Now he applies sealant all around the outside edge of the windshield.

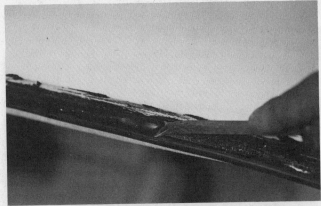

**3** The pro must now cut the remaining rubber off the pinch-weld flange with a scraper and clean the flange all the way around so no rubber remains.

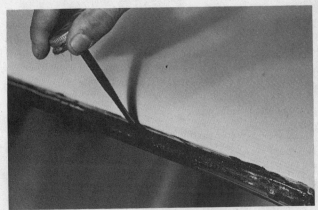

**4** He now brushes a glass primer onto the flange. The windshield will not hold without primer.

**7** With assistance, the pro lays the windshield on the pinch-weld flange, checking to make sure the fit is correct.

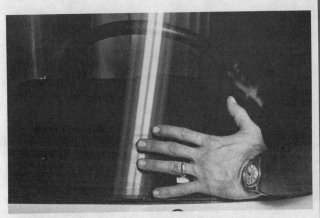

**8** Then he presses the windshield in with his hands to secure the glass and tape in the pinch-weld flange.

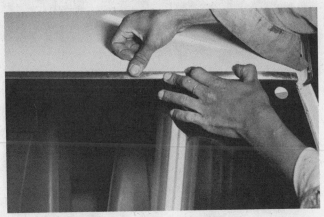

**11** Our pro finishes up by snapping the trim back into place and testing the installation for leaks with the water test (see page 142). Where there is evidence of leaking, he applies more sealant.

Here are the tools the pros use for removing a windshield. **The scraper,** left, is used to rout out all the old rubber from the pinch-weld flange after the glass has been removed. **The trim remover,** center, is used to pry off the trim around the windshield prior to removal. **The windshield knife,** right, is used to cut the rubber holding the windshield in place. It takes skill to use it.

# Sealing window leaks

The main problem with water leaks around doors and windows is finding them. One way is to squirt water from a hose over the outside of the car to locate the leaky areas. We found a bad one in a roof seam over and alongside the back window and in the weatherstripping. Instead of replacing the weatherstripping, we simply applied a sealant underneath it.

Apply the sealant directly at the point where water drips in. Let it dry for about 15 minutes and water-test again. If water is still dripping, once again apply sealant to the spot, let it dry, and test again. Continue this process until the leak is plugged. Use a clear silicone sealant so it will not show on the trim or finish.

Always test around windows with the water coming *down*. If you test with the water shooting *up*, the window will always leak, because weatherstripping is not intended to stop water from below. 90 percent of all door leaks are caused by misaligned doors or windows, not the weatherstripping.

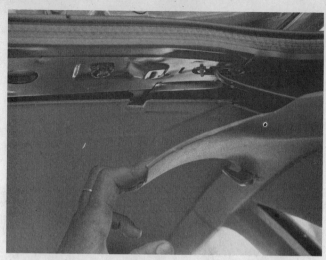

1 To seal a roof leak, remove the top molding and loosen the side panel, giving you access to the whole area.

2 Water test to locate the exact spot where the leak is. Here, the water is dripping from a roof seam.

3 Apply sealant to the leaking area, but be sure it's dry first. If necessary, use a vacuum in reverse to dry out the area after testing with water.

4 Apply sealant under the weatherstripping where it had worked loose. Use your fingers to apply the sealant in curved or out-of-the-way places.

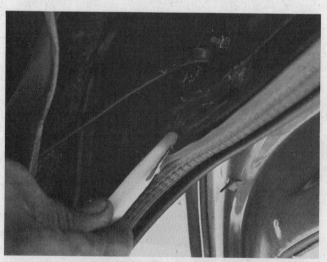

5 Sealant can also be applied with a stick, especially on easy to get at flat surfaces. After letting the sealant dry for about 15 minutes, water test again. Continue this process until final testing shows no further leaking.

CHAPTER 10

# FIXING FIBERGLASS

Fiberglass auto bodies have several advantages over their metal counterparts—they're lightweight, won't rust, and never rattle. But approach fiberglass repair with caution. It calls for many techniques quite different from those in metalwork. Above all, it takes great patience and extra attention to safety.

Fiberglass is made from molten glass drawn out into tiny, threadlike fibers, which are then reinforced with plastic resin and a catalyst and gel-coated to a shiny finish. Since it usually cracks or shatters upon impact, several layers of "glassing" may be needed to achieve the required strength. Also, thorough cleaning of both the outside and the inside of the body panel is very important if you're using bonding strips; their impregnating resin won't adhere if there is dirt between the strip and the surface to be repaired. Fiberglass work requires a rough surface for good adhesion of the filler. So hand sand both sides of the body panel with a fairly coarse grit paper to give it a little tooth.

Don't be overly ambitious. Limit your fiberglass work to small repairs such as cracks or to re-contouring panels. Turn the big jobs over to the pros. You'll see why later on.

Plan ahead. Don't plunge into a fiberglass repair before considering the number of layers, the weather, and the cure time.

Think safety. From start to finish, put safety first. Glass dust, resins, and agents can damage everything from your eyes to your stomach lining. Don't begin before carefully studying the safety tips on page 152.

With the above cautions in mind, proceed with assurance. Fiberglass repairs are tricky. They are also the closest you'll come to actual sculpture work on a car—and therefore can be very satisfying.

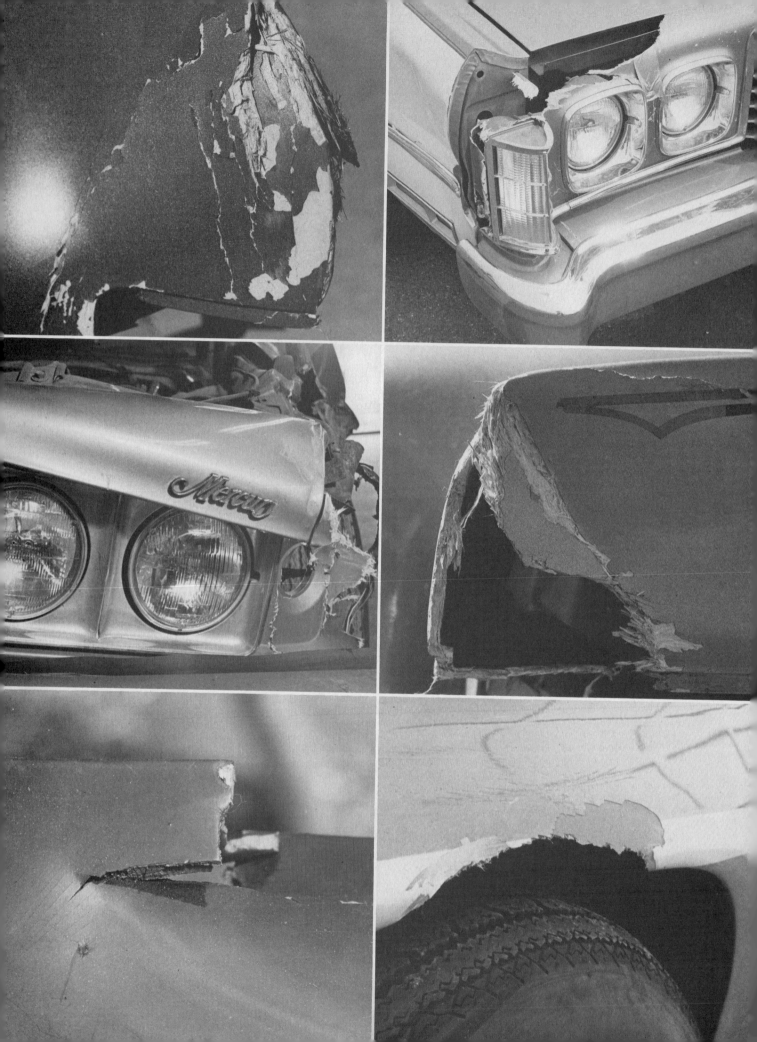

# Job steps Working with fiberglass

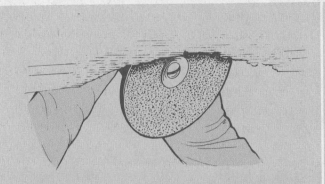

**1** Clean the surface to be repaired by sanding both the front and back with a #24 grit disc attachment on your electric drill.

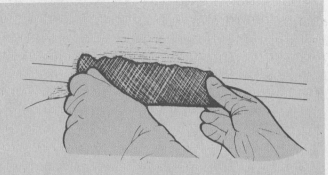

**2** Measure and cut the fiberglass mat to size, allowing a little extra to overlap the good surface on the underside. Be sure to wear plastic gloves.

**3** Mix the ingredients—fiberglass powder, polyester resin, and hardener—which will hold the fiberglass mat to the repair area.

**4** Spread the dough-like mixture thickly on both sides of the surface.

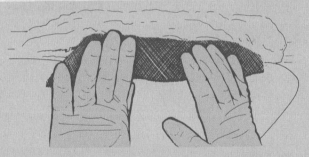

**5** Press the cloth into the mixture. Gently sculpt it to approximate the original contour. After it cures, repeat steps 2 to 5 until the surface is within ⅛-inch of the original shape.

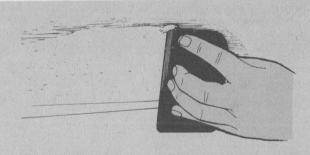

**6** Proceed with the usual surface repair techniques (see Chapter 4) on the newly contoured shape and the surrounding area.

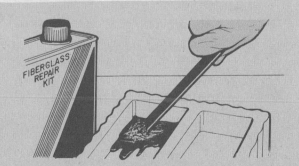

**or:** Use a fiberglass repair kit. You mix and prepare all the materials in the package itself, which doubles as a work tray. These kits are especially suited to

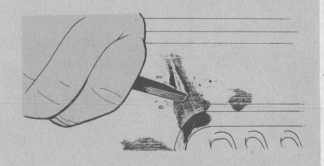

small jobs like repairing this hood crack. Simply grind, chisel, and fill; then finish as usual.

# A small fiberglass job

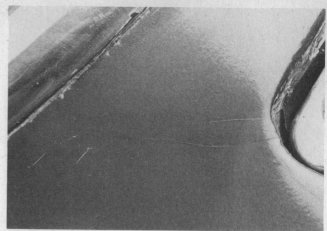

Start small. To get the feel of fiberglass, take a small crack and go to work on it. A good example of a small job is outlined here, along with all the materials you'll need. Everything is available in a kit you can pick up for less than $10.00 and use for many similar jobs. Tip: If you cannot repair a crack as soon as it appears, drill a ⅛-inch hole at each end to prevent spreading. This process is called stop drilling.

**1** A hairline crack ahead of the windshield and running into the grille of this Corvette is the kind of small job you can do with a kit. Because the back of the panel is inaccessible, you won't be able to back up the crack with a fiberglass patch.

**2** With #80 grit paper, carefully remove the paint from an area about two inches on each side of the crack. Try not to abrade the surface.

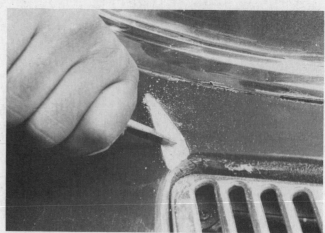

**3** Shape to form a good trough for the mixture of resin, hardener, and fiberglass strands.

**4** Fill with the mixture, then build up the area until it is even with the contour. Be sure to put on gloves for this step. Allow the mixture to harden.

**5** Sand the fiberglass buildup, shaping it to the contour and getting rid of the high spots. Featheredge, feeling the surface frequently for rough or low spots. Then mask the surrounding trim to control overspray, glaze, prime lightly (enough to cover the new fiberglass), apply putty, sand, prime, and paint.

# Mixing fiberglass from a kit

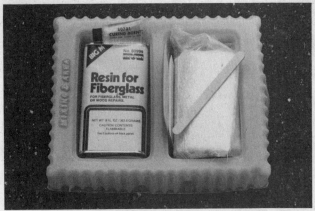

Getting and mixing the ingredients for a small repair is inexpensive and simple. We picked up this compact unit for $8.99, removed the contents, and used the package as our mixing tray. At each step, we kept safety in mind especially that of our hands and lungs. It's a good idea to wear gloves when working with fiberglass.

1 This kit simplifies the job. For one thing, it's self-contained with all the tools you'll need. All, that is, except the safety equipment you've already purchased (see page 152). Most important, the polyester resin is pre-mixed with the fiberglass powder, which you would ordinarily have to buy separately. This is a big time and work saver.

2 Pour the resin sparingly. Too much resin is going to glop up your fiberglass cloth. Remember, you want to keep the work dripless. In this kit, the compartment at the right contains the fiberglass mat you will soak in the resin. Always remember, less is better when you're working in fiberglass.

3 A few drops of curing agent come next. The pros call it a catalyst or initiator, because it starts the chemical reaction making the whole thing gel.

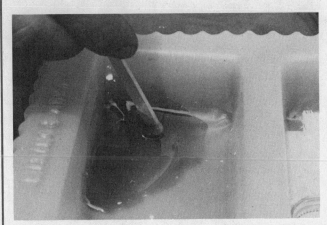

4 Mix the curing agent thoroughly into the resin. This agent not only hardens the mixture, but, mixed properly, will keep it from developing pinholes and other defects in the final painted surface.

5 Now mix in the strips of fiberglass mat. Keep the mixture thick enough so it doesn't run. You'll be glad you did later on when you start applying it.

# A larger 'glass job: shaping, molding, contouring

Now that you've gotten the feel of fiberglass by filling a crack, dent, or hole, you're ready to try something moderately ambitious, like re-shaping a wheel well or door edge. Here is a typical job in the middle range—and about as far as you should go. Turn a bigger job over to the pros. They can cope with the complexities of fiberglass layup and sprayup.

The step-by-step procedures for 'glassing cannot be rushed, require constant checking and re-working, and call for greater attention to safety than for metal-work. Wear goggles, a dust protector over your mouth and nose, and follow the other safety tips on page 152.

**1** The edge of this wheel housing was destroyed by a deep dip into a pothole. As a first step, clean the entire panel with a wax-and-silicone remover. Also clean the underside. Road dirt, oil, and salt buildup can undo the whole job.

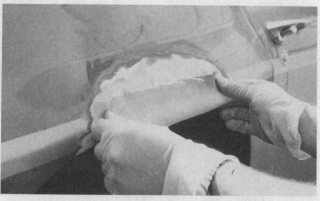

**4** Carefully measure the area to be covered and cut out a piece of fiberglass mat big enough to fit it.

**5** Mix a small amount of fiberglass powder with the resin until it is smooth and uniform in color. At first, it will turn lumpy like bread dough, but don't worry. It'll blend eventually. And don't be concerned that it will dry out too fast, either. When it's mixed, add hardener according to the directions.

**8** When the first layer has cured, cut another same-size patch and repeat steps 6 and 7. Check the cure chart opposite. Make sure the resin soaks through the matting, then begin rolling the cloth under to form a new contour consistent with that of the surrounding fiberglass panel. Be sure to push out all the air bubbles. Use your hand and eye to determine if the contour is smooth and even. Additional layers may be required. Look at the panel from the side. If more layers are going to bring the surface out beyond the original contour, use only one more layer of cloth, making a total of three.

**9** After curing and sanding, apply plastic filler. File with a cheese-grater tool and sand with #40 grit paper, then with #80 grit in a sanding block. Be sure you have feathered the edges for a smooth transition from the repair area.

2 Grind the paint from the repair area with a #24 grit disc. This grinding before 'glassing is essential to assure good adhesion of the fiberglass to the panel. Remove the paint about three inches past the damaged area.

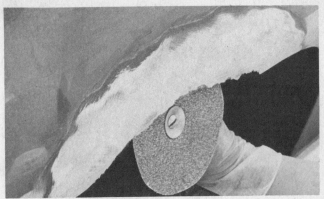

3 Lightly grind the underside of the panel around the damage. Leave the surface rough, but be sure all the old paint has been removed. A clean, rough surface provides good adhesion.

6 Cover the surface to be repaired with a fairly thick layer of the fiberglass-and-resin mixture, using a wooden paint stick. Put on just enough so it covers but doesn't begin to run off or drip. Then press the cloth against it. Where the mixture meets the mat along the edge, apply a little more.

7 To form a new edge on the wheel housing, a step required for this particular repair, let about 1½-inches of mat drop below the original contour line when you apply the first layer. This gives you an edge to begin forming contours in the next step.

10 Prime the repaired area and apply putty.

## How to time a fiberglass cure

Direct, outside sunlight provides the best cure. But temperature and weather will affect the cure time. You are the best judge—by eye and feeling the work—of when a given layer has cured. In general, however, this chart will provide you with useful guidelines.

| Temperature | Sunny | Partly Sunny |
| --- | --- | --- |
| 90° F | ½ to 1 hour | 1 to 3 hours |
| 75° F | ½ to 1½ hours | 2 to 8 hours |
| 50° F | 3 to 12 hours | 8 to 24 hours |

Cure indoors using an infrared heat lamp if the temperature is below 50° or if it's raining. Place the lamp four to six inches from the work for 30 to 40 minutes. Even a small radiant heater will do the job. Or, simply let it cure overnight. As a last resort, use a hair blower on the hot setting. But remember, heat alone will not cure a body patch. Time counts too.

# A big 'glass job

**1** This header panel was cracked in a front-end collision. If you were going to handle the problem yourself, the most practical solution would be to replace the part. An auto body shop, however, is equipped to repair it.

**2** Our pro grinds all ragged surfaces both inside and outside until they are smooth and tapered.

**5** Here is what the panel looks like when the piece of metal is riveted on the back, holding the joint together.

**6** Wearing protective gloves, our pro cuts two pieces of fiberglass cloth. He then mixes a small amount of resin with hardener and brushes it on the damaged area. Now he places the fiberglass over the crack into the resin, pressing it in place.

**9** Next, he removes the screws from the metal holding the joint together, or, if riveted, he grinds off the rivet heads, inserting a screwdriver behind the sheet metal piece. He pries it off gently, then grinds down the rivets. He repeats steps 6 and 7 on the inside of the panel.

**10** He mixes a small amount of fiberglass filler with hardener and applies it in smooth, even strokes over the ground area.

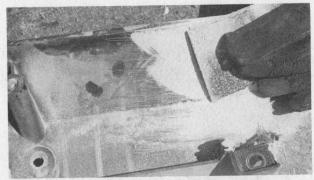

**3** The next step is to sand hard-to-reach places by hand. A pro would always wear protective gloves for this operation.

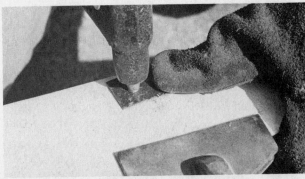

**4** After sanding, he cuts a ¾- by 1½-inch piece of sheet metal and drills a hole in each end. He then fits the sanded edges of fiberglass together and holds them with self-locking pliers. The pro centers one piece of metal over the joint and drills holes in the fiberglass through the holes in the metal. He then inserts a ⅛-inch pop rivet or a self-tapping screw in each hole.

**7** The pro brushes more hardening resin over the cloth, working with an up-and-down motion to eliminate the tiny air bubbles that get into the resin during mixing. Making sure the cloth is saturated, he applies two layers.

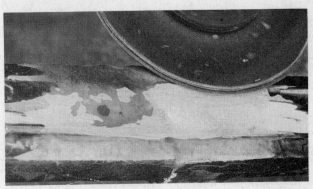

**8** He waits until it has hardened, then grinds down the fiberglass until it is smooth and slightly lower than the surrounding surface. For this he puts on a mask and goggles.

**11** Our pro files down the high spots with a cheese grater file. If there are any lows, he applies further coats of fiberglass filler until these are filled. After filing, the pro sands the filler with #40 grit paper in a sanding block, tapping frequently to get rid of filler particles.

**12** Our pro now applies one thin coat of resin mixed with hardener. When it is hard, he sands it with #80 grit paper in a sanding block. He featheredges with #220 paper and water, then primes, applies putty, and wet-sands with #320 paper. He re-primes to get ready for painting.

# Working safely with fiberglass

Take no chances when working with fiberglass and related ingredients. Polyester resin can irritate the skin and, of course, the stomach lining. The curing agent or hardener is generally a methyl-ethyl ketone peroxide, which produces harmful vapors. We illustrate here the two major protective steps you should take. Wear gloves, especially when you begin working with the resin and hardener. Mask your face and cover your eyes with goggles. Check and re-check the list below until putting it into practice becomes second nature.

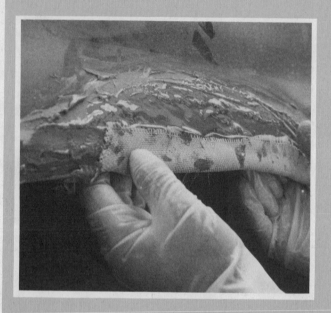 

## Safety checklist

✓ **Wear gloves.** Rubber ones are best when you're manipulating glass. Be sure they cover your wrists and shirt sleeves.

✓ **Wear a mask.** Especially during the 'glassing and sanding steps. First, you're working with a solvent-impregnated material. Second, glass in any form is bad for the lungs.

✓ **Protect your eyes.** Wear goggles, not glasses. 'Glass gets in your eyes, especially during sanding, as do vapors.

✓ **Protect your skin.** Polyester resin and the curing agent can both be harmful to the skin. Keep your hands, wrists, and arms covered.

✓ **Be firm with observers.** Keep them at a respectful distance and make sure they do not edge downwind of the work. 'Glass can get into their eyes, too.

✓ **Watch out for children and pets.** Put newspapers or other protection under your work to catch those pesky strands of fiberglass that can irritate feet and paws. And that resin-hardener-fiberglass mixture looks good enough to eat. If accidentally swallowed, dilute stomach contents with milk or coagulants and call a doctor immediately.

CHAPTER 11

# INTERIOR COSMETICS

It's not enough just to keep your car in top working condition. It must look it, too. After all, you bought your car with an eye for the quality and appearance of its interior, so it's only natural you'll want to maintain that appearance. In addition, a well kept, clean car has more resale value than a comparable one whose interior is marred by ripped vinyl and soiled upholstery.

For general housecleaning, you should remove dirt and dust from upholstery with a whisk broom or vacuum cleaner every few weeks— or oftener if the car receives heavy use. Clean synthetic fabrics with detergent or a colorless spot remover (for strains) and use lukewarm water and a non-alkaline soap for genuine leather and coated fabrics.

Periodically remove the seats and give your interior a thorough cleaning. At the same time, you can do a little preventive medicine by rolling back the floor covering and inspecting the floor for signs of rust. If you find any, remove it and undercoat the floor area to avoid future problems.

Whenever you're working on upholstery and interior trim, keep in mind a few simple precautions. They can save you time and money. Be careful of sharp tools in your hands or pockets when you're working on the interior of your car. Carelessness can result in ripped upholstery. Also, use the upholstery tool and other appropriate tools when removing and replacing interior sections—and avoid using excessive force on them.

When you have to remove upholstery panels in the course of a repair, it's better to remove the panel completely—not just loosen it. In working around a loosened panel, you're apt to tear the fabric or at least get it dirty.

When using spot removers, always follow directions to the letter. And, if you're using an inflammable cleaning agent, be sure the area is well ventilated.

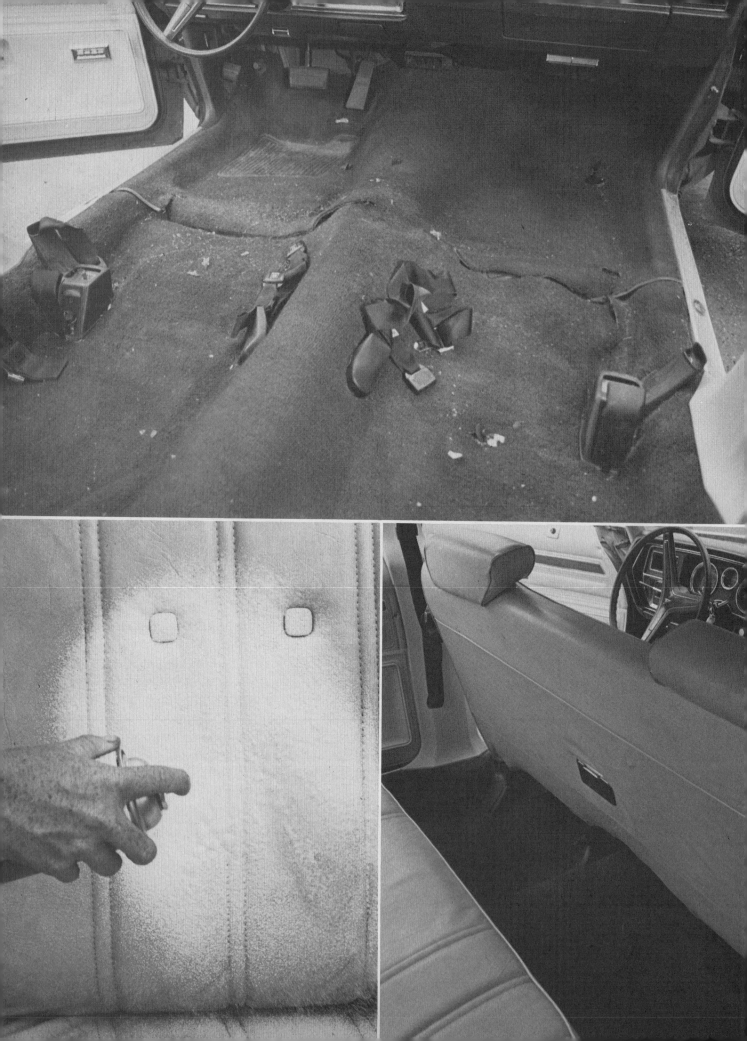

# Job steps Maintaining your car's interior

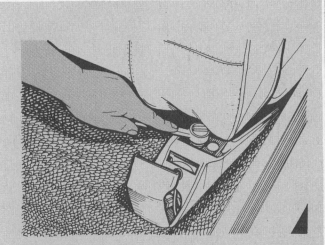

**Remove the front and back seats** together with the seat belts and seat-belt fasteners, clearing the interior of the car.

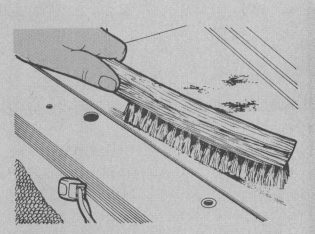

**Roll back the floor covering** and inspect the floor for signs of rust. Remove any rust, make repairs, if necessary, and undercoat the area.

**Shampoo the floor carpeting** and clean the seats and all other interior upholstery thoroughly. Be sure to use the right cleaners for the right fabrics.

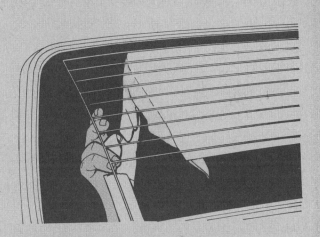

**Install a defroster/defogger mechanism**—a nice safety touch for the rear window in winter driving.

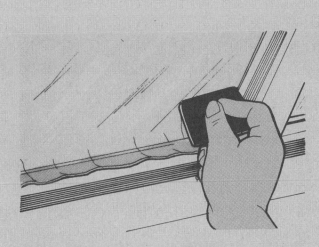

**Apply a tint film to your car windows**—another way to make the interior a more pleasant and safe place to ride in.

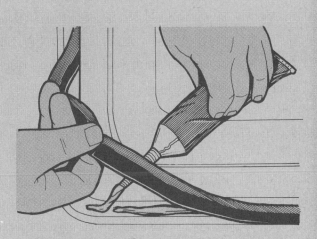

**Replace aged or damaged weatherstripping**—a must for helping to keep out water leaks and wind whistles.

# Removing seats

1 To remove the front seat, pry off the outer cover and remove the bolts under the rear of the seat on both sides with a wrench. First use the seat adjustment mechanism to move the seat to its maximum forward position to make the job easier.

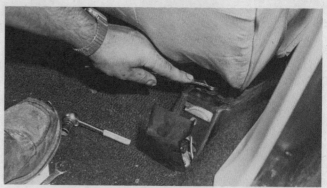

2 Remove the bolts in front of the seat on both sides. They are usually located under the carpeting, so you'll have to fold back the floor matting or carpeting. Move the seat to its maximum rearward position to make the removal of the front bolts easier.

5 Pull the rubber boot off the seat belt cover, if there is one, and remove the bolts anchoring the belts to the floor. The seat will come out even if these bolts are not disconnected, but you should remove them anyway before shampooing the carpet and lubricating the seat tracks.

6 With an assistant, lift the front seat up and out of the car door. Since door openings vary depending on the make of car, you will have to experiment to find the best way to take the seat out of your car door.

## Looking for rust

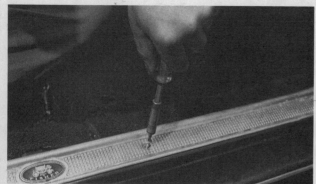

1 As a really smart preventive measure, you should periodically look under the floor covering or carpeting in your car for signs of rust. Generally, carpets and floor coverings can either be simply pulled out or removed by unscrewing the metal plate shown here with a Phillips-head screwdriver.

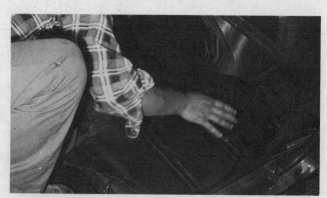

2 Pull away the carpeting and any liners that may be underneath so you can examine the car floor. Check carefully for signs of rust, even very small spots. If you are lucky and don't find any traces of rust, clean the area, spray on undercoating, and replace the carpeting.

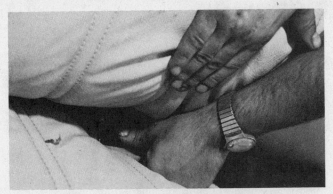

3 Push down on the plastic seat belt guide and pull the top portion of the seat up so there is enough room to pull the whole seat belt through from the rear.

4 Adjust the seat to its maximum forward position, then pull the safety seat belts through from the back.

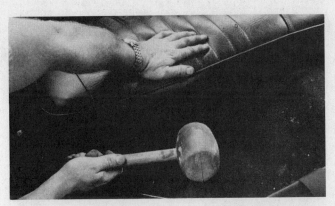

7 Remove the rear seat cushion by pushing back on the front of it to unlock it from the metal holding clips. This can be done by pushing back with your knees or by using a rubber mallet to hit the front edge of the seat toward the rear in order to release it. When it is loose, lift up the front and remove the seat.

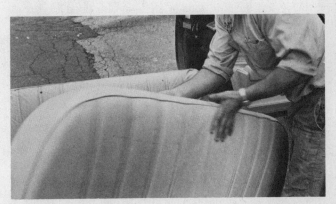

8 The backrest is hung on a hinge at the top and held tight at the bottom with screws or bolts. Remove them and lift the backrest up in the front and off the hooks at the top. It can then be removed. The interior is now clear and you are ready to inspect the floor for rust, to undercoat and lubricate the front seat tracks, and to shampoo the carpeting.

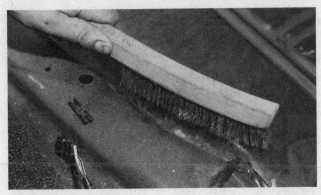

3 If you spot any rust at all, you must remove it—all of it. When the rust spots are superficial and no real damage has yet been done to the metal, you can just wire brush the area until all the rust is gone, apply undercoating to the bare metal, and then replace the floor covering.

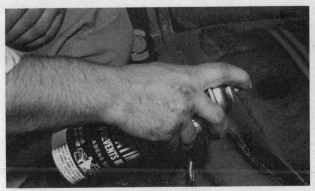

4 In some cases, you will find that the rust is more extensive and has already etched out a depression or a hole in the car floor. Depending on the depth of the rust, you can either grind it out and fill and patch the damage, or in more serious cases pop-rivet a patch over the area. Then apply undercoating to the repair and replace the floor covering.

# All about cleaners and cleaning

## Fabrics

There are three types of fabrics used in a car's interior: synthetics (nylon, rayon), genuine leather, and coated ones (vinyl, mylar). It's a good idea to vacuum or brush (with a whisk broom) your upholstery every few weeks. If your car receives heavy use, you may want to clean off the accumulated dust and dirt more frequently. Be careful about using a whisk broom on fabrics that have raised tapestry patterns because you may damage the fine threads. Use a vacuum instead.

## Cleaning synthetic fabrics

Synthetic fabrics can be cleaned with detergent (for general cleaning) and with volatile cleaners (for difficult stains). Detergents will usually do a good job on most stains and on dirt. Volatile cleaners are used for dissolving tough stains like grease, oil, and other road grime. Be sure any detergent you use is the correct one for the fabric you're cleaning, because the wrong one may damage the color or finish of the fabric.

When you are using a volatile cleaner to remove stains or grime, be careful not to apply too much and use a clean cloth to apply it. Remember the solvent is supposed to do the work, so don't rub too hard or too vigorously when you apply it. Clear the area you want to clean of all loose particles of dirt. Take a clean cloth—cheesecloth is OK—and dampen it with the solvent. Let some of the cleaner evaporate so the cloth is only slightly damp. Then, using a circular, lifting motion and light pressure, rub the stained area. Work from the outer edge of the stain in toward the center until the whole area is cleaned. Change to a clean spot on the cloth after every few strokes.

When you have finished applying the cleaner, use a clean white blotter to soak up the excess solvent. Continue blotting until no more cleaner soaks into the blotter surface. Then wait for several minutes to let the cleaner evaporate from the area. Make sure you do not apply too much. It should never sink through to the padding under the upholstery because some cleaners will attack and damage the sponge rubber frequently used as padding.

On a really stubborn stain, you may have to repeat the application and blotting procedures a couple of times. If a ring forms on the fabric while you are removing a stain, clean the entire area as you would the area of the stain. Always let cleaned upholstery dry completely before you use it.

Most important, strictly follow the directions accompanying any cleaner. Keep the work area well-ventilated when using volatile cleaners and avoid prolonged breathing of the vapors.

To clean synthetic fabrics with a detergent, mix the detergent with warm water until you have a bucket of thick suds. Apply the solution to the surface of the upholstery, using light to medium pressure when scrubbing. Rub the area with a second dampened cloth to remove the detergent and all soiled material. Then clear the area of excess moisture with a clean dry cloth. Allow the upholstery to dry partially. Then inspect to see if another application of detergent is needed. When you are satisfied that the upholstery is thoroughly cleaned, let it dry completely.

On broadcloth, it is not advisable to use cleaning solutions containing water since they tend to destroy the finish of the cloth.

## Cleaning leather and coated fabrics

The surface of leather and coated fabrics should be wiped occasionally with a dry cloth to clean off collected dirt. Mix water and a nonalkaline soap and apply thick suds to the material with a piece of gauze or cheesecloth. Wipe the area clean with a damp cloth. Then dry the material with a clean, dry cloth. Don't use volatile cleaners, furniture polish or polishes used for auto body finishes, or household cleaning or bleaching agents for cleaning these fabrics. On leather surfaces, a nonstaining conditioner may be used. Don't use neat's-foot oil, because it will change the color of the leather.

## Cleaning carpets

First, brush or vacuum the carpet after removing the seats. If this does not clean it sufficiently, remove it, vacuum it thoroughly, and apply a rug shampoo. Clean approximately one square foot of the carpet at a time, removing as much of the cleaner as possible as you complete each area. When you have finished, use an air hose to fluff up the carpet pile, then allow it to dry. When it is completely dry, you may want to use the air hose on it again.

If the carpet is not terribly soiled, you may shampoo it while it is still in the car using foam upholstery cleaner. If you must use a volatile cleaner on a carpet to remove a stain, use it sparingly since it may remove some of the coloring.

## Removing upholstery stains

**Blood** stains cannot be removed by using hot water or soap and water. This will only set the stain, rendering it impossible to remove. Instead, rub the stain with a clean cloth that has been dipped into cold water until no more of the stain will come out. Be sure to use a clean portion of the cloth as you continue to rub the stain.

If the cold water alone does not remove the stain, apply a small amount of household ammonia in water to it, cleaning it away with a wet cloth after about a minute. If the stain remains, try a mixture of cornstarch and cold water. Make a paste and apply it to the stain. Let the paste dry and then pick it off. The paste should absorb the stain as it dries and the stain will come off with it. For a bad stain, you may have to use several applications of the cornstarch solution.

**For candy** stains other than chocolate, rub the affected area with a cloth soaked in very hot water. If some stain remains, you may want to use a volatile cleaner on it. For candy stains from fruit or cream-filled candies, wash the area with a cloth soaked in lukewarm water and suds from a neutral soap, then scrape the area while still wet with a dull knife. For chocolate stains, rub the area first with a cloth dipped in lukewarm water. When the spot dries, lightly apply a volatile cleaner and blot the area with a clean blotter to remove the cleaner and stain.

**Chewing gum:** Apply a piece of ice to the gum to harden it and then scrape it away with a dull knife. If particles remain, moisten them with a volatile cleaner and scrape them away while wet with a dull knife.

**Fruit, liquor, wine, ice cream:** Generally, these stains are best removed by treatment with very hot water. If this does not work, rub the spot lightly with a volatile cleaner.

**Grease and oil:** First remove as much of the grease or oil as possible by scraping it away with a dull knife. Then rub the stains lightly with a cloth dipped in a volatile cleaner and blot away stain and excess cleaner.

# Cleaning and lubricating the interior

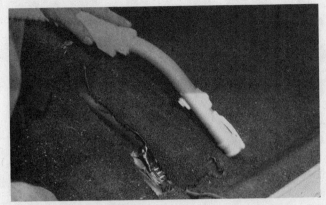

**1** With the seats removed from the car and any rust problems on the floor corrected, it's a good time to give the interior a thorough vacuuming. You'll be amazed at the amount of junk—and loose change—you'll find in the area under the seats.

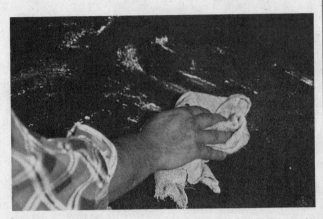

**2** Shampoo the carpeting with one of the several brands of carpet shampoo on the market. In most cases, you spray on a foam, scrub it into the carpet, and wipe it off with a clean cloth.

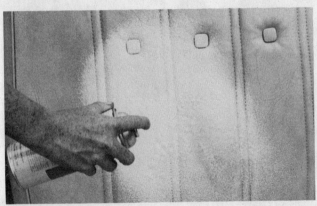

**3** This is also an excellent time to clean the vinyl seats, since they are out of the car. Spray on a good commercial vinyl cleaner, following the directions on the label. If stains persist, you may have to use more than one application to get the seats really clean.

**4** Now, clean the rest of the interior. Any detergent that degreases will do the job. You may also want to use metal or chrome polish on all interior hardware to finish up in style.

**5** Clean and then lubricate the seat tracks. Generally, the best lubricant is either white or plain grease.

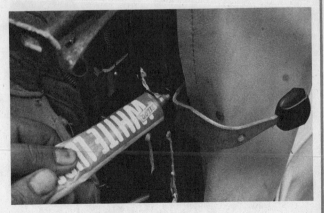

**6** It is also a good idea to lubricate various other moving parts of the seat system, such as the seat adjuster mechanism controlling the forward and backward movement of the front seat.

# Installing a defroster/defogger

**1** Disconnect the battery. This is very important whenever you are working on a car's electrical system.

**2** Position the switch in the bracket and snap it into place. Mount the switch assembly under the dash (allow for knee clearance) using the two screws supplied.

**3** Strip the insulation and crimp a spade terminal on one end of the six-foot length of black wire.

**7** Using the black wire left over from step 4, strip the insulation, and crimp a ring terminal to one end. Attach the ring terminal end to a ground convenient for attachment to the element at the rear window.

**8** Clean the inside of the window thoroughly with window cleaner and then with ammonia and water. Polish the glass with a clean, dry cloth. Be sure the glass is free of film, moisture, and all decals.

**9** Lay the element on a flat work surface with the colored line marked side up. Peel off and reattach the two vertical paper protecting strips so the element side bars are just covered.

## Tinting car windows

People who live in the sunbelt area of the country, or in any particularly sunny place, may want to apply a tint film to their car windows. Tinted glass keeps out a great deal of sunlight, thereby keeping your car cooler when it must be left out in the sun for any length of time.

Tinted glass also cuts down glare from oncoming lights, reflected lights, and sunlight. This gives you a safer and more comfortable ride, especially on long journeys which tire the eyes. You should, however, check the laws in your state regarding tinted glass on cars. Some states have regulations prohibiting the use of such glass for windshields.

**1** Cut the tint film ¼-foot larger than the glass opening, using scissors or a razor blade. You can trim the film to the glass size after installation, using the window frame as a guide. Remember, the finished installation must be less than the glass opening.

**2** Clean the glass thoroughly with window cleaner and a squeegee. Use a razor blade to remove any specks or paint. Then remove the protective backing from the film. Start by pulling the backing from the film at one corner. You don't need to remove the backing completely at this time.

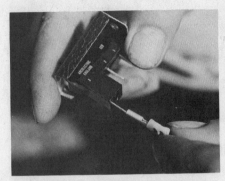

**4** Connect this to terminal number 3 on the switch and route the wire back under the dash to a body screw that can serve as a ground. Install a ring terminal and ground the wire. Save the excess wire.

**5** Strip the insulation and crimp a spade terminal to one end of the 17-foot red wire and attach it to the number 2 wire on the switch. Route the red wire under the carpet to the rear window for connection to the heating element.

**6** The defrosting unit can be mounted with its power terminals leading up or down. Route the red wire to above or below the rear window accordingly.

**10** Center the element on the inside of the window and secure it with masking tape. Mark it with tape or a marking pencil.

**11** Line up the terminal tabs with the element side bars so the bars correctly cross the tabs. Peel the protective paper from the tabs, stick the tabs to the glass, and pull the side bars from the backing.

**12** Strip and crimp the spade terminals to the black and red wires and attach them to the terminal tabs, securing the side bars to the tabs. Be sure you have enough length for each wire to reach its terminal.

**3** Spray the glass with water—it must be wet. Put the film, cut to size, on the wet glass with the partially removed clear backing toward the interior. Hold the film with one hand while you strip away the backing with the other.

**4** Turn the film over so the adhesive side faces the glass. While the film and glass are still wet, the film can be moved on the glass for exact positioning. Then squeegee the film as hard as possible with a wet, soft rubber squeegee. Work from the center out to remove excess water and bubbles.

**5** After you have worked out all the water and air bubbles with the squeegee, run it along the edges of the window and tuck in the edges under the weatherstripping. Now trim around the edges with a razor blade.

# Installing weatherstripping

Weatherstripping, which is used to close the gap between moving and stationary panels, keeps out water, dust, and air from the car's interior. It can be attached to panels in several ways, depending on the make and model of the car. It may be connected by adhesives, screws or clips, or by inserting it in a specially designed groove built on the panel or in a screw-on retainer. In most cases, adhesive is used with clips or screws.

Aged or damaged weatherstripping must be replaced to prevent leaks and whistles. Use caution when removing weatherstripping attached by plastic retainer clips, since they are easily damaged.

A thin, flat, dull knife, like a putty knife, is an excellent tool for removing the old adhesive from the pinch-weld or flange prior to applying adhesive for the new weatherstripping.

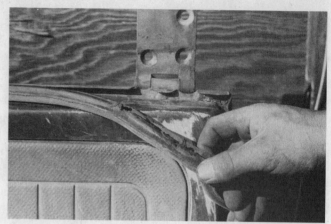

**1** Remove the old weatherstripping by prying up at one end and pulling it off. Then take off all the old adhesive and residue with a dull knife.

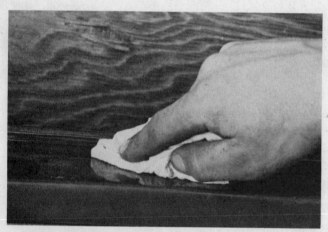

**2** Clean the bare pinch-weld or flange metal with a degreasing solvent. This is a good time to check the flange for irregularities and the clips for indications of damage. Make repairs and replacements where necessary.

**3** Apply the weatherstripping adhesive to the bare metal. Be sure to purchase the adhesive especially made for this job. Let the first coat dry on the metal.

**4** Apply a second coat of adhesive and bond it immediately. Don't pull the stripping too taut around the corners or you may end up with an inadequate seal. Test the installation by using the water test (see page 142, Chapter 9) or the brown paper test (see the Body Shop on this page).

Here is a good way to check whether you have a proper seal in your replacement weatherstripping.

After the weatherstripping has been installed, pull a piece of brown paper (torn from a paper bag) through the opening between the window and the stripping with the window closed shut. Check the feel of the drag on the paper for tightness. If the installation is good, it will be hard to pull the paper through. If the paper goes through easily, the seal is poor. If you find places where the paper pulls through easily, it means the weatherstripping is not adhering evenly.

CHAPTER **12**

# LITTLE TOUCHES

So your car's body is finally shipshape. Now you'll want to think about those little touches that cause heads to turn, protect the appearance you've worked so hard to get, or just plain make your car safer and more pleasurable to ride in.

To protect your car's paint job against the perils of the parking lot, you can install adhesive plastic moldings to large panel areas such as doors. They are easy to apply and even look good. For further protection, you can apply clear plastic or chrome strips to the edges of the doors. They conform to the door shape and protect against chipped paint while you're shopping at the supermarket.

You can protect your new paint job by attaching conical rubber bumpers just below the side molding. They not only protect the car's paint, but also protect the other person's car from collecting chipped paint from your car door. For another protective touch, apply a plastic film to the rocker panels to protect them from stones and gravel tossed up by the tires.

You should wash your engine with a heavy duty cleaner every once in a while. It makes it look nice and new and you don't get greasy every time you get near it.

To brighten things up, you may want to add pinstriping to your car using pressure-sensitive pinstriping tape. It's easy to apply and gives a lot of pizazz. You should also know how to install a new car antenna and how to make small repairs on the vinyl roof.

You should learn how to fix headlights and sidelights, if for no other reason than pure safety. And for any number of reasons, you may want to bolt a trailer hitch onto your car. You can install the lighter duty hitches yourself, but for a Class Three hitch—an equalizing one—you'd be better off taking the job to a pro.

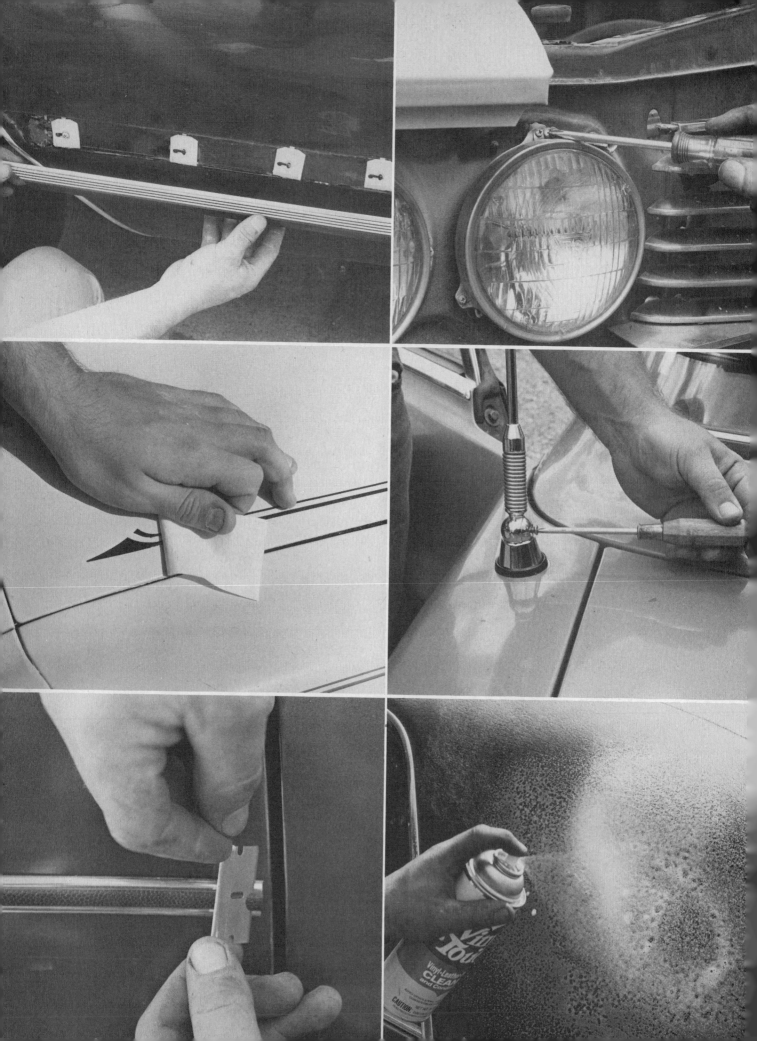

# Job steps Adding some extras

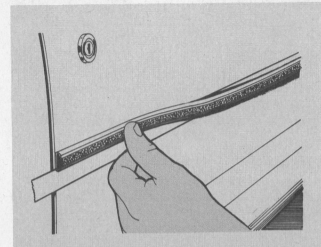

**Apply adhesive side moldings** to protect the paint. Measure and cut to size. Lay down masking tape as a guide and press it on firmly.

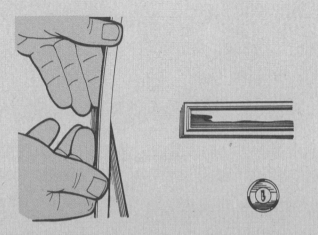

**Snap on protective chrome** strips around the edge of the car doors. Hold the strip to the door edge to test for length. Cut to size and press on.

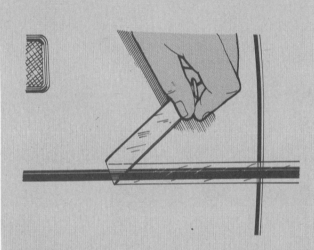

**Add pinstriping.** Clean the surface first. Apply either stick-on or decal-type pinstripes. Eyeball it for straightness.

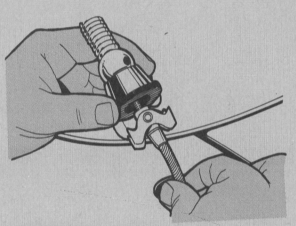

**Replace antenna.** Disconnect the battery. Remove the old antenna and mark the wires for easy reconnecting. Tie on the new guide and feed it through the fender. Tighten the assembly, then reconnect the wires and battery.

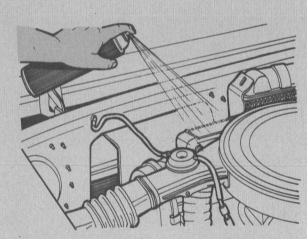

**Clean your engine.** Spray cleaner on the engine and the underside of the hood. Hose off and apply silicone to the distributor wires.

**Replace headlights.** Remove the headlight housing door and retaining ring. Loosen the screws and lift the light out. Unplug the wires at the back of the light.

# Protecting the car door

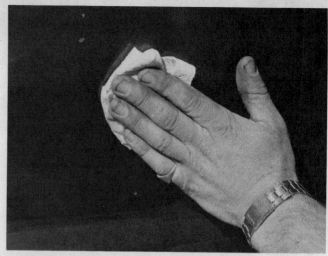

Chips on your car door are one common result of another car door hitting it in a parking lot. To prevent this, you can apply an adhesive molding along the side of the door or add a plastic or chrome strip to the door edge. To prevent your door from damaging someone else's, you can attach conical rubber bumpers below the side molding strips.

1 Before you apply adhesive moldings, wash the car door with a wax-and-silicone remover. The moldings will not adhere if any wax remains on the surface.

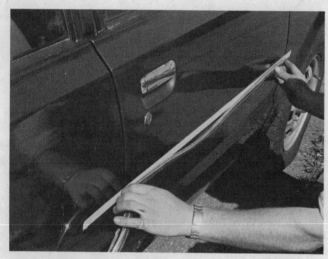

3 Measure the length of molding you will need by holding it against the car.

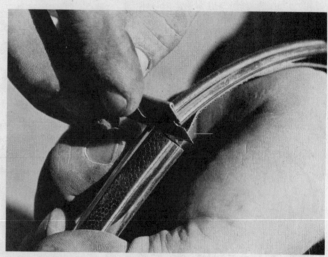

4 Cut the molding with a razor blade.

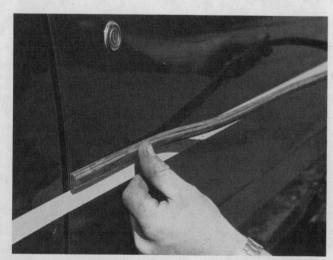

6 Place one end of the molding down first. To ensure that it will lie flat, press slowly along its length as you pull the other end taut.

**To protect the door edge,** you can attach a clear plastic or chrome strip. The strip is flexible and conforms to the shape of the door. It snaps on and doesn't require any adhesive.

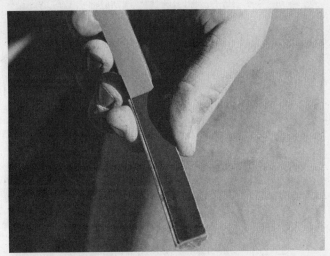

2 Place a piece of masking tape along the side of the door to use as a guide for placing the molding.

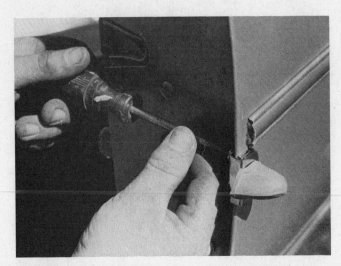

5 Peel the protective paper from the back of the molding strip.

**Conical rubber bumpers** screw on below the side molding strip. They help prevent the door from chipping the surface of another car door.

# Chip-proof your finish

You can apply a transparent plastic film to the rocker panels to protect them from stones and gravel kicked up by the tires. The product is a 10-mil clear plastic film with adhesive on one side. Gravel bounces off it without chipping the paint underneath and road tar can be wiped off with any solvent. You can remove it without harming the surface below.

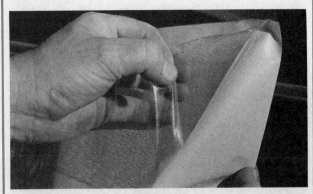

1 Clean the area to be protected such as the rocker panel or the lower edge of the door, with a wax-and-silicone remover. Peel the protective backing off the clear plastic.

2 Apply the clear plastic to the area by pressing it down. Handle the plastic carefully because any dirt or dust coming in contact with the adhesive backing will stick to it.

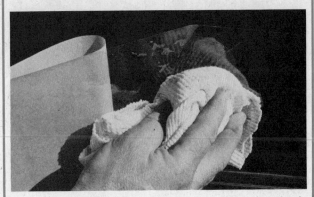

3 Continue to pull off the backing and press the plastic down. To make sure it adheres, rub it with a clean cloth, pressing and pushing towards the sides to remove any air bubbles.

# Cleaning your engine

Industrial-type cleaning compounds such as "Gunk" are useful for cleaning away grease and grime accumulated on the engine without any backbreaking work on your part. Following the directions on the can, you just spray the cleaner on, let it stand for about ten minutes, and hose away the dirt and grease. There is no scrubbing, no fuss, no mess. If the engine is really covered with grime, use two applications. You may even want to clean up the mess that's been accumulating on your garage floor over the years.

**1** Degrease your engine by spraying an industrial degreasing compound on it. Take care to mask off the distributor beforehand. Your engine will look better, and working on it will be a lot more pleasant.

**2** Clean the underside of your hood too. However, if there is a layer of asbestos there, do **not** spray industrial cleaners on it. Clean off any grease and mud that may have built up on the walls of the engine compartment.

**3** Wash the cleaner and dirt off with a good blast of water from your hose. Take the masking off your distributor, start your engine, and let it warm for a few minutes. This will dry out the engine.

**4** After the engine has been cleaned and dried, spray silicone on the wires leading from the distributor to the spark plugs to keep them soft. You should do this in any case from time to time as a regular maintenance procedure.

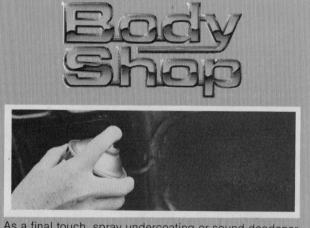

**Body Shop**

As a final touch, spray undercoating or sound deadener under your hood. You may already have material under the hood that acts as a sound deadener, but this material also retains water splashed up from the road. This promotes rust, so you may want to remove the material and use spray undercoat, which is waterproof, instead.

Remember to clean the hood first to remove all the dirt and grime before you apply the undercoating.

# Applying pinstriping tapes

**1** Here is an assortment of pressure-sensitive tapes which let you add the zing of pinstriping to your car even if you're not a master painter. These tapes are good looking, permanent, and, above all, easy to apply.

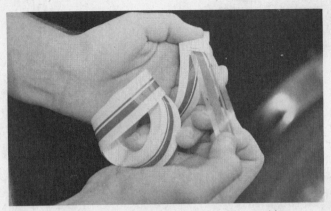

**2** First clean and mark your car with chalk, masking tape or crayon in the pattern you desire. Then peel away the paper backing tape. The pinstriping tape shown here is the double-stick type, the easiest to apply in terms of straightness and alignment. This tape is available in single and double stripe configurations. The one applied here is a parallel thick and thin one.

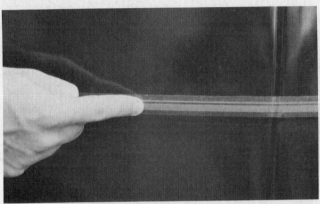

**3** Stick the cellophane strip onto the surface, aligning the colored stripes to the pattern or lines you have made. Press your forefinger firmly along the tape to secure the stripes to the body. Remember to use firm pressure.

**4** Now peel back the clear cellophane-like portion and the striping will adhere to the car's surface. After a few days, the stripes will become permanent— they won't lift off or fall off.

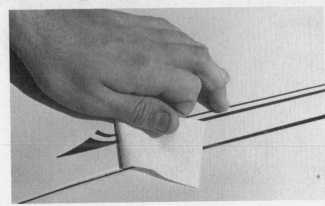

**5** Decorative end pieces (arrows, points, and the like) are available in tape to finish off your pin-striping in style. Just peel off the protective backing, place in position, apply pressure, and pull away the cellophane, leaving the decorative end affixed.

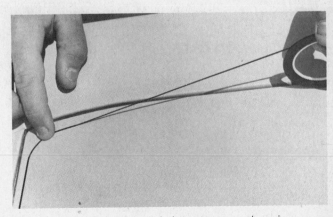

**6** Helpful hint. When negotiating curves or changing the direction of the tape-dispensing hand, press down with the finger tip in small increments. In conjunction with the hand dispensing the tape, this lays out the radius of the curve.

# Replacing a radio antenna

**1 CAUTION:** Before you begin, disconnect the battery ground cable to avoid getting a shock or shorting out other dashboard wires. Disconnect the old antenna cable from the radio lead under the dashboard. Mark the lead with a piece of tape to distinguish it from other wires. Tie one end of a long guide wire to the end of the old antenna cable. To prevent the wire from being pulled through, tie the other end to the center of a paint stick.

**2** To remove the old antenna base assembly from the fender, loosen the metal fitting by turning it counterclockwise with a wrench. Then remove the fitting and rubber gasket, making sure the threaded metal pipe underneath doesn't fall inside the fender.

**3** To pull the threaded pipe out of the fender hole, use a small screwdriver to push the swivel hooks into a vertical position. Then pull out the pipe assembly.

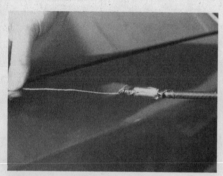

**4** Pull the old antenna cable out through the fender hole. When the entire cable is out and several inches of guide wire are showing, untie the guide wire from the old cable.

**5** Tie the guide wire securely to the connector end of the new cable. Feed the new cable through the fender hole by pulling the guide wire from the inside of the car. The metal fitting at the other end of the new cable will prevent it from being pulled through the fender hole.

**6** The new antenna has a spring on its base for flexibility. The end of the new antenna mast is a ball that fits into the socket base where it is held by two screws. Remove these screws and the ball. Loosen the screw at the bottom of the socket all the way, then tighten it about two turns.

**7** Move the swivel hooks at the bottom of the socket to a vertical position and insert them in the fender hole. Use a screwdriver to position them horizontally. Tighten the socket screw all the way so the hooks grip the underside of the fender and the new base assembly is firmly attached to the fender surface.

**8** Remove the guide wire from the connector end of the new cable. Plug the new cable into the radio lead under the dashboard, then reconnect the battery ground cable.

**9** Place the ball end of the mast in the socket and tighten the screws slightly. Extend the antenna to check its position, then tighten the screws when the adjustment is complete.

# Attaching a trailer hitch

Trailer hitches come in three classes or types. A Class One hitch attaches to the bumper and is capable of pulling the least weight of the three. The photos show how to attach this type. A Class Two hitch attaches to the frame of the car and can pull more weight. A Class Three hitch also attaches to the car frame but it should be installed by a pro. It is an equalizing hitch which spreads the weight it is pulling over the entire chassis.

**1** Attach the hitch brackets to either side of the bumper, then place the tow bars on the brackets.

**2** On each bracket, push a bolt up through the bottom, through the tow bar, and through the upper bracket. Don't tighten the bolts.

**3** To protect the bumper from scratches, you can slip a piece of corrugated cardboard between the hitch brackets and the bumper.

**4** Align the tow bar so it is equidistant from the bumper. Then tighten the bolts gradually, working on one bolt and then the other until both are tight.

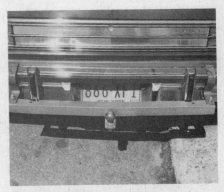

**5** This tow bar is attached securely. Brackets are made to fit each type of bumper so be sure you buy brackets made for your model car.

# Repairing a vinyl roof cover

**1** Vinyl is difficult to repair because it was stretched when it was put on the car and the sun causes it to shrink. Professional repair jobs are no better looking than using a do-it-yourself kit. The only way to get a perfect vinyl top is to replace it.

**2** Before you begin the repair, clean the vinyl with a vinyl cleaner and conditioner. It is important to get the vinyl as clean and soft as possible before you attempt to stretch the edges of the tear so they will meet.

**3** Coat the underside of the torn flap and the outer edges with vinyl glue, which is available in aerosol cans or squeeze bottles. Stretch the edges of the tear so they meet as you press the torn piece down.

# Installing a headlight

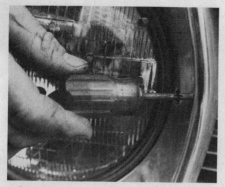

**1** Open the hood of the car. Remove the screws on the headlight door with a Phillips screwdriver.

**2** Remove the headlight door.

**3** Don't confuse the adjusting screw (left) with the retaining ring screw (right). You can change a sealed beam headlight without realigning the lamp if you are careful not to loosen the adjusting screws.

**4** Use a magnetic screwdriver when loosening the retaining ring screws because they are placed in so far they can drop behind the headlight. Remove the sealed beam headlight and retaining ring by turning it clockwise. Unplug the wires at the back of the bulb.

**5** Plug in the new lightbulb, then replace the retaining ring.

**6** Place the keyhole opening on the retaining ring over the screws, then turn it counterclockwise so the screws fit securely in the small end of the hole. Tighten the screws and replace the headlight door.

## Replacing a turn signal or backup light bulb

To replace the light bulb in a stoplight, a turn signal light, a parking light, or a backup light, you will have to locate it. If the lens retaining screws are visible from the outside of the car, you can reach the bulb by removing the screws and the lens. If no screws are visible, reach in through the trunk or engine compartment and remove the bulb by twisting it counterclockwise.

To install a new bulb, align the pins on the base with the proper slot in the socket. Insert the bulb in the socket and turn it clockwise to lock it in place. If the bulb doesn't turn, it is not aligned correctly. Remove the bulb, turn it one-half turn, and insert it again. If necessary, replace the lens.

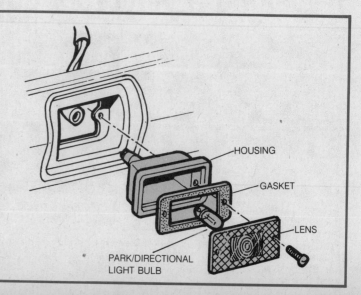

HOUSING

GASKET

LENS

PARK/DIRECTIONAL
LIGHT BULB

CHAPTER **13**

# PAINTING

Painting is an important part of bodywork because a car is always judged by the appearance of the final coat of paint. This topcoat can be decorative as well as functional depending on how you approach the paint job.

The first and most common reason to paint is to refinish a part of the car that has been damaged. Painting a spot repair requires several applications of paint that must blend into the original finish.

Second, you may want to refinish the entire car. You can do this simply because you want to change the color. Or you may want to enhance its appearance before you sell it. Or you may want to restore a deteriorated finish. Refinishing the entire car must be preceded by masking, a time-consuming but necessary task.

And last, you may want to let your car reflect your personality. You can decorate the car with anything from small, thin pinstripes to an entire mural.

Before you begin to paint, you must find out what kind of paint is on your car because different paints require different methods of application. Then, to get a quality paint job, one that is smooth and adheres well, you must prepare the surface. The color coat, whether it covers the entire car, one panel, or is added as a decoration, will not fill or cover any surface imperfections. It will magnify them.

Painting requires a combination of skill and a thorough knowledge of paint materials. Skill can be acquired only through practice. The more often you paint, the easier the job will be. Paint materials are constantly being improved and upgraded by the paint manufacturers so it is important to keep up-to-date.

# Job steps Painting

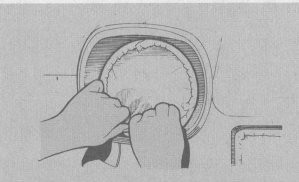

**1** Mask all areas of the car not to be painted, such as headlights and bumpers, with paper and masking tape.

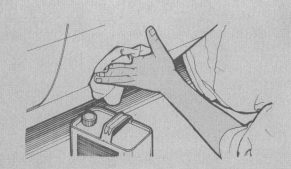

**2** Clean the car with a wax-and-silicone remover to remove all dirt and wax.

**3** Apply three or more coats of primer surfacer, depending on the condition of the repaired surface. Allow each to flash dry. When the last coat is dry, sand thoroughly with #400 grit paper wet or dry.

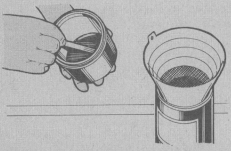

**4** To thoroughly mix the paint, pour it into another container. Put some thinner in the bottom of the first can and stir until no pigment is left on the bottom.

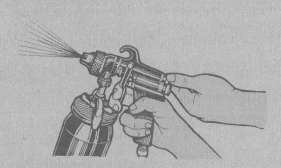

**5** Reduce the paint following the directions on the label. Strain the paint into the cup, then adjust the spray gun.

**6** Apply the paint in long, steady strokes, each overlapping the previous by 50 percent. Apply four or five coats, letting each one flash dry.

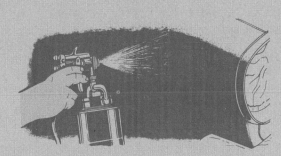

**7** Mix the final or mist coat by adding one part paint to five parts thinner. Apply this coat at slightly lower spray gun pressure.

**8** To get a very smooth finish, wet-sand the last coat of paint with #600 grit sandpaper and lots of water. Use a squeegee to remove the sludge so you can check for smoothness.

# All about preparing the surface

The appearance and durability of any finish depend to a large extent on the condition of the surface over which the paint is applied. You must take enough time to prepare the surface properly so the finished job will look professional.

## What is the surface?

The surface is the condition of the auto body part to be painted just prior to the application of color coats. To get the surface smooth and level, you have to fill and sand it. You also have to treat the surface to get good adhesion for the top coat. Remember, the color coat will not fill in rough areas, so the finished job will be no smoother than the surface over which the paint is applied.

## Preparatory steps

If possible, wash the car with soap and water. Then use a wax-and-silicone remover to get rid of any wax, grease or other surface contaminants. Gasoline is not a good wax remover because it leaves a film. Don't use a synthetic reducer to clean an acrylic enamel surface. Apply wax-and-silicone remover to the surface and remove it while it is still wet. Use new cotton cloths to wipe it off because laundered used cloths may still contain residue.

Remove whatever you can in the way of moldings, name plates, letters, mirrors, in fact, any object not to be painted. Tape what you cannot easily remove.

## The old finish

Check the condition of the old paint surface. It must have good adhesion and be rust-free. To test for adhesion, sand through the finish and featheredge a small spot. If the thin edge does not break or crumble, you can assume the old paint will stay on when the new color is applied. Developing rust can be detected by a roughness or pitting on the surface. The paint on those areas where either poor adhesion or rust is found must be removed to bare metal. If the panel has rusted to the point where bare metal cannot be reached, use a metal conditioner.

You now have to determine whether the old finish is acrylic lacquer, lacquer, alkyd enamel or acrylic enamel. The easiest method, if the car has not been repainted, is to consult a paint production color book at a new car dealer, an auto body supply store or a body shop. You can make a test to determine the type of finish on your car with lacquer thinner, which reacts differently when rubbed on various finishes. It dissolves lacquer very

Drawing courtesy Ditzler Automotive Finishes/PPG Industries

Bare metal
Original primer
Original paint
Repair primer coat
Repair paint 1st coat
Repair paint 2nd coat
Top coats (feathered)

**Featheredging,** or sanding an area so the edges taper from bare metal up to the top coat, is necessary to prepare the surface for painting.

Featheredged area

Bare metal

Old paint

**On a surface with good adhesion,** you can featheredge or taper the edge of the paint to the bare metal.

Old paint

Bare metal

**On a surface lacking good adhesion,** the edge of the paint will not taper but will crack, leaving a ridge along the paint edge.

easily, dissolves acrylic lacquer only with considerable rubbing, and does not dissolve alkyd enamel, acrylic enamel or catalyzed finish at all. Manufacturers have changed original factory finishes from standard baking enamels to acrylic enamels, and from nitrocellulose lacquers to acrylic lacquers.

## The new finish

Now you have to decide what finish to apply. If the car has the original factory paint job, you can use either lacquers or enamels. You may have problems if the car has had a number of paint jobs. The paint buildup can be very heavy, and more paint added on top may cause the finish to crack. To be safe, take down the old finish to bare metal.

## Sanding the old finish

If the old finish is lacquer and it's in good condition, very little sanding is necessary. You can cover it with either

When a spot is properly featheredged, all previous coats of paint and undercoats as well as the bare metal are visible.

lacquer, alkyd enamel or acrylic enamel.

If the old finish is acrylic lacquer, it must be thoroughly sanded with #400 grit sandpaper used either wet or dry. After sanding, you may apply acrylic lacquer, alkyd enamel or acrylic enamel paint.

If the old finish is enamel, it must be thoroughly sanded with a fine-grit sandpaper to provide adhesion. Now you can apply a new coat of enamel. Blending is difficult with enamels, so use them only when you are painting an entire panel, not for making a spot repair. When applying lacquer over the original factory enamel, the surface must be sanded with #400 grit or finer sandpaper. A sealer may have to be used over some enamels before lacquer can be applied. Remember, all bare metal must be primed.

## A guide to factory finishes

**All Chrysler Corporation, Ford Motor Company, and American Motors cars:**

1955 and earlier: standard baking enamel.

1956–1958: Mostly standard baking enamel, but some test colors are super enamel.

1959–1962: All super enamel.

1963–1964: Super and acrylic enamel.

1965 and later: All acrylic enamel.

**All General Motors cars:**

1955 and earlier: Nitrocellulose lacquer.

1956–1958: Lacquer; but more acrylic used each year. Check the identification plate.

1959–1972: All acrylic lacquer.

1973 and later: Mostly acrylic lacquer with some acrylic enamel.

## Stripping to metal

When a car has many layers of paint, it is often necessary to remove paint buildup completely before a new finish can be applied. You can tell if your car's body needs to be stripped to the bare metal by examining the surface. Look for cracks or deep chips or sand a damaged spot. You may not be able to featheredge the spot if there are too many layers of paint.

When you work with paint remover, do it outdoors or in a well ventilated area. Do not work in bright sunlight. The paint remover will dry before it has a chance to saturate the old paint.

A car needs from two to four applications of paint remover and scrapings, sometimes more, depending on the paint buildup. Then wash the car thoroughly to get rid of all the remover. Any residue will affect subsequent applications of paint. Dry the car immediately with clean cotton cloths. Bare metal starts to rust very quickly if left wet.

**1** Remove all chrome trim and name plates, taking out any screws or nuts. If necessary, insert a screwdriver under each one and carefully pry it up.

**2** Brush on a medium to thick coat of paint remover over the entire surface to be stripped. Let it dry for about 15 minutes.

**3** A chemical interaction will cause the paint to bubble up. When this happens, use a metal scraper to remove the paint. You can score the paint surface with the scraper to help the remover reach the paint below. But do it carefully so you don't damage the metal.

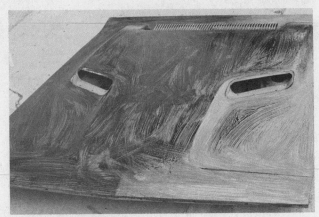

**4** After you have scraped off all the paint you can, there will probably still be some adhering to the surface. Apply a second coat of paint remover and let it dry.

**5** Scrape again when the paint has bubbled. You may have to repeat these steps several times. Put on rubber gloves and use coarse steel wool on very difficult spots. When all the paint is removed, wash the car.

# Where to find the paint code on your car

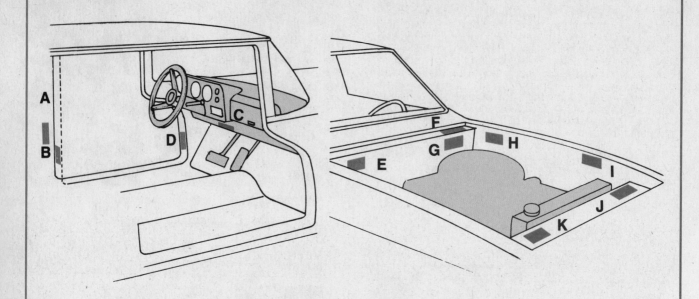

## American cars

On the patent plate or identification plate located on most cars, you will find a code number identifying the type and color of paint used. Any body shop or auto body supply store can interpret this code or tell you how to obtain this information if your car has no way to identify the paint.

### GM group

On all GM cars except the Corvair and Corvette, the identification plate is on the upper left or right side of the firewall, under the hood (G).

On the Corvair, the plate is on the cross rail in the rear engine compartment.

On the Corvette, the plate is on the instrument panel brace below the glove compartment (C).

### Ford group

All Ford cars have the identification plate on the rear of the left front door (A or B).

### Chrysler group

On the Chrysler, the plate is on the cowl top panel on the left side under the hood (F).

On an Imperial, the plate can be in one of several places: on the left front body pillar post (D), on the left side of the firewall under the hood (G), on the left wheel housing (I), or on the radiator yoke (J).

On a Dodge, the identification plate is on the left-front-fender side shield or wheel housing (H).

On a Plymouth, the plate can be in one of several places: on the right or left side of the cowl panel (G), on either front-fender side shield (H), or on the right side of the radiator side panel (K).

### Kaiser Jeep Corporation

On a Kaiser Jeep, the plate is on the upper right-hand side of the firewall, under the hood (E).

## Foreign cars

**Alfa Romeo.** The identification number is stencilled under the trunk lid.
**BMW.** The plate is on the inside rear front fender.
**Citroen.** The identification number is on a round brass tag affixed to a plate on the right front firewall.
**Datsun.** The identification number is on the firewall.
**English Ford.** The patent plate is located under the hood inside the right front fender.
**Fiat.** The identification plate is on the rear firewall on 600 models; on the right front firewall on other models.

**Mercedes-Benz.** The identification plate is on the inside left front door post.
**Peugeot.** A number is stencilled in the engine compartment on the right front fender.
**Porsche.** The identification plate is on the left door post.
**Renault.** A number is stencilled on the firewall in front of the battery case.
**Saab.** The identification plate is on the firewall.
**Sunbeam.** The index numbers are stamped on the chassis identification plate.

**Toyota.** The identification number is on the left side firewall.
**Triumph.** The identification plate is on the firewall of the Spitfire and TR-1200 models; on the left hand A-post under the hood on TR Sports 6.
**Volkswagen.** The identification number is on a sticker under or behind the spare tire.
**Volvo.** The plate is on the right side of the firewall on regular models; on the left side of the firewall on sports models.

# The spray can

A spray can is like an internal pressure spray gun: the paint and a gas are mixed inside the can. The gas propels the paint out of the can and atomizes it.

**Mixing:** If the spray can is not used for sometime, the paint sinks and the propellant rises. Before you begin to spray, shake the can vigorously. Inside the can a small metal ball acts as a paint stick. You can hear the ball move as it breaks up the paint and mixes it with the propellant. Hold the can upside down as you shake it. Point it away from the car in case any paint leaks out.

**Clearing the nozzle:** To keep the nozzle from getting clogged with paint after each coat, turn the can upside down and spray. If the nozzle does become clogged, take it off and soak it overnight in a little thinner. If the nozzle becomes too clogged to use, you can replace it with one from another spray can. To avoid mixing colors when you do this, spray for a few seconds aiming away from the car.

**An optional handle:** If you are going to do a lot of spraying, you may want to purchase a handle with a trigger mechanism made especially for the spray can. This handle makes holding the can and spraying more comfortable.

**Safety:** Exercise caution when you use a spray can. The paint is flammable so don't use a spray can near heat, sparks or an open flame. And spray only in a well-ventilated area. Do not breathe in the vapor. Avoid getting any spray in your eyes. If you get any paint on your skin, wash it off immediately.

The contents of a spray can are packaged under pressure so don't puncture the can or incinerate it. And be sure to store the can at room temperature.

**Turn the can upside down** and spray after each coat of paint; only propellant will come out. This cleans the nozzle so paint doesn't clog it.

**Take the nozzle off** if it does become clogged and soak it overnight in a small amount of thinner. This will dissolve the paint.

**To facilitate spraying,** you can buy a handle to attach to the spray can. Pulling the trigger on the handle is more comfortable than keeping your finger on the button.

## Abrasive guide

**To remove paint,** use a #16 or #24 grit disc with an electric or pneumatic disc grinder or a 3-inch #24 grit disc on a 3-inch disc holder made for a ¼-inch electric drill.

**For sanding plastic filler,** use #40 grit sandpaper dry with a sanding block or a flexible holder. Then finish the job with #80 grit paper used dry.

**For featheredging,** use #80 grit sandpaper dry, then finish with #220 or #320 grit used wet or dry if you are sanding by hand. If you are using a power sander or a sanding pad attachment in an electric drill, use the paper dry.

**For sanding putty,** hand sand with #220 or #320 grit wet-or-dry sandpaper using a sanding block. On large areas, start with #220 grit and finish with #320.

On small areas, you can use #320 grit for the entire job. Use the paper wet to achieve greater smoothness and prolong the life of the paper. However, with wet sanding it takes more time to wash away the sludge and to allow for drying.

**For sanding primer,** use #400 grit sandpaper either wet or dry. Using the paper wet will result in a smoother finish.

**For sanding the color coat,** wet-sand only with #600 grit.

# A spot touch-up

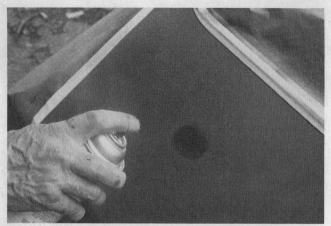

**1** Mask the surfaces not to be painted (see p. 184), then apply primer to the damaged area.

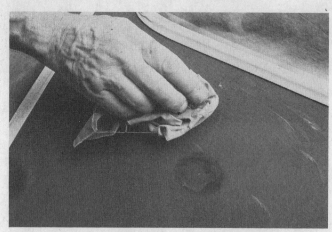

**2** Apply fine rubbing compound to the painted surface surrounding the primed area to bring the old finish up to its original shine.

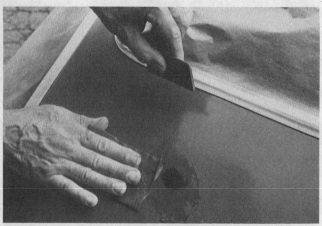

**5** Gently wet-sand the primed area with #400 grit sandpaper until it is smooth. Use a squeegee to wipe off the water, then check the surface. Dry it completely.

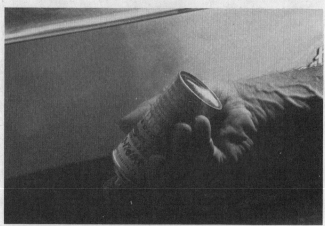

**6** Hold the color spray can away from the panel in case any paint leaks out, then shake the can of paint vigorously until you can hear the ball moving freely.

## Painting a panel

**1** To spray paint a large area such as a panel separated from adjacent areas by molding, start applying the paint at the top of the panel.

**2** Continue working your way down the panels, making sure each stroke overlaps the previous one by about 50 percent.

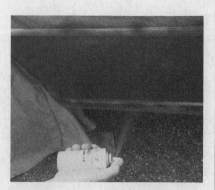

**3** Apply the next coat by working up and down. Repeat several times until the surface is completely covered, allowing each coat to flash dry before applying the next.

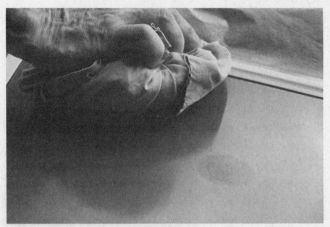

3 Rub back and forth, not in circles, until the compound is completely dry. Wipe with a clean rag. Don't rub too hard, because compounding can remove the paint.

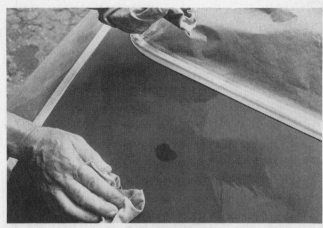

4 Clean the panel with enamel reducer. Apply the reducer with one cloth and wipe it off with a second. Make sure to wipe off the reducer before it dries.

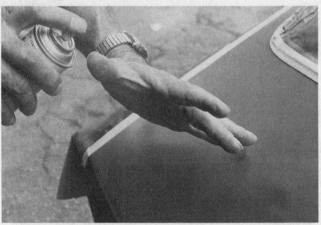

7 Hold the spray can six to eight inches from the surface. Use a ruler or your hand spread as a guide.

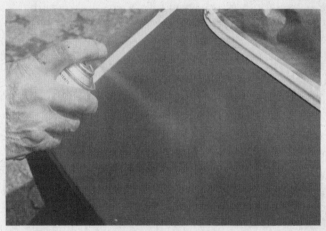

8 Apply four double coats of paint to the panel, allowing each to dry before applying the next one.

Drawing courtesy Ditzler Automotive Finishes/PPG Industries

Original spot with primer coat

First color coat

Second color coat

Third color coat

Fourth color coat

Mist coat

**To blend a spot repair** into the old finish, each coat should cover a larger area than the previous one.

9 After each coat, turn the spray can upside down and press the button for a few seconds to keep the opening in the valve clean. Shake the can well before you apply each coat. Allow to dry overnight before you apply compound.

# All about paints

Paint is composed of two parts, the volatile portion which evaporates and the film-forming portion which dries as a thin coat of color.

The non-volatile or film-forming portion is made up of a binder and pigments. A binder is a carrying medium; pigment is the color. The function of the volatile part is to dissolve the binder, making it possible to apply the paint.

As the coat of paint (and the undercoat) dry by evaporation, shrinkage occurs. If you sand or compound without allowing sufficient drying time, all the scratches and imperfections you have covered will reappear.

## Types of paint

**Enamel** is an extremely durable, lustrous paint that dries to a high-gloss finish requiring little or no compounding. The main disadvantage of enamel is that it requires a long drying time. Enamel dries in two stages. First, the solvents or reducers evaporate from the paint film. Second, the remaining paint hardens by oxidation, the absorption of oxygen from the air into the paint. Oxidation can cause enamel to turn lighter in color as it ages.

**Lacquer** paint usually contains an ingredient called nitrocellulose, which makes it dry quickly. It is probably the easiest paint to apply. Lacquer flash-dries between coats and is completely dry as soon as the solvent or thinner evaporates from the film. It is also very durable. To achieve a high-gloss finish equal to that of enamel, it is necessary to compound the final coat.

**Acrylic** is neither lacquer nor enamel but a finish made from synthetic polymers. Often added to lacquer and enamel, it is similar to lacquer in that it dries by solvent evaporation. Special solvents are used to reduce acrylic. An acrylic finish requires rubbing or polishing to obtain a high luster, but it is durable.

## Acrylic lacquer

**Acrylic lacquer,** lacquer paint with acrylic added, is recommended rather than lacquer because of its greater durability. With lacquer, you apply four or five double coats, while acrylic lacquer may require six or seven. Some lacquers may be sanded, compounded, and polished in two to four hours. But acrylic lacquer, because it retains solvent more than lacquer, should be allowed to dry overnight before sanding or compounding or you may lose the gloss.

## Thinners and reducers

Thinners and reducers dilute paint that would otherwise be too thick to spray. Thinners are used to dilute lacquer, and reducers with enamel. Never use a thinner with enamel or a reducer with lacquer or the paint will curdle.

The ingredients in thinners and reducers act to dilute the paint so it can be applied with a spray gun. Once on the surface, a thinner or reducer should keep the paint in solution long enough for it to flow out and assume a level surface, but not so long that it sags or runs. It must evaporate completely and leave a smooth, durable finish.

When using solvents, remember that two variables—temperature and humidity—affect drying time. Hot, dry weather results in the fastest drying time; cold, humid weather requires the longest drying time. For best results, painting should be done in temperatures of 60°F and above.

## Preparing the paint

When working with any kind of paint, always follow the directions on the label. Before opening any can of paint or solvent, read the directions even if you feel you know how to apply the paint. Each manufacturer uses a somewhat different paint formula and provides specific directions for use. Never

**In addition to paint, solvent, and a spray gun,** you will need masking tape and paper, a paint paddle, a strainer, and a protective mask.

use one manufacturer's directions for another manufacturer's paint. And don't assume all brands of the same type of paint require the same preparation steps.

Avoid the use of cheap thinners in high-quality paint. Make sure you use the right thinner or reducer for the particular paint you are using.

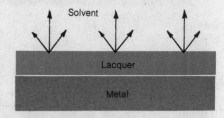

**Lacquer dries** by the evaporation of the solvents and is quick drying.

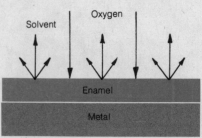

Drawing courtesy Ditzler Automotive Finishes/ PPG Industries

**Enamel dries** in a two-step process: first, by the evaporation of the solvents, second, by oxidation.

## Differences in paints

Enamel paint dries slower than acrylic, lacquer or acrylic lacquer. It dries to a full gloss and needs little polishing.

Dust in the work area is a more serious problem with enamel than with acrylic or lacquer because enamel requires a longer drying time.

Acrylic, lacquer, and acrylic lacquer need rubbing or polishing after drying to attain their full gloss.

Follow these basic steps in paint preparation to achieve a successful paint job. First, stir the paint thoroughly to get a uniform mixture of pigment, binder, and thinner. Failure to do this will make it difficult if not impossible to get a good match to the old paint.

Second, reduce the paint with the right type of thinner and use the correct amount as indicated in the directions on the label. Always keep paint and thinner at room temperature.

Last, strain the reduced paint through a fine mesh strainer. Commercial strainers are available at hardware stores.

## Equipment

In addition to paint, thinner, and spray gun, there is some additional equipment to help you do a professional-looking job. A tack cloth, made of especially prepared cheesecloth, really picks up the dust and lint rather than just moving it around when you wipe the car with it. You will need old rags and cloths for various jobs. Cotton is better than polyester or a blend because it is more absorbent. You will need a paint paddle or stick for mixing, and a paint strainer. You should always wear gloves, safety goggles, and a mask when painting.

**Here are two types of protective masks.** At left is a dust mask. At right, one which keeps out fumes and dust with a removable filter of cotton and charcoal.

| Paint repairs: what to use | | |
|---|---|---|
| **New paint over old paint** | **Recommended?** | **The reason why** |
| Lacquer over lacquer | Yes | When lacquer is used over an old lacquer finish, the thinner in the new paint will partly dissolve the old paint so it blends with the new. For this reason, lacquer can be used for a spot repair over an old lacquer finish. |
| Enamel over lacquer | For a complete paint job only | Enamel will not blend in with lacquer so it is not recommended for a spot repair or for refinishing one panel. Enamel can be used for a complete refinishing job. |
| Acrylic over lacquer | No | Even if you use a sealer over the lacquer, the acrylic paint will crack after it's exposed to the weather. |
| Acrylic lacquer over acrylic lacquer | Yes | For spot repair, this is the best paint to use because it will match the color of the old paint and will have the durability of the old so it will stay matched. |
| Enamel over acrylic lacquer | For a complete paint job only | Use enamel for a complete paint job only. For a spot repair, use acrylic lacquer. |
| Lacquer over acrylic lacquer | No | The durability of lacquer is not equal to that of acrylic lacquer so the difference between the two paints will become evident. |

## Safety

Before you start to paint, set up the area to avoid the hazards of toxic materials and accidents. Almost all paint materials, including paint and solvents, are flammable. Fumes from evaporating thinners, when confined in a small area, can be ignited by sparks. So follow these safety procedures:
● Provide adequate ventilation to remove all fumes.
● Keep all solvent containers closed except when pouring from them.
● Handle all liquids, especially solvents, with care to avoid spilling them. If you do spill thinners on your clothes, change them immediately.
● Don't smoke or light matches in the area where you are painting or mixing paint and solvents.
● Follow all safety codes when using electrical equipment.
● Wash your hands thoroughly after working with paints and solvents, especially before you eat or smoke.
● Keep the floor free of tools that might cause an accident.
● Keep the floors clean. If something is spilled, wipe it up right away.
● Keep used cloths or rags in a covered metal container.
● Throw away all used paper products at the end of the day. Don't store them.
● For personal safety, you want to wear safety goggles. These are clear plastic glasses that keep out dust, splashed liquids, and other harmful matter. You can wear safety gloves, if you wish, to protect your hands from corrosive liquids.
● Masks filter out dust and fumes. Some masks are just for dust. Others keep out fumes and they come with several filters of cotton and charcoal. The filters should be changed as often as indicated by the manufacturer.

# Masking the entire car

Masking (covering those areas not to be painted) is an extremely important step in preparing a car for painting. If you do it carelessly, you will wind up pulling off some of the paint when the masking tape is removed. The tape must be so placed that it does not touch the metal being painted. It is better to show a little chrome or glass, up to 1/16-inch, than to have the tape pressed right on the metal. A complete masking job will take longer than the painting. Before you begin, wet-sand and wash the car and dry it thoroughly.

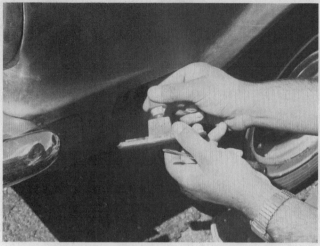

1 It is often easier to remove a part than to paint around it, so remove side marker lights and anything else that can be removed easily. Be careful not to bend or break any parts.

4 To make a masking apron, put masking paper on a flat surface—the roof of the car will do—and tape along one edge of the paper.

5 Cover the windshield with a masking apron, placing the taped edge of the paper over the masking tape outlining the windshield.

8 Now mask the windows, folding the edge of the paper to conform to the masking tape frame at the window's edge.

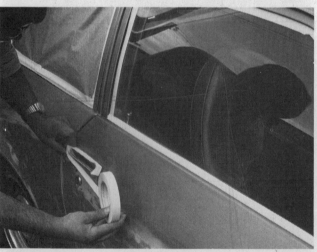

9 Wrap tape around the door handle and press it down. Be sure to tape any chrome still exposed.

2 Remove the windshield wiper blades and arms. Wrap tape around the pivot shaft and then tape the top if necessary.

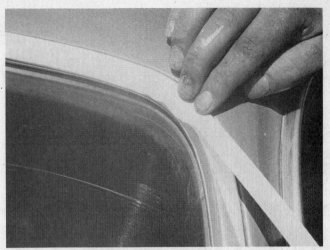

3 Place a piece of tape on the windshield chrome, running your finger along the edge. Press it to conform to the rounded corners, taking care not to stretch it.

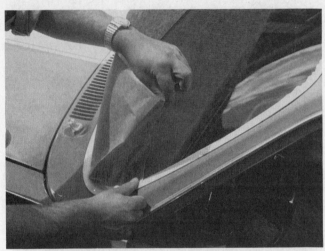

6 Fold excess paper in at the corners. If necessary, use another piece of paper, overlapping the two by three or four inches. Then tape the edges where they meet.

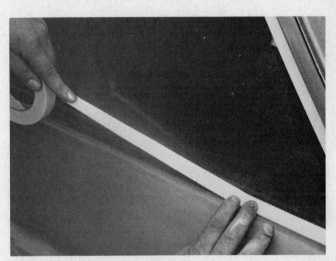

7 Lay masking tape along the outside edge of the windows. Press it down with your finger as you go. Again, don't stretch it.

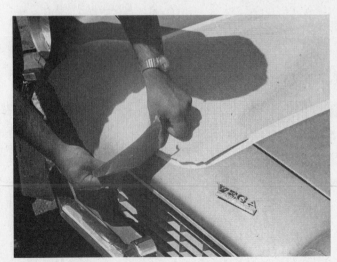

10 Outline with tape any part of the car's surface not to be painted. Then cover that area with paper, tearing or folding the edges to conform to the shape of the area.

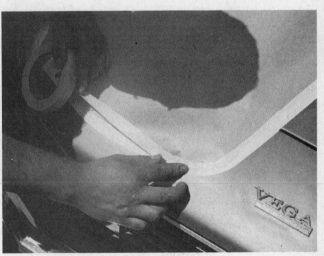

11 Tape the edge of the paper to the outline tape you applied in step 10.

**(continued)**

## Masking the entire car (continued)

12 Tape around the edges of the headlights, making sure the tape does not touch the surface to be painted.

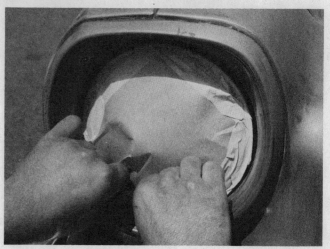

13 Cover the headlights with paper, taping the edge to the tape already on the lights.

## Masking tape and paper

Masking is a slow, tedious job that must be done with great care. Use the right materials. They will help make the task easier and the final paint job more satisfactory. Masking tape is better than other adhesives because it adheres well to most surfaces, resists solvent, is waterproof, will not fall off when it becomes wet, and can be removed without leaving a residue. Of the available widths, ¾-inch is the most common for masking, but ¼-inch is useful for masking small areas such as the nameplate, for turning angles, and for following curves.

### Masking paper

Masking paper, which is heavier than newspaper, protects areas of the car not to be painted. If you use newspaper, turn the edges under to increase strength. You can also use brown paper bags. Just make sure there are no pockets or folds that can fill up with paint. Masking paper is also somewhat more water resistant than other papers. It is available in several different widths. To mask an entire car, you may want to use both the 4-inch and 12-inch widths.

### Masking aprons

To make masking aprons, put masking tape along one edge of a piece of paper. Place the tape so half of it adheres to the paper and the other half will stick to the area to be masked. You can make masking aprons yourself. An auto body shop will have a dispenser for these. The dispenser holds both the paper and the tape. One edge of the paper is taped as it comes out.

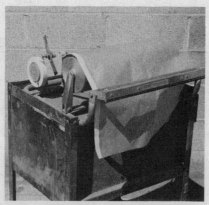

**Most auto body shops** have a dispenser to automatically lay masking tape along one edge of the paper to form a masking apron.

### Tips on masking

Here are several tips on using masking tape to ensure proper adhesion. If the tape does not adhere, it will not keep the paint out.

When you apply the tape, try to keep your fingers off the adhesive side so you don't get grease and dust on it. Make sure the surface you are taping is clean, dry, and free of dust, wax, silicone, and lubricants. Don't stretch the tape as you put it down. To tape a curve, place one edge along the curve, then gather the excess tape on the other side and press it down firmly. Make sure the tape does not touch anything to be painted. It is better to see a bit of the surface being masked—up to 1/16-inch—than to have any tape on the surface to be painted, because when the tape is pulled off, it will also pull off some paint.

Remove the masking tape as soon as the paint is no longer sticky. Don't wait overnight. Pull the tape away from the painted surface at a 90° angle. Do not apply or remove tape in cold weather. The air temperature should be at least 60°F. Store masking tape in a cool place. Never leave it on a radiator, exposed to sunlight or on top of a can of solvent. Heat, sunlight, and solvent can affect the adhesive.

14 Put tape around the edges of the taillights, then cover the inside area with masking paper as you did with the headlights.

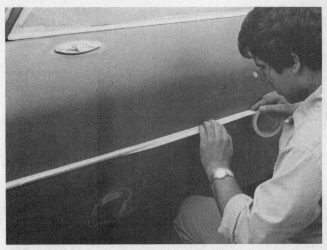

15 Carefully apply a length of masking tape over the chrome trim, making sure the tape does not touch the metal. Don't stretch the tape.

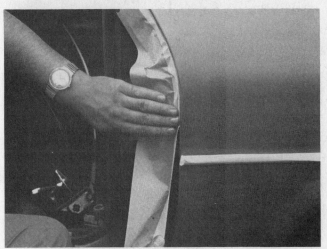

16 Put a masking apron on the rear door post, placing the tape along the outside edge of the post.

17 Put a piece of tape around the front grille, then cover the entire grille with masking paper.

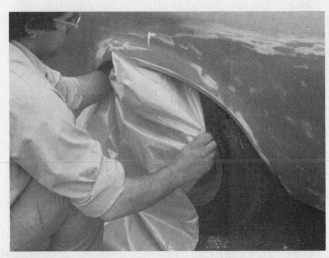

18 To protect the wheels from paint, cover each with a plastic garbage bag.

19 Now entire car is masked and ready to be primed and painted.

# The spray gun

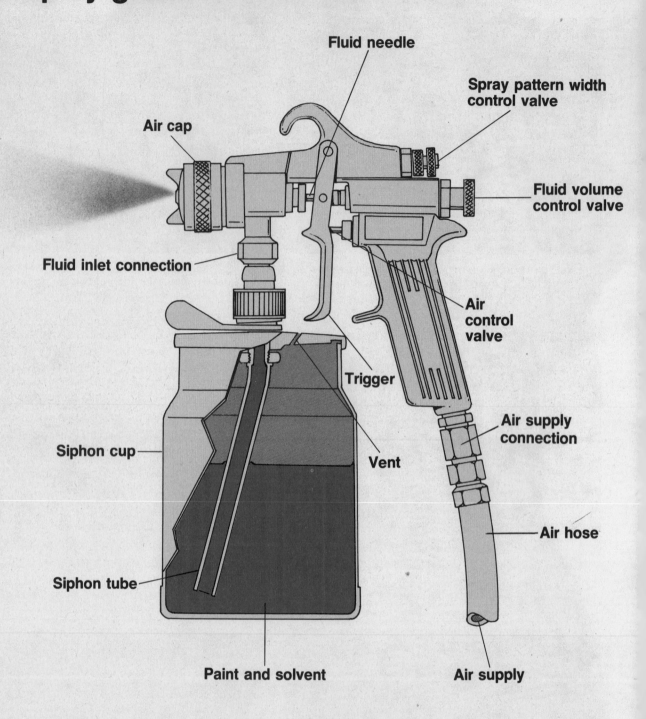

Fluid needle

Spray pattern width control valve

Air cap

Fluid volume control valve

Fluid inlet connection

Air control valve

Trigger

Air supply connection

Siphon cup

Vent

Air hose

Siphon tube

Paint and solvent

Air supply

A spray gun uses compressed air to atomize sprayable material and apply it to a surface. Air and material enter the gun through separate passages and are mixed and ejected at the air cap in a controlled pattern.

There are several types of spray guns. An external-mix gun mixes and atomizes air and material outside the air cap. This type can be used to apply almost all materials and is the only one suitable for fast drying materials such as lacquer. An internal spray gun mixes air and material inside the cap before expelling them.

A suction-feed gun is one in which a stream of compressed air creates a vacuum, allowing atmospheric pressure to force material from an attached container to

the spray head of the gun. This gun is usually limited to quart size containers.

A pressure-feed gun has an air cap not designed to create a vacuum. Material is forced to the spray head by pressure from a tank or pump.

A spray gun is a precision instrument that, if handled carefully, will produce good results for a long time. Clean the gun and the paint cup immediately after each use, but don't immerse the gun in thinner or the lubricants in the packings will be destroyed. Lubricate the air valve and the packings occasionally. For the gun to work properly, keep the air vent in the lid of the cup open and free of particles at all times.

## Regulating the spray

Photos courtesy of DeVilbiss Co.

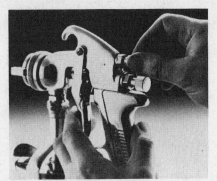

**To get the desired spray width and shape,** manipulate these two valves at the back of the gun.

**The top valve** is the air control valve. It controls the flow of air entering the spray gun.

**The bottom valve** is the fluid control valve. It controls the amount of paint material leaving the gun.

## Parts of the spray gun

**The air cap** (above) at the front of the gun directs compressed air into the paint stream to atomize it and form it into a spray. The cross section of this spray is called the spray pattern.

**The spray-pattern width control valve** is adjusted to control the amount of air passing through the air horn orifices. This, in turn, controls the shape of the spray pattern.

**The fluid tip and the fluid needle** (below) together direct and control the flow of paint material as it leaves the gun.

**The fluid-volume-control valve** controls the amount of paint material leaving the spray gun.

**The air control valve,** operated by the air-fluid control trigger, controls the flow of air entering the gun.

**The air supply connection** at the base of the spray gun handle is attached directly to the hose leading to the supply of compressed air.

**The air hose** is the connection between the supply of compressed air and the spray gun.

**The fluid inlet connection** connects the gun directly to the paint cup.

**The siphon cup** holds the paint which has been reduced with solvent. You must thoroughly clean it after each use.

**The siphon tube** extends from the spray gun into the paint cup. It allows the paint material to flow up to the fluid nozzle.

**The vent** in the lid of the siphon cup allows air at atmospheric pressure to enter the cup.

**The air-fluid control trigger** (above) controls the action of the material leaving the gun or it can cut off the material flow completely. This trigger also allows air to flow before the fluid nozzle is opened and after it is closed to ensure atomization of every drop of paint material. By pulling the trigger halfway, only air will come out.

**The orifices** (below) are holes in the air cap. Air from the center, auxiliary, and air horns mixes with paint from the fluid orifice.

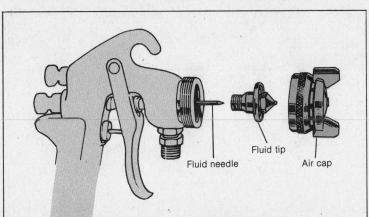

Fluid needle

Fluid tip

Air cap

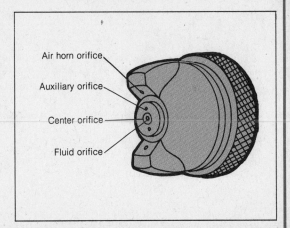

Air horn orifice

Auxiliary orifice

Center orifice

Fluid orifice

# The air compressor

To use a spray gun, you need an air compressor to transfer the paint from the container, atomize it, and create a spray pattern on the panel. The effectiveness of the compressor can be altered by the quality of the air transformer, the compatibility of the gun, and the diameter of the hose.

## Air transformers

An air transformer, which may be called a regulator-extractor on your rig, removes oil, water, and dirt from compressed air and regulates the pressure of the air leaving it and passing through a hose to the spray gun. Never allow water to accumulate in an air transformer. Drain it every day by means of a valve located on the bottom of the tank.

Since the quality of a coat of paint depends on a steady supply of clean air at the spray gun, a transformer is essential for a commercial air compressor.

## Renting a unit

You can buy or rent a small, portable air compressor for home use. Both electric- and gasoline-powered models are available. If you choose an electric model, be sure you have enough wattage to run it. Not all compressors will run on house current.

When renting or buying a compressor, make sure the spray gun and compressor are compatible. The compressor should supply slightly more air than actually needed and have the capacity to keep the required quantity of compressed air flowing to the gun.

Don't economize on the spray gun. The better it is, the better the paint job will be. Make sure the air capacity of the tank is sufficient to supply air

**Rental compressors for use in the home** vary in size. This one has a 21-gallon tank, a one-horsepower motor, and produces up to 100 pounds of pressure per square inch. The motor turns off when the pressure reaches 100 and automatically turns back on when it drops to 60.

for the entire job you are doing. You will, of course, need more air to paint the side of a car than you will to paint one fender. And make sure the motor is large enough for use with a spray gun. A one-horsepower model will do the job. You can rent a transformer separately. It is well worth the slightly higher cost.

## Choosing the right compressor

The four determinants of an air compressor's capacity are:
- The horsepower rating, or HP. The

greater the HP, the more powerful the compressor and the potential for air delivery.
- Pounds per square inch, or psi, the pressure at which the air is delivered.
- Cubic feet per minute, or CFM. This indicates the compressor's air volume output. The higher it is, the more paint you can spray in a given amount of time.
- The tank size. This tells the amount of air-storage capacity.

## Air hoses

Air hoses come in ¼-, $^5/_{16}$-, and ⅜-inch

## Setting up a rented compressor

1 Before you turn on the compressor, make sure all the connections between the hose, the regulator, and the compressor are tight.

2 On the regulator-extractor, the bottom gauge indicates the pressure in the tank. The top gauge is set to the pressure you want at the spray gun.

## Guide to air pressures

There are general guidelines on what pressure to use. However, different situations may call for different pressures.

All pressure adjustments are made at the regulator or transformer. The gun should be empty and the trigger pulled back all the way. Here are some guidelines:

Lacquers, for a spot repair: 30 to 35 psi.

Lacquers, for overall refinishing: 40 to 45 psi.

Lacquers, for the final blend or mist coat: 20 to 25 psi.

Acrylic enamels, for overall finishing: 45 to 65 psi.

Alkyd enamels, for painting a panel or for a complete refinishing job: 45 to 55 psi.

### Table of air pressure drop at spray gun

| Size of air hose inside diameter | 10-foot length | 15-foot length | 20-foot length | 25-foot length | 50-foot length |
|---|---|---|---|---|---|
| ¼-inch | Lbs. | Lbs. | Lbs. | Lbs. | Lbs. |
| At 40 lbs. pressure | 8 | 9½ | 11 | 12¾ | 24 |
| At 50 lbs. pressure | 10 | 12 | 14 | 16 | 28 |
| At 60 lbs. pressure | 12½ | 14½ | 16¾ | 19 | 31 |
| At 70 lbs. pressure | 14½ | 17 | 19½ | 22½ | 34 |
| At 80 lbs. pressure | 16½ | 19½ | 22½ | 25½ | 37 |
| At 90 lbs. pressure | 18¾ | 22 | 25¼ | 29 | 39½ |
| 5/16-inch | | | | | |
| At 40 lbs. pressure | 2¾ | 3¼ | 3½ | 4 | 8½ |
| At 50 lbs. pressure | 3½ | 4 | 4½ | 5 | 10 |
| At 60 lbs. pressure | 4½ | 5 | 5½ | 6 | 11½ |
| At 70 lbs. pressure | 5¼ | 6 | 6¾ | 7¼ | 13 |
| At 80 lbs. pressure | 6¼ | 7 | 8 | 8¾ | 14½ |
| At 90 lbs. pressure | 7½ | 8½ | 9½ | 10½ | 16 |

TABLE COURTESY OF THE DEVILBISS CO.

inside diameters. The larger the hose, the less restriction there will be and the smaller the drop in air pressure between the compressor and the gun. The amount of drop varies with the inside diameter of the hose and with its length. A 5/16-inch diameter hose is recommended for use with a spray gun.

Enamel and lacquer paints require different levels of air pressure at the spray gun. The amount of pressure to use with each is indicated on the label. Because of air pressure drop, the regulator must be set at a greater pressure than that actually leaving the gun.

**This is a commercial air compressor** like those used in auto body shops. The tank capacity is 50 gallons.

**An air transformer** is a separate device used to remove oil, water, and dirt from the compressed air.

3 Before you begin to spray, make sure the vent hole in the cap of the spray gun is free of dirt or paint particles. Air must be able to pass into the siphon cup through this hole.

4 Adjust the size of the spray pattern by turning the spray-pattern width control valve at the back of the spray gun.

# How to handle a spray gun

Using a spray gun properly involves more than just pressing the trigger and hoping the right amount of paint will go where it is supposed to. It is a skill requiring practice. You can buy or rent different types of guns. A siphon gun is the one to use for auto work. Its trigger controls both the air and the fluid. Not all siphon guns are meant for car painting, however. Make sure the one you get is specifically designed for this task.

## Reducing the paint

All paint must be reduced with either thinner or reducer to the proper consistency. The amount of solvent to add is always indicated on the label. Use exactly that amount. And don't try judging consistency by the way the paint runs off the paddle. This is not an accurate test because the appearance of the paint is affected by air temperature. Automobile paints are manufactured to spray best at varying consistencies. Read and follow the directions on the label to get the best possible job. Use a measuring cup for this or the cup that comes with the spray can.

## Temperature

Both the air temperature and that of the car can influence the smoothness of the finish. So if you are painting indoors, let the car sit inside long enough to reach room temperature. Spraying warm paint on a cold car or vice versa affects the flow of the paint. If you are going to paint outdoors, pick a dry day with the temperature in the seventies or higher.

## Thickness of the paint film

The thicker the coat, the longer it will take for the paint to dry. The reason is that the solvent will have to travel from a greater depth to reach the surface

## How to spray

**A thin, rough, dry coat** results from holding the gun too far away, not enough paint or too much air coming out, paint thinned too much, painting too fast or strokes which do not overlap enough.

**A heavy coat with sags and ripples** is a result of holding the gun too close, paint too thin or too thick, low air pressure or a stroke that is too slow or overlaps too much. This is sometimes referred to as piling on.

**A medium coat of paint** with good flow-out will result from a properly adjusted gun held at the right distance from the surface, properly reduced paint, the correct mixture of air and paint, and strokes of the right speed overlapping by 50 percent.

where it evaporates. With enamels, the thicker the film, the greater the distance the oxygen must penetrate. And penetration is further inhibited in thick coats by a skin that forms on the surface as the paint dries.

The correct way to paint is to spray a coat that will stay wet on the surface just long enough for the proper flow-out and no longer. A thicker coat of paint is not necessary and may even cause sags and wrinkles. Also, the longer the paint takes to dry, the greater chance it has of penetrating the old coat, causing additional problems.

## Adjusting the gun

The amount of paint sprayed on the surface with one stroke of the gun will depend on several factors: the type and amount of solvent used, the flow of material, the width of the fan, the air pressure at the gun, the distance from the gun to the panel, and the speed of the stroke.

The first step in using a spray gun is to adjust the fluid-volume control valve and the spray-pattern-width control valve at the back of the gun. The spray pattern of a properly adjusted gun is an elongated ellipse with a uniform distribution of paint over the entire area.

## Distance from gun to car

Spray guns work best when they are held at a distance of six to eight inches for lacquers and eight to ten inches for

Drawing courtesy Ditzler Automotive Finishes/PPG Industries

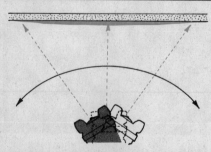

**The incorrect way to use a spray gun,** swinging it in an arc, will result in an uneven coat, because the gun is farther away from some of the surface areas.

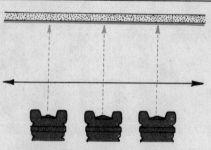

**The correct way to hold a spray gun** is to keep it parallel to the surface being painted. This will result in an even coat.

**When the spray gun is held at an angle** to the surface, some of the areas will get more paint than others, causing an uneven coat of paint.

**The correct width spray pattern** will result in a uniform distribution of paint on the surface.

**Too wide a spray pattern** will disperse the paint, and cause too much overspray, and dry rough surfaces.

**Too narrow a spray pattern** will concentrate the paint in a small area and cause a build-up of paint.

enamels. If the gun is held closer, the force of the compressed air causes the wet paint to ripple. If the gun is held farther away, more solvent evaporates, causing a dry paint film and paint loss due to overspray.

## Learning the stroke

To achieve an even coat, move the gun parallel to the surface you are painting. This requires a steady movement of the entire arm without flexing the wrist. Hold the gun so the spray meets the surface at the right angle. If you tilt the gun away from the surface, the spray pattern will be uneven. Don't swing the gun in an arc. This varies the distance between the gun and the car, making the paint wetter when the gun is close to the surface and drier when it is farther away.

To get proper coverage, each stroke should overlap the previous one by 50 percent. If you are working horizontally from top to bottom, aim the center of the spray pattern at the lower edge of the previous stroke. The stroke should start beyond the beginning of the area to be painted and continue beyond the other end to ensure proper coverage without producing paint buildup at the ends. The strokes should reverse direction each time. If the first stroke is from left to right, the second should be

from right to left. Use steady, deliberate strokes.

Learn to use the trigger correctly. The farther back the trigger is pulled, the greater the material flow. To avoid buildup at the end of each stroke, release the trigger just before the stroke is completed. Pull at the start, release at the end, so you are turning off the gun at the end of each stroke.

Spitting is caused by air leaking into the fluid passageway. This could mean a number of things: not enough paint in the cup, the gun held at too great an angle, dirt lodged between the fluid tip and the gun, or a loose fluid tip.

## Some tips

Make each stroke as long as you can. The longer the stroke, the smoother the finish. Try to extend each stroke from one end of the panel to the other.

To make sure you cover the edges of a panel, you can spray around them first. Then paint the entire area with parallel strokes.

If you are painting an area such as a

hood that is so large that, standing in one place, you can't reach the whole thing, spray from one side to the middle. Then walk around the car and spray from the middle to the other side. Don't spray in from the sides. And expect the strokes to meet in the middle.

**To clear the gun** from paint clogging it, hold your hand or a rag over the air cap and pull back the trigger all the way. This will force most of the paint in the gun back into the cup.

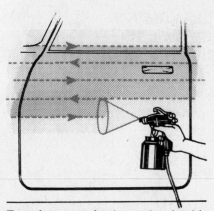

**To paint properly,** the stroke should start before the area you are spraying begins and stop after it ends. The strokes should go in the opposite direction with each pass, and each stroke should overlap the previous one by 50 percent.

## Spray problems

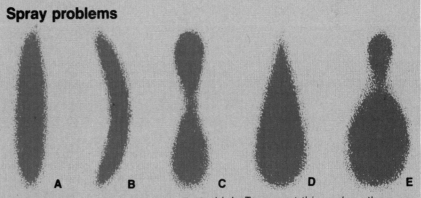

A   B   C   D   E

**When the gun is properly adjusted** and held at the correct distance from the panel, the spray pattern is an elongated ellipse with a uniform distribution of material over the entire area (A). A crescent-shaped pattern (B) is a result of restricted air flow caused by dried paint in the air horns. To correct this, soak the air cap in thinner and clean it. A split spray pattern (C) is caused by air pressure which is too high. To correct this, reduce the pressure. A spray pattern wider at the top or bottom (D) results from dried paint around the fluid tip. To correct this, remove the air cap and fluid tip and clean them. A pattern heavy in the middle and splattered on the edges (E) results from pressure which is too low. To correct this, increase the pressure.

# Cleaning the spray gun

Painting pros, who use a spray gun constantly, completely disassemble and clean it once a week. For those who use one comparatively rarely, it is essential to clean it after each use. All you need to clean it is a wrench and the same solvent you used to reduce the paint.

Between frequent uses of the spray gun, it is always a good idea to keep the air cap immersed in a thinner.

**1** Take off the fluid inlet connection.

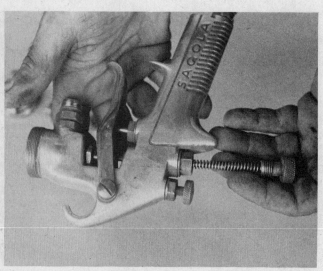

**4** Take out the needle valve.

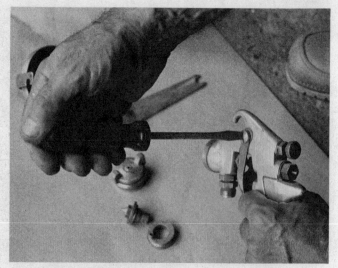

**5** Remove the air-fluid control trigger.

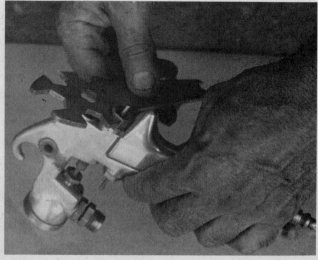

**8** Take off the fluid-volume control.

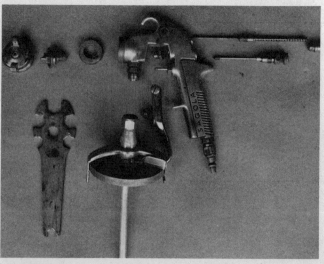

**9** Now the spray gun is completely disassembled.

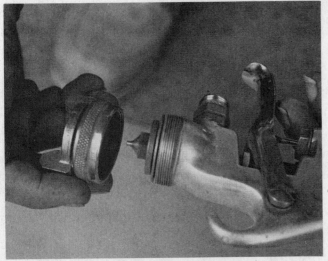

**2** Remove the air cap.

**3** Unscrew the nozzle.

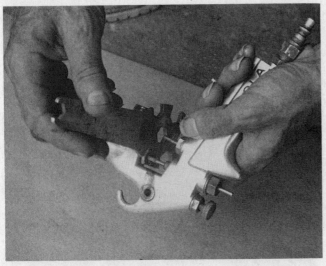

**6** Take off the air-control valve.

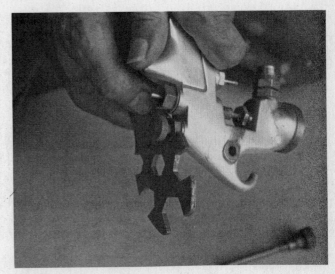

**7** Remove the spray-pattern valve.

**10** Clean all the parts with solvent.

**11** Clean the gun body also.

# Painting like a pro

You can paint your car just like the pros if you take your time and follow these steps. Once you have carefully masked the car (see page 184) and mastered the spray gun, you're all ready to paint.

When painting, follow the directions on the paint label exactly as stated. Each manufacturer makes his paint slightly different in content, so to get a professional looking job follow the directions for the type of paint you are using. Add the right amount of thinner, mix the paint thoroughly, apply single or double coats as indicated, and allow the suggested drying time. And follow the safety precautions recommended on the label. Wear a mask while spraying and paint in a well ventilated area or outdoors. Don't smoke or light a match near paint materials.

1 Gather the necessary painting equipment: paint thinner, spray gun, strainer, and paint paddle or stick.

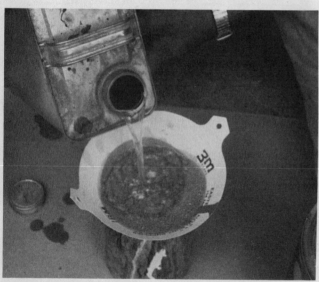

4 Measure the thinner according to the directions on the label and add it to the paint through the strainer.

5 Attach the spray gun to the paint cup, making sure the gun is screwed down tightly.

---

## A glossary of painting terms

**Acrylic.** A clear chemical added to lacquer and enamel paint to provide durability, and to retain color and gloss.

**Adhesion.** The term used to describe how well paint sticks to the surface to which it is applied. Surface preparation has a strong influence on adhesion.

**Air compressor.** A machine used to compress air from atmospheric pressure to a higher pressure.

**Air dry.** The ability of paint to reach its complete hardness under normal atmospheric conditions.

**Air transformer.** A device used with an air compressor to prevent oil and water from getting into the air line. It also regulates pressure.

**Atomize.** To break up paint into fine particles by forcing air into it. This is done at the nozzle of the spray gun.

**Bleeding.** An old color showing through after a new topcoat has been applied. It occurs mostly with reds and maroons and can be prevented by using a special bleeder-sealer.

**Blushing.** A milky, misty, or dull appearance in lacquer and acrylic paint occurring immediately after spraying.

2 To mix the paint thoroughly, make sure the stick touches the bottom of the can and picks up the pigment. Stir until the paint is uniform in color. Some pros remove all the paint from the can, pour in a little thinner, put the cover on, and shake well. Then they stir again, adding this to the thinner.

3 Pour the paint through a strainer to keep out particles that might clog the spray gun.

6 Insert a piece of wire in the vent hole in the top of the spray gun to make sure it is open. The hole must be open to let air in.

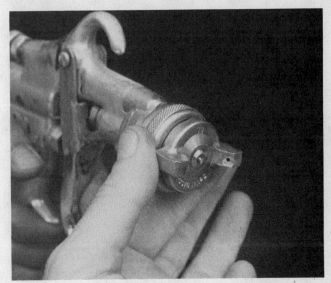

7 Remove and clean the air cap which directs the compressed air into the paint stream to atomize it.

**(continued)**

---

It is caused by the condensation of moisture on the wet paint.

**Clear.** A finish that has no pigment or color in it.

**Coverage.** The amount of surface a given quantity of paint will cover.

**Crazing.** A breakdown in the finish in the form of small cracks in all directions.

**Curing.** The final drying stage where a paint achieves its full strength and durability through chemical change.

**Double coat.** A single coat of paint followed immediately by a second coat without allowing any drying time between. The second coat is often applied in the opposite direction to the first. One is sprayed horizontally and the other vertically.

**Drier.** A catalyst added to paint to speed up the drying time.

**Dry spray.** A sprayed coat with insufficient liquid in it which often turns out rough and dull. It is caused by too fast a solvent for the temperature, holding the spray gun too far from the surface so too much solvent evaporates before reaching the surface, or by maintaining too high an air pressure.

**Enamel.** A type of paint that dries in two stages; first by evaporation of the

## Painting like a pro (continued)

**8** Use a small brush and paint thinner to clean out the air cap. Make sure all the holes are free of paint.

**9** Use the same small brush and paint thinner to clean the fluid nozzle.

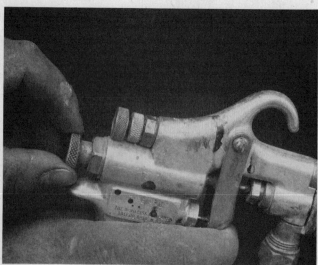

**11** Adjust the spray gun by turning the two knobs at the back of the gun. The upper one is the pattern control, the lower one the fluid control.

**12** Test the spray before working on the panel. This spray is adjusted properly for a good mix of paint and air.

## A glossary of painting terms (continued)

solvent, and then by oxidation of the paint film.

**Evaporation.** The transformation of solvents from liquid into gas and the escape of the gas from the paint into the air.

**Featheredge.** The tapering with sandpaper or special solvents of the edges of any broken area on the surface.

**Fish eyes.** Bubbles in the paint film caused by silicones remaining on the surface.

**Flash.** The first stage of drying where some of the solvents have evaporated, causing the paint film to look slightly duller than the wet gloss.

**Glazing putty.** A substance similar to but thicker than primer-surfacer. It is used to fill surface flaws.

**Gloss.** Surface luster or brightness due to the reflection of light.

**Hiding.** The ability of paint to cover or obscure the surface to which it is applied.

**Holdout.** The ability of an undercoat to resist penetration by the top coat.

**Humidity.** The amount of moisture in the air.

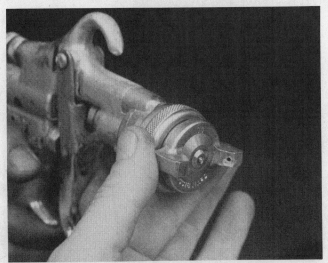

**Body Shop**

To get professional results from a spray gun, you must clean and maintain it. Clean it after every use. Paint should never be allowed to dry on any of the parts. To clean the gun, wash out the paint can with thinner. Put the gun back on and spray thinner so the spray mechanism is cleaned out. To make sure the air cap is free of paint which could dry and clog it, put it in the bottom of the can, cover it with thinner, then let it soak overnight.

**10** Replace and adjust the air cap. The fan can be horizontal or vertical depending on the position of the air cap. You never have to turn the gun.

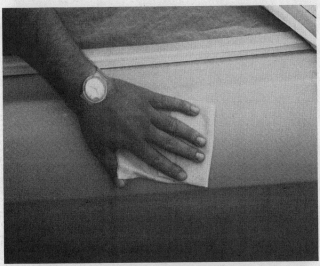

**13** Just before you begin to paint, use a tack cloth to wipe off any dust or lint from the panel.

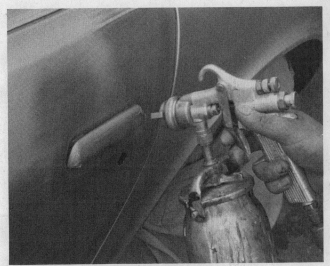

**14** Begin by spraying around the door handle, making sure the paint covers the area.

**Lacquer.** A type of paint that dries by evaporation only. A quick-drying paint.

**Masking.** The covering of areas on the car not to be painted.

**Metal conditioner.** A chemical cleaner that removes rust and corrosion from bare metal and helps to prevent further rusting.

**Metallics.** A group of paints which have metal flakes added.

**Mist coat.** A final coat of paint that has been thinned considerably with solvent and is very wet.

**Orange peel.** A pebbly surface looking like the skin of an orange. Caused by paint that is applied so dryly and thinly that the droplets won't flow together.

**Original finish.** The paint applied to the car at the factory by the car manufacturer.

**Overlap.** That part of the spray applied over paint applied in the previous stroke.

**Oxidation.** The combining of oxygen from the air with the paint. This is the chemical process by which enamel paint continues to dry and harden.

**Paint film.** The layer of paint on the surface.

**Pinholing.** Small holes or pock marks that form in the topcoat or undercoat.

## Painting like a pro (continued)

**15** Then paint along the edges of the panel.

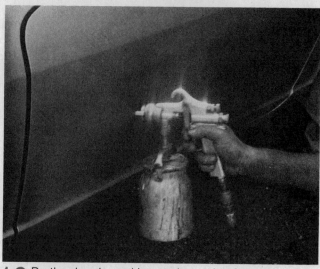

**16** Do the door by making strokes going from left to right, overlapping each.

**19** Don't get too close to the panel as you paint or the coat will be too wet and may run. And keep your speed steady.

**20** Don't stand too far away from the panel or the paint will be too dry and look dusty.

## A glossary of painting terms (continued)

**Prime coat.** An application of primer or primer surfacer to the bare metal to get better adhesion of the topcoat.

**Primer.** An undercoat applied to bare metal to promote the adhesion of the topcoat.

**Primer-sealer.** An undercoat applied over the old finish to promote adhesion of the new coat and to provide holdout, the ability to prevent the topcoat from sinking into the old finish.

**Primer-surfacer.** An undercoat promoting the adhesion of the new paint and also filling in minor scratches and nicks to bring surface areas up to the level of the adjacent painted surface.

**Reducer.** The solvent used to thin enamel.

**Retarder.** A slow-drying solvent that slows down the rate of evaporation. Never used alone, it is added to the solvent being used.

**Sand scratches.** The marks made in bare metal or on the old finish caused by using too coarse a grit sandpaper. Also, marks in the finish coat due to lack of filling or sealing.

**Shrinkage.** Automobile paint contracts or shrinks as it dries. If surface

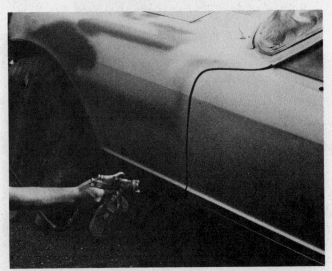

**17** To paint the rocker panel, squat down to get an even distribution of the spray.

**18** Make sure you paint the fender bead where it curves in. Keep the gun at the same distance from every section of the curve.

## Portable sprayers

**If you have a touch-up job to do** and you can't buy paint in a spray can in a color matching your car or you don't need the volume of paint in the spray gun, use a portable sprayer.

The sprayer has two containers: a metal can for the propellant and a plastic jar for the paint and thinner.

To use a portable sprayer, mix the paint and thinner according to the directions on the label. Use the amount and type of thinner indicated and mix thoroughly. Strain the thinned paint through cheesecloth or pour it through a strainer. Fill the plastic jar and screw it onto the top.

To use the sprayer, keep your finger on the knob with a steady pressure—do not use an off-and-on motion. To clean the sprayer after you have finished, pour a small amount of the same solvent used to thin the paint into the plastic jar. Spray once and the nozzle will be clean.

The sprayer should be used for side applications only. The jar will drip if it is held at an angle greater than 45 degrees.

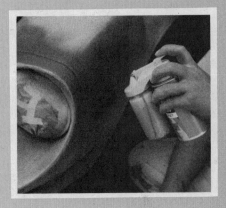

flaws such as scratches have not been properly filled, the paint shrinks into them and they show in the topcoat.

**Silicone.** An ingredient used in polish and wax, making them water resistant, heat resistant, and smooth and sleek to the touch.

**Single coat.** To paint a surface in individual strokes, with each stroke overlapping the previous one by 50 percent.

**Solids.** The part of the paint that stays on the surface after evaporation, thus forming the coat.

**Solvents.** A liquid added to paint which dilutes it enough so it can be applied to the surface. The term includes reducers and thinners.

**Spray gun.** A tool using compressed air to atomize sprayable material and apply it to a surface.

**Tack cloth.** A cheesecloth that has been dipped in diluted varnish to make it tacky. It is used to pick up dust and lint from the car's surface.

**Thinner.** The solvent used to thin lacquer and acrylic.

**Weathering.** The deterioration of the painted surface due to exposure to environmental conditions.

# Painting a soft nose

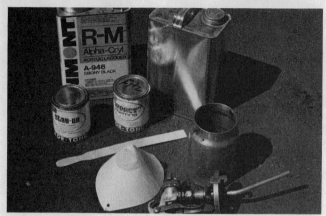

1 To paint any flexible plastic body part such as a nose, bumper or bumper filler, you will need, in addition to the usual paint materials, a special primer and an additive for the paint.

2 Before priming, wash the panel with a wax-and-silicone remover. Sand the repaired area with #320 grit paper, then pour the primer into the paint cup through the strainer. Apply two coats of primer, allowing five to ten minutes drying time between. Allow the second coat to dry thoroughly.

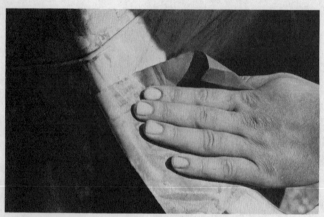

3 Wet-sand the entire panel with #400 or #500 grit paper, depending on the condition of the surface.

4 To paint a flexible or soft part, you can use either acrylic lacquer or acrylic enamel paint, but you must add a flexible agent. With acrylic lacquer, use equal parts of paint and additive. With acrylic enamel, use two parts paint to one part additive. Measure the paint and pour it through the strainer.

5 Now measure the special additive following the directions on the label and add it to the paint by pouring it through the strainer. Then reduce this mixture with thinner following the directions on the label.

6 Spray paint the soft, flexible body part, in this case a nose. Apply several coats, allowing each one to flash dry before applying the next.

# CUSTOM PAINTING TECHNIQUES

Ever since the Model T came out "in any color you like as long as it's black," owners have been individualizing their cars. In the '50's, hot rodders used bright colors, flames, and pinstripes. In the '60's, metallic, candy, and pearl paints were developed. Vans have become increasingly popular during the '70's, and their large, flat surfaces are ideal for sophisticated techniques.

Custom painting techniques and materials are now available to individual car owners, making a custom paint job possible for anyone with sufficient time and talent. Remember though, that a beginner must have the patience to spend a few hours practicing just to do a routine paint job well. And a custom paint job requires even greater patience, plus some skill and luck. Practice on a piece of masonite, glass or even cardboard before you start on your car.

For custom painting, only lacquers are recommended. They are fast-drying, so additional coats can be applied quickly and extensive and complex use of masking materials is possible. The drawback is that lacquers require special treatment to achieve a high gloss. While you can usually apply lacquer right over enamel, you may first want to use a sealer over your car's original paint job. See the discussion in this chapter on the proper use of sealers.

Special paints used for custom effects are candies, pearls, and metallics, all of which contain particles in suspension. Candy paints are translucent top coats which add depth to the base color, sometimes a metallic. They are difficult to handle because you cannot sand them to remove irregularities. Metallics take their name from the metal particles suspended in the paint, while pearls are so called because of the particles of mother of pearl (in a synthetic form) used to produce the iridescent effect. While spraying, keep the particles in suspension by putting several large ball bearings in the paint cup and agitating it every few seconds. To achieve a high gloss, wet-sand with water and #600 grit paper and wipe with a wet cloth. Then spray on a coat of thinned-down clear acrylic (85% thinner, 15% acrylic) and finish off by compounding.

## All about the airbrush

The airbrush is a precision tool that makes possible almost infinite control over the mix of paint and air that comes out of the nozzle. This allows subtle shading plus gradual blends of one color into another. In addition, because of its small size and ease of handling, the airbrush lets you put paint exactly where you want it, even in tight corners which would be unreachable with a production paint gun. Once you become familiar with it, the airbrush will become the essential tool for creating the exotic painting effects shown on the following pages.

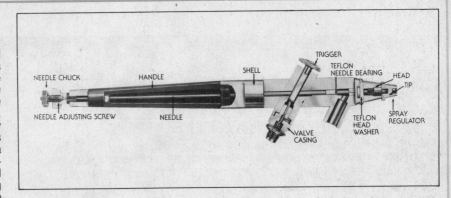

### Cleaning and maintenance

Keep your airbrush and jar and/or color cup clean at all times and do not leave dried paint in the airbrush too long. After using the airbrush, you should remove the needle to clean it. Use the proper solvent and make sure the needle is replaced properly and that it is snug against the tip. Don't jam it. A residual stain will remain on the needle. Polish it by holding it flat on a worktable and running a pink eraser over the length while slowly rolling it toward yourself. Be sure to remove the eraser particles.

1 To clean the color chamber, remove the cup or jar. Then insert a bristle brush or cotton swab into the hole that the jar fits into and turn it.
2 Another method of cleaning the airbrush is to back flush it. Fill the jar with clear water or thinner. Pull back on the lever and push down for full air passage while your finger or a soft cloth covers the tip. Place the airbrush underneath a tabletop to prevent color splattering your work.
3 Use a bristle brush to swirl clean water over the inside surfaces of the color cup until all the paint is cleaned away.
4 If the needle is stuck, carefully loosen the chuck, then grasp the end of the needle with pliers and twist counterclockwise. Inspect the needle for hardened paint, which may be removed with thinner or extra fine sandpaper.
5 It is not always necessary to discard a bent needle. Place it on a firm surface and run your fingernail across it from the body outward toward the tip while you turn it slowly.
6 Before you soak the airbrush in solvent, remove the valve assembly with pliers, turning counterclockwise. To protect the brush and the knurl on the valve, put tape or aluminum foil on the pliers.

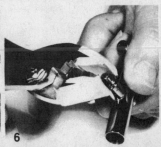

# How to paint a mural

Mural painting is the most recent addition to the custom painter's bag of tricks. Due to the increasing popularity of vans with their large, inviting surfaces, murals are becoming more numerous on the roads every day. But, to bring off a rather complicated work of art like the one illustrated here, you will need more than just a willing attitude. In fact, much more. In addition to the standard techniques of shading, blending, and masking, the mural requires sizeable doses of artistry and planning.

Start with a design. Draw it yourself or trace it from another source. Magazines are rich in possible ideas. Once you settle on a drawing, the next step is to blow it up to van size. The original for our mural, shown below, was eight inches high. We traced it onto ½-inch gridded paper, then transferred it, line by line, onto 3-inch gridded paper, a 6X enlargement. This made it 48 inches high, just right for the side of a van. The image was transferred to the van by tracing the design with the sheet firmly pressed against a spray-mask film. If you are going to use

## Surface preparation

Surface preparation is essential before beginning any custom painting job. If the surface is bare metal, see the steps for priming and painting such a surface in this chapter. Remember that you will be using acrylic lacquers, so the primer will be lacquer as well. This will prevent problems such as solvent penetration, which occur when lacquer is painted over enamel. If you are going to paint over the original factory enamel, you must first seal the area to be painted. Here is the best way to proceed:

1 Degrease the entire area using a commercial wax-and-silicone remover. Several applications may be necessary to get rid of all the old wax and silicone from previous waxings and buffings.

2 Using water and clean rags, wash the area to be painted to remove the degreaser film. If water still beads up on the surface, degrease and wash once again.

3 After removing any trim, mask around the entire area with masking tape and paper. Tape where the panels are joined (at the seams) or at a door or molding.

4 Wet-sand the area to be painted with #400 grit paper to make the surface rough enough so the sealer will adhere. Wipe the surface first with a clean rag, then with a tack cloth to remove dust.

5 Apply two coats of clear sealer over the area to be painted. Two layers prevent solvents in the lacquer art work from penetrating the enamel base coat. For more on sealers, see p. 62.

more than one or two colors, you might want to have several copies of your large-scale design made by a commercial copying service. This will allow you to work with each color separately.

Be sure to key the color masters together so they fit exactly. On the following pages, we illustrate and explain the steps Carl Caiati took in producing this mural, "The Book of the Dead."

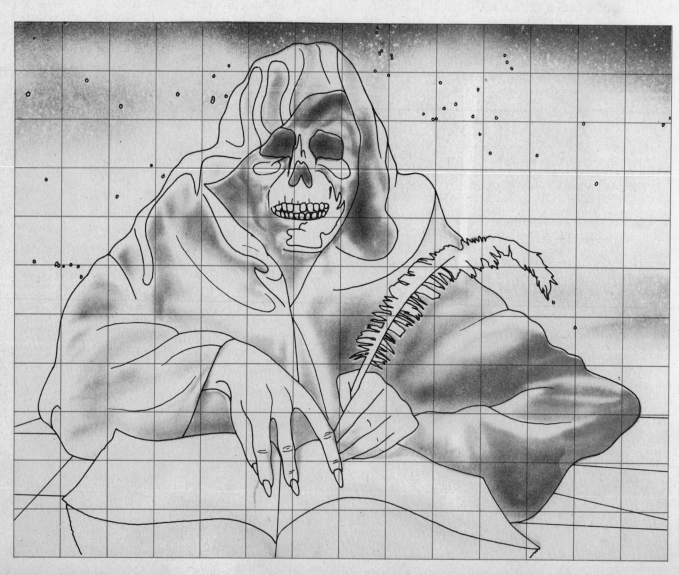

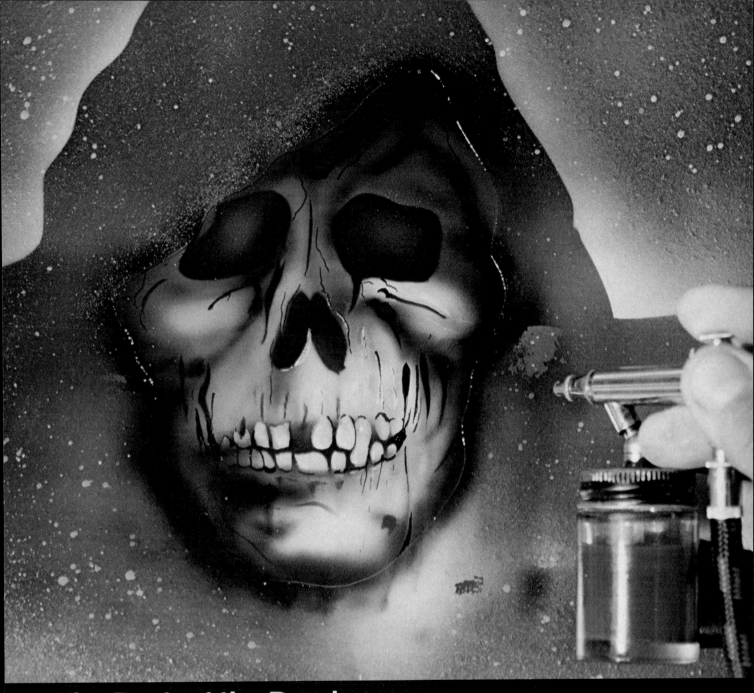

# The Book of the Dead   A mural painted by Carl Caiati

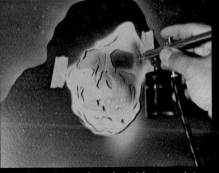

**1.** After the background for the mural is prepared, the area in which the figure is

**2.** Cut the lines of the facial features into a stencil and tape it over the area of

**3.** Use the airbrush to add the facial outlines, then remove the stencil. The

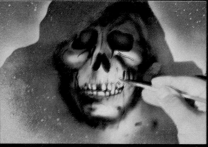

**4.** Add shadows to the face with an airbrush using different shades of red and brown. Good airbrush technique requires practice. Try every freehand brush stroke on a practice surface before starting on the real project.

**5.** Use white to highlight dark features. Sable dagger brushes are used for the really fine work. Again, practice before beginning on the final project.

**6.** Repeat the steps you used on the face to create the hands. Airbrush black paint through a stencil to produce the outlines.

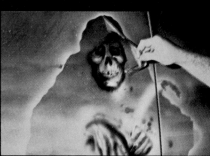

**7.** Airbrushed shadows and hand-painted highlights and details finish the hands. Always do the larger patches first, then the smaller details.

**8.** The cloak is next. Cut around the edges of the figure with a razor or Exacto knife. Use a light touch to avoid scratching the paint underneath the masking.

**9.** Peel away the masking from the cloak area. Wipe off the exposed surface with solvent to remove gum and dirt before painting. Remask the finished areas of the mural (the face and hands) to protect them from overspray.

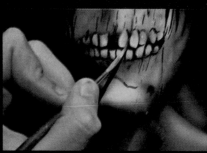

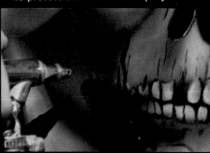

**10.** Airbrush the soft folds of the cloak with a freehand technique. Shading and blending of the colors into each other require a lot of practice before attempting the real thing.

**11.** When the cloak is finished, peel away all of the masking material and clean the surface. Details are now added with a round sable brush.

**12.** Add more tone colors with the airbrush to blend the face and the cloak together. At this point, the choice of final details is left to the artist.

**13.** More final details are added to the quill with a fine sable brush. These details require a very light hand, so step back often and make sure not to overdo it.

**14.** When the last detail is finished, let the mural dry completely. Then spray the entire surface with several coats of clear lacquer to protect it and provide an evenly reflective finish.

## Three-dimensional effects

A painter must know how to do dimensional shading for op-art, cubistic or geometric paneling, and murals. Practice applying shading techniques to the rectangle, which is the basic shape for achieving the cube and other more complicated 3-D straight-line forms. It can be used with other shapes and other airbrush techniques to form interesting combinations. Such practice will familiarize you with this versatile tool and enable you to get the most out of it. Hint: In assigning the lighted and shaded surfaces of a 3-D shape, a good rule is to have the imaginary source of light at the upper left-hand corner.

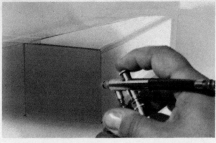

1. This box consists of three rectangles — front, top, and side — Lay out the box on stencil paper so that it tapers toward a point in the distance. Cut the rectangles out and save them. Airbrush the whole shape with a light wash of color. Replace the side and top stencils and spray the front with a darker color.

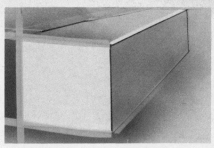

2. After the front has dried, replace the stencil on the front of the rectangle and remove the panel from the side.

3. Airbrush the side of the rectangle with a dark, even coat of the base color.

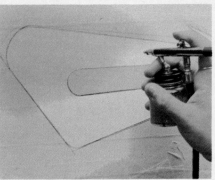

4. For a sharper image, add a highlight along the bottom edge of the side rectangle.

5. If you wish, add more tone to the side panel for greater contrast. Remove the stencil to reveal the finished box.

## Shading and blending

Shading and blending are the forte of the airbrush. The easiest way to achieve them is to apply a series of thin coats of paint. A light coat of one color slightly covered with a light coat of another will produce a blend of the same intensity as a medium coat of a single color. Practice varying the amount of air and paint being sprayed to achieve the desired effect. The following steps show the method used to shade and blend a design for a rainbow effect.

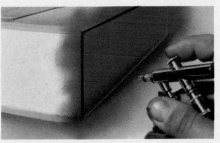

1. Mask the area on which to place the design with 2″ tape. Then draw the design on the tape (use a straightedge), cut along the design, and remove the tape from the area to be painted. Apply the first color in several coats. The first coat should cover the widest area, the next coat a slightly smaller area, and so on so that the paint is thickest in the middle and fades out to the edges.

2. Add green and blend it into the yellow, using several coats.

3. Blend the blue into the green using the same blending technique described above. Darken the extreme end of the blue area using additional coats.

4. Add red and blend it into the other colors. Shade the red darker toward the end. After the paint has had a chance to dry, use a tack cloth to wipe off the overspray.

5. Use a tack cloth to wipe off the overspray after the paint has dried. Then remove the tape to reveal the finished product.

# Stencil art

A wide variety of interesting and complex patterns may be created from simple stencils found in the home or readily available. Shown in the following photos are stencils made of cut cardboard and circular, gummed labels from the stationery store. Drafting templates and French curves, also from the office supply store, make good stencils. Any simple geometric shape may be cut from cardboard and used repeatedly to produce a wide variety of beautiful effects. Use your imagination!

**1.** This fan stencil was made by folding a piece of cardboard down the middle and cutting out the pattern.

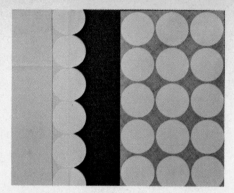

**2.** Use circular, gummed labels to make this one. Draw a line on a piece of cardboard with the distance from the edge equaling half the label diameter. Place the labels side by side along the line. To prevent sticking, place another row of labels against the exposed ones, adhesive sides together.

**3.** Use the stencils repetitively in overlapping patterns to provide a variety of interesting effects.

**4.** For optimum effect, keep the spray passes equal in density.

**5.** Overlapping patterns and a change of color resulted in the design at left. Move the stencil after each airbrush pass to achieve a fish-scale pattern (right).

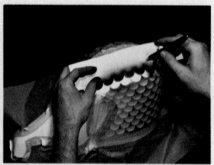

**6.** Here the gummed-label stencils are used to apply the fish-scale effect to a motorcycle gas tank. Make small marks at regular intervals to help keep the rows of scales even.

**7.** A combination of index cards is used to add another kind of fish-scale design to the gas tank.

**8.** Voila! the finished tank shows a nice combination of techniques: fan, fish-scale, and index card. For making ribbons and scrolls, see the following pages.

## Pinstriping

Freehand pinstriping is an old art requiring the talents of a fine craftsman, so don't try it unless you have years of practice. We present here an alternate method for doing pinstriping using various widths of masking tape. To develop the feeling of movement, horizontal striping can narrow to an apex near the front of a van or car. Here is how striping techniques were applied to the Badger Co's. Star Bus.

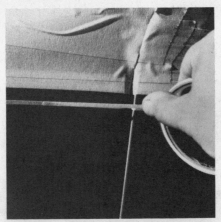

**1** After the panel is masked off, tape is laid out to mask the line. To lay a straight line, secure one end of the tape and pull the roll as shown.

**2** For curves and circles, follow the curve with the tape while affixing it with the forefinger. Developing this technique requires practice.

**3** Lay down parallel stripes of ⅛- to ¼-inch tape, decreasing the distance between each pair of lines. An undercolor stripe will stand out when the area is sprayed and the tape removed.

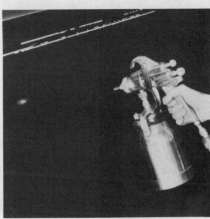

**4** A coating of black is applied, overcoated with hazed green and red Murano for depth.

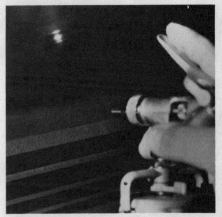

**5** If a contrast color line is desired, spray the masked off panel prior to removing the pinstripe tape.

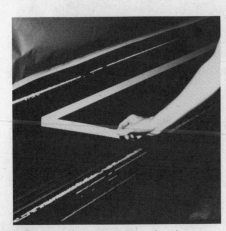

**6** Remove the tape to reveal a clean, crisp line. If the tape was secured firmly, the edges will be perfect.

**7** The finished job shows the results of time and care in planning and execution.

## Flames

Flames originated in the hot rod era of the 1950's and are still frequently used as designs on custom cars. You can create them with stencils, but where they cover wide areas and work their way over curved surfaces and body lines, it's best to use tape. ⅛-inch is easy to work into the clean curves essential for stylized flaming. Here is one basic pattern and the end result.

**1** Lay out the pattern with ⅛-inch masking tape.

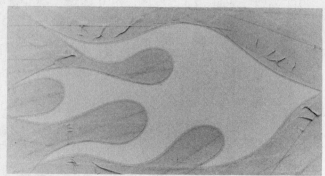

**2** Use wider tape (½-, ¾-, 1-inch) and paper on the outer areas.

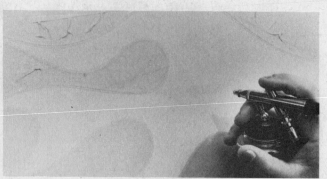

**3** Airbrush a neutral base color over the whole area.

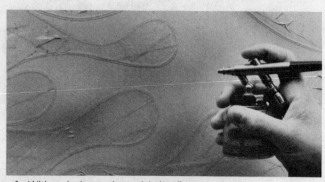

**4** With a darker paint, add shading.

**5** Strengthen and outline the edges with deep tones.

**6** Peel off the masking before the paint dries completely and you have the finished flame.

# Ribbons and scrolls

Ribbons and scrolls are exacting effects but the results are worth the effort. Your use of spray-mask and your work with the airbrush must be careful and precise, since success depends on 3-D effects and shading. The most important advice is to plan with care and take your time.

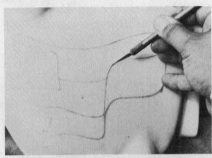

**1** This scroll was painted on a motorcycle side cover. Start with a layer of spray-mask and, when it has dried to a film, draw your design.

**2** Cut away the foreground ribbon sections with a hobby knife and peel away. Caution: Be very careful when working with sharp instruments.

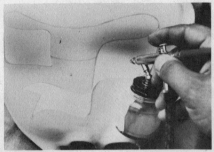

**3** Apply the base color. Vary the amount to achieve the illusion of depth. Now comes a coat of candy paint for shading.

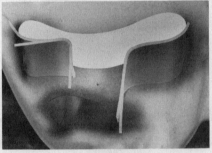

**4** The remaining area to be painted is then cut and peeled. The edges of the adjoining painted areas are masked with ⅛-inch tape.

**5** The remainder of the painted area is masked off with 1-inch tape and a darker coat of the original color is applied.

**6** Dark contour shading is sprayed on, always using a light touch.

**7** The finished painting. The result is an individualized vehicle.

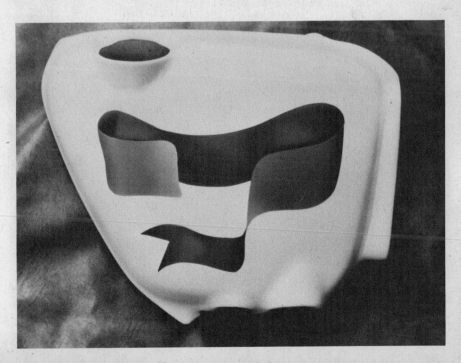

# Wood grain effects

Wood grain looks terrific when it is used with restraint. An entire car or van in grain would probably be a bit too much, so limit yourself to a panel or two. Use Metalflake's Eerie-Dess or water-base acrylics as a covering color and, while it's still wet, wipe it away with a special squeegee. You can govern the length of grain by a rocking motion of your hand.

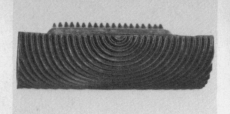

**1** This is the wood grain squeegee. As you wipe it across the painted surface with a rocking motion, the rubber edges give it a grained look.

**2** Mask around the area to be grained and apply a coat of Eerie-Dess or acrylic with the touch-up gun or airbrush.

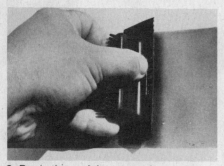

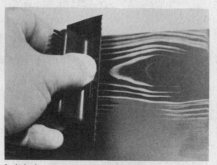

**3** Begin the graining procedure at one edge immediately after applying the Eerie-Dess. Angle the squeegee as shown.

**4** It is important to hold and manipulate the squeegee properly. It is held by the handle and moved horizontally across the coated surface with a slight rock to one side.

**5** Then rock in the opposite direction. A gradual rocking motion results in a long grain pattern while rapid rocking allows for a tighter grain.

# Freak drops

Freak drops are basic airbrush effects achieved by using the tool in a unique manner. The paint is allowed to burst out of the airbrush in circular globs instead of in an atomized spray, and then a quick blast of air forces the drop to spread hair-like branches out from its circumference. Experimenting with overthinning the lacquer and varied controlled airburst procedures will provide a variety of effects.

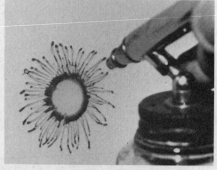

**2** Concentrate a blast of air straight into the center of the blob, exploding the circumference as shown.

**1** To produce the freak drop, deposit an ample circle of lacquer.

**3** By spraying air while the lacquer is still wet, the design can be manipulated, varied or distorted as shown.

# A professional finish

Urethane is a chemical-resistant automobile finish that can be applied over lacquer finishes—some over any lacquer finish, others over new finishes only. The label indicates on which surfaces urethane can be applied. Urethane creates a rock-hard finish needing no polishing or compounding to produce a high shine, but it can be compounded to remove dirt particles. A fairly new development for protecting a car's finish, urethane is applied after painting, color sanding and compounding are completed. Applying urethane is a job for the pros because of the toxic quality of the fumes. And wearing a air-supplied respirator is essential.

This hard finish protects against chips and scratches and, since it is waterproof, guards against surface rust. It is especially good for vulnerable areas such as the front of the hood and the rocker panels. The most practical time to apply urethane is when the car is new, before any surface damage has occurred. Urethane is applied in three separate coats. The top coat must dry for 16 hours.

1 Our pro measures the correct amount of urethane enamel according to the directions on the label and pours this into the spray gun paint cup.

2 He adds the hardener, which makes the urethane dry faster, in a proportion of one part hardener to four parts urethane.

3 With a paint paddle, the pro mixes the urethane and the hardener together. He mixes them completely before beginning to spray.

4 He sprays the urethane and hardener mixture onto the panel as he would spray paint. Urethane creates lots of fumes, so it is absolutely necessary to wear a protective respirator.

5 Our pro applies a double coat of urethane to vulnerable areas such as the rocker panels. He lets each coat flash dry before applying the next. The third and final coat needs 16 hours to dry.

# Blending a spot repair

Before making a spot repair, mask the areas surrounding the repair. To blend a spot repair into the original finish, apply several coats of paint, each one covering a larger area than the previous one. Allow each coat to flash dry before you apply the next one. The final "mist" coat should be very wet, one part paint to five parts thinner. It should extend well onto the old finish.

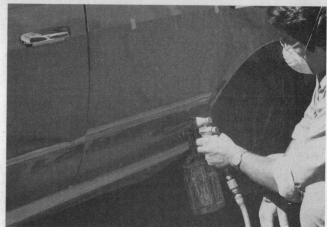

**1** Reprime the area after feathering and sanding the putty and the area has been washed clean of sludge and dried thoroughly.

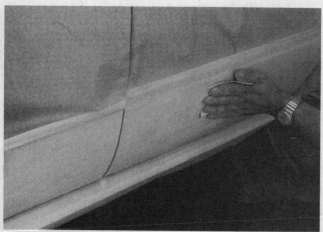

**4** Sand the primed area with #400 grit sandpaper used dry, then wipe with a clean rag.

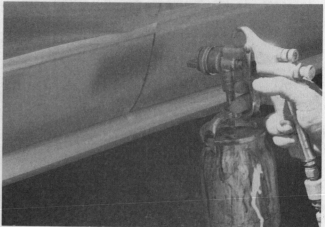

**5** Paint with a light pass over the primed area only. The acrylic lacquer used here dries very quickly at a temperature of 60 degrees and above. Apply six more coats, making sure to extend the area being painted a little more with each coat. Allow a few minutes drying time between each coat.

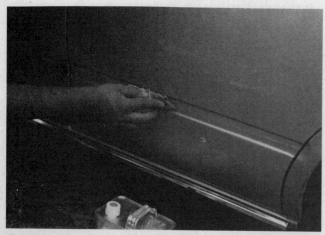

**8** Before you replace the adhesive moldings, clean the area on the panel underneath them with a wax-and-silicone remover to take off any remaining adhesive.

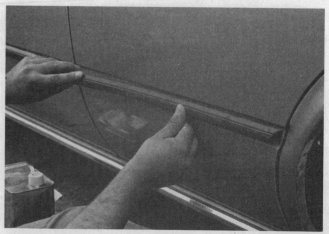

**9** Spray adhesive on the back of the molding strip and align the strip carefully. First use light pressure, then press firmly. You can put several pieces of masking tape vertically over the molding strip to hold it until the adhesive dries.

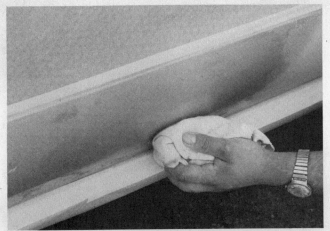

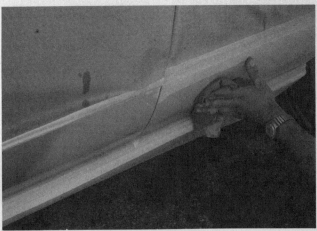

2 Apply fine rubbing compound to the painted area surrounding the primed area to bring the old paint up to the original shine. Rub the compound in with one cloth, then wipe if off with a second.

3 Clean the compounded area with enamel reducer and a clean cloth. Work fast, then wipe the area dry.

6 The final coat should be a mist coat using one part color to five parts thinner. Apply with slightly lower pressure. This coat should wet the painted area and the overspray should blend into the old finish around the repair area. These two films should be the same color when wet, allowing you to check your color match immediately.

7 Remove any masking tape and masking paper. To apply compound, put several drops on the painted surface and buff it with a back-and-forth motion. Keep the buffer moving and use a light touch.

## Gloss coat

To add a shine and protect the paint on your car, you can apply clear acrylic paint as the final coat. If you are painting an entire panel such as a fender or a door, you can use straight acrylic. If you are painting only part of a panel and want to blend the new paint to the old, mix four parts clear acrylic to one part paint. Whichever way you use the clear acrylic, reduce it with thinner following the directions on the label.

1 Mix four parts clear acrylic and one part paint for the final coat of clear acrylic and paint. Measure the paint and pour it through a strainer.

2 Measure the correct amount of clear acrylic and add it to the paint by pouring it through the strainer. Reduce this mixture with the amount of thinner recommended on the label.

# All about metallics

Metallic paint contains small flakes of metal suspended in liquid. The metal particles combine with the pigment to impart varying color effects. The effect depends on the position the flakes assume within the paint film.

## Reflecting light

The position of the metal flakes and the thickness of the paint affect the overall color of the painted surface. The flakes reflect light, but some light is absorbed by the paint. The thicker the layer of paint, the greater the light absorption.

## Light color

When metallic paint is sprayed on dry, the metallic flakes are trapped at various angles near the surface. Light reflection is not uniform, and, because the light has less film to travel through, little of it is absorbed. The result of non-uniform light reflection and a minimum of light absorption is a painted surface with a metallic appearance and a light color.

## Dark color

When metallic paint is sprayed on wet, the metallic flakes have sufficient time to settle so they lie parallel to and deeper within the paint film. Light reflection is uniform and, because the light has to go farther into the paint film, light absorption is greater. The result is a painted surface which appears deeper and dark in color.

## Matching metallics

When matching metallics, you have to figure out how the original finish was sprayed—whether it was applied wet or dry or somewhere in between. If the finish is in good condition, the job of matching will be easier. As the ravages of time and weather take their toll, it becomes more difficult to match a new coat of paint to the old. Mix the paint thoroughly when matching metallics. In this paint, the pigment settles below the binder and the metal flakes settle below the pigment. The paint must be thoroughly stirred both before and after the thinner is added, because any pigment or metal flakes left in the bottom of the can or spray cup will change the

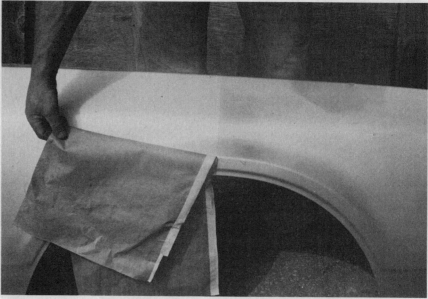

**If an original metallic finish** was applied somewhat dry (left) and the new paint is applied somewhat wet (right), the new paint will be darker than the original finish because of the way the metal flakes arrange themselves in the paint film and how they reflect light.

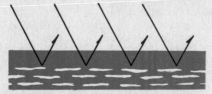

**Metallic paint sprayed wet** is dark in color because the flakes have time to settle parallel and deeper in the paint film.

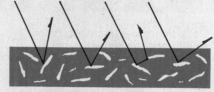

**Metallic paint sprayed dry** is light in color because the flakes are trapped at various angles near the surface.

color of the paint as it is sprayed onto the surface.

Lift the pigment and metal flakes from the bottom of the can with a stick or paddle. To make sure no particles are left in the bottom, pour the contents into another can. Continue to pour the paint back-and-forth between the cans until the paint is mixed. Then remove all the paint from the almost empty can. Pour in a little thinner, put the cover on, and shake well. Open the can and stir, making sure no pigment or metallic particles are left on the bottom. You may have to repeat this a few times until the inside of the can is clean.

Then add the thinner according to the directions on the label. Mix the

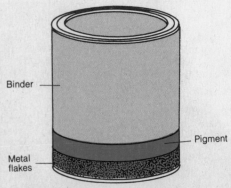

**Metallic paint is composed of binder,** pigment, and metal flakes. The pigment settles below the binder. The flakes settle below the pigment.

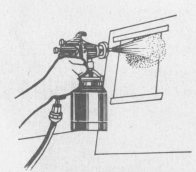

**To match the color exactly,** make a test card by spray-painting a piece of cardboard.

**Hold the test card** against the car to see if it matches. If it is too dark or too light, you can make several adjustments.

## Mixing paint

Whether the paint your are using is metallic or not, you must mix it thoroughly. You cannot match the original finish if the paint has not been properly mixed.

**1** Stir the paint with a paddle, always reaching to the bottom of the can. Then pour the paint back and forth from the can into another container.

**2** Add a small amount of thinner to the empty paint can and mix until you can see the bottom.

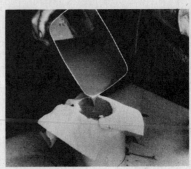

**3** After reducing the paint according to the directions on the label, strain it through several layers of cheesecloth or pour it through a commercial strainer.

paint again after the thinner has been added. Follow the manufacturer's instructions exactly when measuring and mixing the paint and thinner. When adding thinner, remember that weather conditions will affect the color, because drying time affects the position of the metal particles. High humidity means a longer drying time; the less humidity, the shorter the drying time. The higher the temperature, the faster the drying; the lower the temperature, the slower the drying. Also, the better ventilated the area, the quicker the drying. A stuffy area with stale air will slow down drying.

## Making a test card

To make sure the paint will match the car's finish, you can make a test card. First compound the finish to bring it up to its original shine. Then find a piece of thin cardboard, the kind shirt laundries use, rather than corrugated cardboard. Tape the cardboard to newspaper or another protective backing and prop it up so you are spraying horizontally. Spray paint the cardboard, then hold it against the car to see if it matches. You may have to make several test cards before you achieve a good match.

## Correcting the color

If the test card does not match the finish, there are various ways to adjust the degree of wetness or dryness for a better match. Make as many adjustments as you need to get the right color. If the test card is too dark, you can lighten the color by making two adjustments on the spray gun. Turn down the fluid feed valve so less paint flows out and move the fan adjustment to get a wider pattern. To get a lighter color, move the spray gun farther from the surface, speed up the stroke, and increase the flash drying time between coats.

If the test card is too light, you can darken the color by opening the fluid feed valve, allowing more paint to flow out. You can also move the fan adjustment to decrease the pattern. While spraying, you can darken the color by moving closer to the surface, slowing down the stroke, and allowing less drying time between coats.

When you have a test card matching the original finish on the car, use the same techniques, settings, and adjustments you used on the card to paint the car.

# Painting a vinyl top

If the vinyl top on your car is dirty and somewhat worn from the constant beating it takes from weather and pollution, you can clean and paint it and make it look like new. There is a paint made especially for vinyl. It has the consistency of heavy cream and is applied with a sponge applicator. The entire job, including cleaning the roof, masking the car, and painting, takes less than two hours—the perfect maintenance job for a Saturday afternoon.

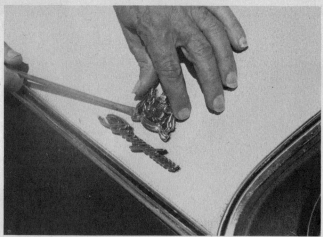

1 Before you clean the roof, remove the nameplate and the insignia by inserting a screwdriver under each and prying it up gently.

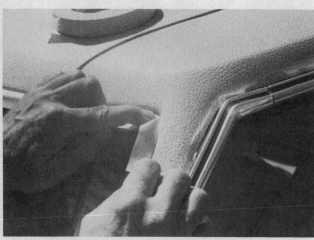

4 Put masking tape along all of the chrome trim surrounding the vinyl. Don't stretch the tape. Gather it at the edges where it goes around corners of the trim and press it down.

5 Following the instructions on the label, shake the paint well. Pour some into a container large enough for the applicator.

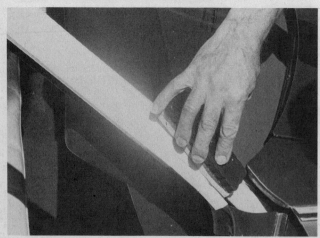

8 If the vinyl continues down the doorpost, you will have to paint that as well. Open the door and carefully apply the paint with the applicator.

9 It helps to use a brush to get paint into the drip-molding area. But make sure you mask the lower part of the car with paper to prevent spattering.

**2** With a strong detergent or scouring powder and a brush, thoroughly clean the vinyl top. A brush is better than a sponge because it scrubs out the dirt lodged in the crevices of the vinyl. Don't use a soap which will leave an oily film.

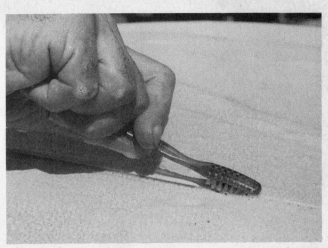

**3** To get the dirt out of narrow areas and seams in the vinyl, use a toothbrush and scrub along the length of the seam. Wash off the cleanser with a hose, then dry the car thoroughly.

**6** Apply the finish using long, overlapping strokes going in one direction, front-to-rear or rear-to-front. Apply two smooth, even coats. Allow each to dry thoroughly.

**7** You can use the sponge to apply paint right up to the edge of the vinyl, but a brush is more useful to cover the edges.

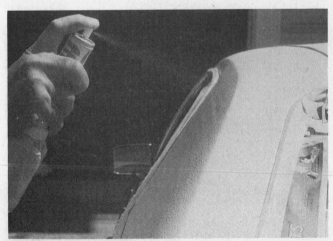

**10** You can apply the vinyl paint with a portable sprayer instead of the sponge applicator. If you decide to spray, mask the windows and the lower part of the car to avoid getting paint on these areas. Vinyl paint is also available in an aerosol can.

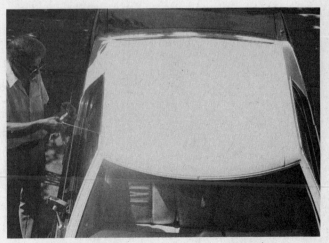

**11** After allowing the vinyl paint to dry somewhat, about half an hour, you can remove the masking tape and paper. For a very high shine, allow it to dry for two days, then apply one of the no-buffing, clear liquid vinyl floor waxes.

# Color sanding
# for a high shine

To bring the final color coat up to full luster, use #600 grit waterproof sandpaper and lots of water. This is called color sanding. It gets rid of the spray dust and orange peel inevitable in the topcoat of any spray-painted surface. The result is a clean, smooth finish.

Both the sandpaper and the surface have to be very wet, so dip the paper into a bucket of water and hold a sopping wet sponge above the area you are working on. As you sand, continuously squeeze water onto the area. Run a squeegee across it occasionally to get rid of the sludge and to find out how smooth the surface is.

1 To wet-sand, you need #600 grit waterproof sandpaper, a squeegee, a sponge, and a bucket of water. Wet-sand before the finish is compounded.

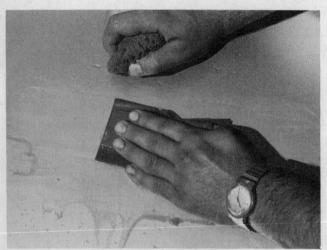

2 Before you sand, thoroughly wet the surface. Water should be dripping off the car. Use a squeegee as backing for the sandpaper to avoid unevenness. Continue to apply water as you sand.

3 Run the squeegee across the surface to make sure the imperfections have been sanded off. If the finish is metallic, be careful to sand evenly or you will create light and dark areas. Check the surface frequently. As soon as it is smooth, stop sanding.

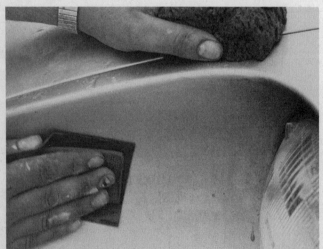

4 Never sand on a ridge or high spot. Sand along one surface up to the ridge, then along the other side.

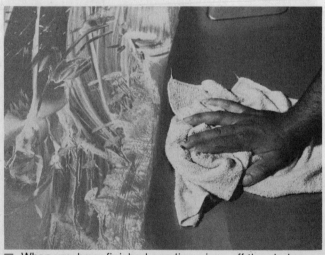

5 When you have finished sanding, rinse off the sludge with water and dry the surface. It is now ready to be compounded.

# HIGH SHINE

Since most people judge the condition of a car by the appearance of the topcoat, you'll want to keep your car as clean and shiny as possible. There are many different products to help you do this.

Compounds, polishes, and cleaner-waxes clean and add a shine or gloss to the topcoat. Paste waxes and silicone polishes protect the topcoat from pollution, water, and road grime.

Compounds are abrasives that remove some of the old paint, leaving a smooth and even surface. There are rubbing compounds and polishing compounds. Rubbing compounds have coarser abrasive particles than polishing compounds. Compounds are used to produce a gloss on a new lacquer finish, to bring an old finish surrounding a repair up to its original color, and to restore the luster on an aged finish.

Polish is a cleaner containing either a very fine abrasive or a cleaning liquid. Some polishes also contain silicone, which makes the finish more weather-resistant but also makes it more difficult to repaint. Polish is used to restore a slightly dulled old paint job that is not in bad enough condition to require compounding.

Paste wax forms a protective coating on the surface. Many waxes now contain silicone to add more protection. Wax is applied only after the surface has been thoroughly washed with soap and water and compounded if necessary. New paint jobs should not be waxed for at least 30 days or as long as is recommended on the paint label. Old finishes that have been restored with polish or compound can be waxed for greater protection.

Cleaner-wax has a mild abrasive added so the surface can be cleaned, smoothed, and waxed in one operation. Cleaner-wax can be used on an old finish after it has been washed with soap and water to remove all dirt and dust so they will not be rubbed into the finish.

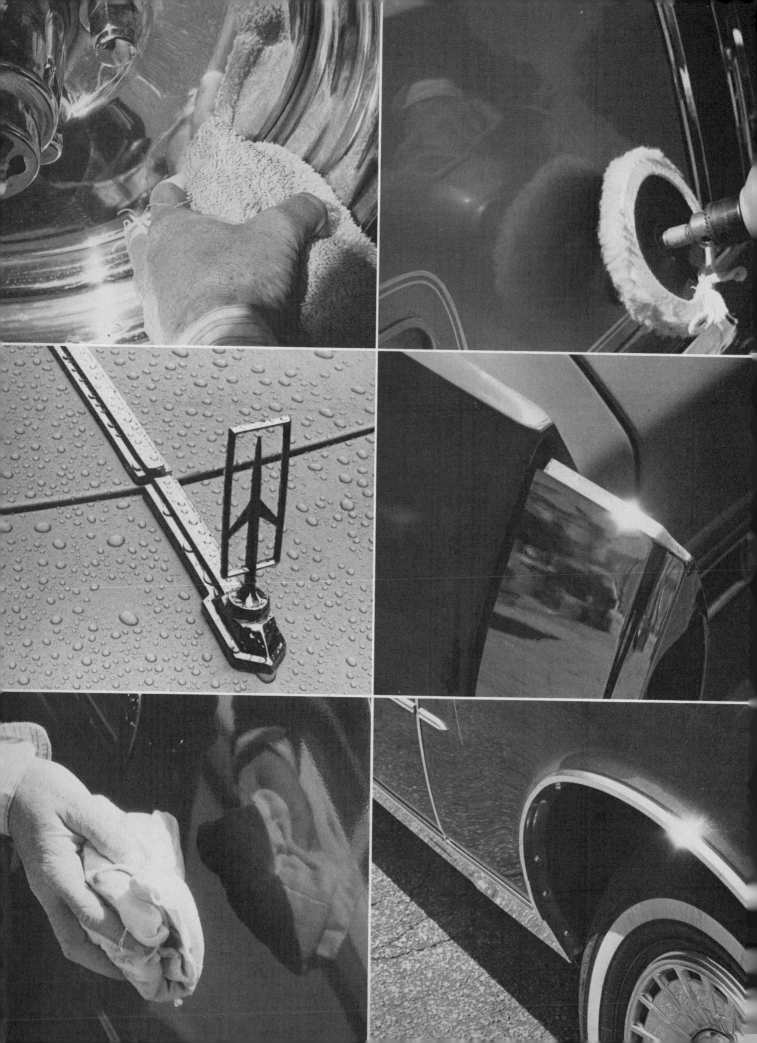

# Job steps Getting a high shine

## A new lacquer finish

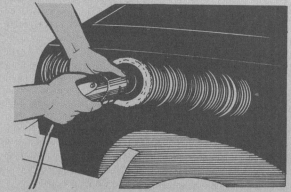

**1** After a new lacquer finish has dried overnight, compound by machine with rubbing compound thinned with water. Work one small area at a time.

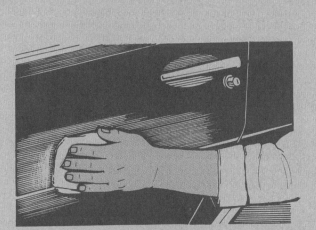

**2** Compound all ridges and edges by hand. Compounding removes some paint and since there is less paint on the ridges and edges, it might take all the paint off these areas.

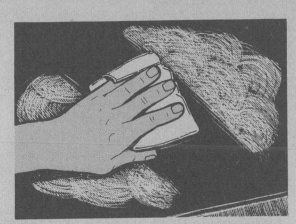

**3** Apply polish to give some protection to the surface until it can be waxed—at least 30 to 90 days later or the time specified on the label.

## An older finish

**1** On an older finish, wash the car with soap and water and dry it thoroughly.

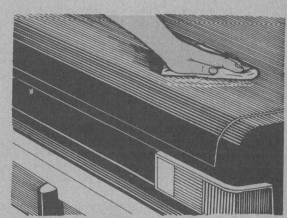

**2** Compound by hand with extra fine rubbing compound thinned to a creamy paste. Work small areas at a time so the compound doesn't dry.

**3** Apply paste wax with a clean, slightly damp cloth. Wipe it off immediately with another clean cloth. Shake and turn the cloth frequently.

# Steps to a high shine

### After refinishing with lacquer:
● Wet-sand the finish with #600 paper, rinse, and dry thoroughly.
● Compound by machine with rubbing compound thinned with water.
● Apply polish for some protection.
● To wax, wait the length of time specified on the lacquer paint label.

### For a spot repair with lacquer:
● Before repairing, prime then compound the old finish surrounding the primer. Work the compound into the edges of the primer also. This brings the old finish up to the original color.
● Spot repair with lacquer (page 214).
● After painting, compound again with polishing compound.

### After refinishing with enamel:
● Wait for the finish to completely dry and harden (the length of time is specified on the paint label).
● Do not wet-sand.
● Apply polish or wax.

### To clean an older finish that is dull and dirty:
● Compound by hand with extra fine rubbing compound thinned with water to a creamy paste. Apply a small amount to the surface with a dry cloth. Rub with considerable force initially, then ease up gradually as the compound dries and produces a gloss. Clean with a clean, dry cloth.
● Apply a good paste wax.

### To clean an older finish that is in good condition:
● For a fast shine, apply polish.
● For a shine that is smoother and lasts longer, use cleaner-wax.

## Compound

Compound, when rubbed against a surface, will remove part of the paint. As this paint is removed, the surface becomes smooth and even. There are two types of compounds, rubbing and polishing. They contain a form of abrasive fine enough to give your car that desired mirror-like finish. Available in either paste or liquid form, compounds are used to produce a gloss on a new lacquer finish, to bring an old finish surrounding a repair up to its original color, and to restore the luster on an aged finish.

Compounds can be further defined. There are machine and hand rubbing compounds and machine and hand polishing compounds. Rubbing compounds have coarser abrasive particles than polishing compounds.

Hand-rubbing compound is coarser than machine-rubbing compound. It is used on small spot repairs, but it can be used on an entire car. It is applied with a damp rag to one small area at a time in a straight back-and-forth motion, not in circles. It is then buffed by machine or by hand.

Machine-rubbing compound is made for use with a portable polisher, buffer or buffing attachment on a ¼-inch drill. It is finer than hand compound because the machine provides more power. This compound should be thinned with water before it is applied to the surface.

A new lacquer finish is always compounded because it has a dull, uneven appearance as a result of the rough texture of the spray. After it has dried overnight, wet-sand it with #600 grit waterproof sandpaper and water. Apply the compound. If you are com-

**Compounding removes orange peel** and spray dust from the final coat of paint. Compound has been applied to the hood of this car and buffed to a high shine on the front right side part only.

pounding an entire panel, you can use a slightly more abrasive compound than if you are only compounding a spot repair. Be careful not to compound through the old paint around the repair.

For older finishes, acrylic and nitro-cellulose lacquers and aged enamels, there is an extra fine polishing compound which has a mild abrasive to remove stains and minor scratches. Before you use it, wash the car with soap and water and dry it thoroughly by hand. Apply compound thinned with water to one small area at a time. Dry buff it to a high shine by hand with a soft cotton cloth, or use a machine with a polishing bonnet. Use a soft touch. Move the buffing machine in a straight back-and-forth motion. Compounding by machine creates heat due to friction. Keep the machine moving because you can rub through or burn the

## Machine compounding

Machine rubbing compound must be thinned with water before it is applied to the surface. Apply it in a small area because the compound should not be allowed to dry. Machine compounding generates heat, so don't keep the machine in one place and don't press too hard. Also, make sure the machine is rotating at a speed appropriate for the surface—about 1200 rpm for nitrocellulose lacquer and about 3000 rpm for acrylic lacquer. Clean the polishing pad often so you don't rub dried compound into the surface.

**1** Thin the compound with water and mix it until it is smooth. Apply it to a small area with a brush or a squeeze bottle. Don't let the compound dry.

**2** With a compounding bonnet on the buffer, run the machine in straight lines. Compounding generates heat, so don't keep the machine in one place or press too hard.

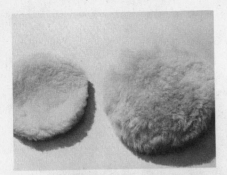

**Bonnets made of lamb's wool** are attached by a drawstring to a holder for a ¼-inch drill. A compounding bonnet (left) has short lamb's wool. A polishing bonnet (right) has long lamb's wool and is softer.

paint if you keep it in one place too long. Check the bonnet and clean it often so you don't rub dried compound into the surface.

Here are some compounding hints: Do not machine-compound on ridges or edges; do them by hand. You can put masking tape over the ridges while you are machine-compounding. Then take the tape off and compound around the ridges by hand. Apply compound to a few small areas at a time so the compound doesn't harden before you rub it in. Compound gives little protection to the surface. It is for cleaning and shining only. A compounded surface should be polished to give it some protection until you can wax it. New paint jobs should not be waxed for at least 30 days. Check the instructions on the paint can for the exact waiting time. Older finishes can be waxed immediately.

## Polish

Polish is a cleaner containing either a fine abrasive or a cleaning liquid. It removes grime and dirt from the topcoat. Some polishes also contain silicone which gives added protection against weather conditions. Polish is used to restore a slightly dulled, older paint job or after a new lacquer finish has been compounded. Polish cleans and leaves a shine on the surface. It is not as deep or as long-lasting as compound and wax. Polish is used for a quick shine.

Before polish is applied, the surface should be washed with soap and water and dried thoroughly. Some polishes are made for application by hand, others by hand or machine. If you use a machine, keep it flat against the surface. Don't tilt it. Polish any ridges or edges by hand. Polishing by machine creates some heat so keep the buffing machine moving constantly.

## Wax

Wax is applied to a surface to help keep it clean and to protect it from weather conditions. It provides a durable finish. Wax can be used on a new finish after it has cured for 90 days or the length of time specified by the paint manufacturer and on an old finish after it has been compounded.

Liquid wax is easier to apply than paste wax. It requires less rubbing, but doesn't provide the durability of a paste wax.

## Cleaner-wax

Cleaner-wax is a product containing wax and a polishing compound, consisting of very fine abrasive particles. It will smooth the surface and wax it at the same time. Cleaner-wax is used to restore a dull, old finish needing more than a wax but less than compounding.

Before cleaner-wax is applied, the surface should be washed with soap and water and dried thoroughly. Apply cleaner-wax with its own applicator, a sponge or a clean rag, in a circular motion to an area about four feet square, or one panel at a time. Let it dry slightly until it forms a haze. Then wipe it off with another clean rag.

## Polishing machines and polishing pads

If you use a power tool or a buffer attachment on a ¼-inch drill, make sure the machine does not rotate at too high a speed causing you to burn through the finish. All machines have a small plate attached to them giving specifications. Check the revolutions per minute. For compounding after refinishing with nitrocellulose lacquer, use 1200 rpm; for compounding after refinishing with acrylic lacquer, use 3000 rpm.

Polishing machines or power drills come equipped with a holder for the pads and bonnets. Some are fastened with a special nut through a hole in the center. Others are tied on with a drawstring. Pads and bonnets come in different diameters. They have to fit the holder. Compounding pads or bonnets have short lamb's wool. Polishing pads or bonnets are made of long lamb's wool and are softer. The pads and bonnets should be cleaned often so you don't rub dried compound or polish into the surface.

**3** Do not machine compound any edges or ridges. Do them by hand after the panel has been compounded.

**4** With a clean polishing bonnet, dry-buff the area that has been compounded (on the left) to get rid of the swirls. Use a light pressure and let the pad do the work.

## Buffing pads and bonnets

Buffing pads and bonnets must be kept clean so you don't rub dried compound into the surface. To clean a pad, you can use a special tool, a wheel attached to a handle. You hold the wheel against the pad as the machine is running. Wear safety goggles as you do this to keep particles of compound out of your eyes. To clean a bonnet, remove it from the holder and rinse it with water. Put the bonnet back on and spin off the excess water. Make sure the bonnet is dry before you buff.

# Shining a new lacquer finish

All new lacquer finishes must be compounded to remove orange peel and spray dust from the surface. The lacquer should be allowed to dry overnight before compounding is begun. A new finish can be compounded by a combination of machine and hand; machine-compounding for the large areas and hand-compounding for the ridges and edges. Apply compound to a few small areas at a time. Never allow the compound to dry.

After the surface is compounded, dry buff it, then apply polish to protect the surface until it can be waxed. Wax cannot be applied for 30 to 90 days or the length of time recommended by the paint manufacturer.

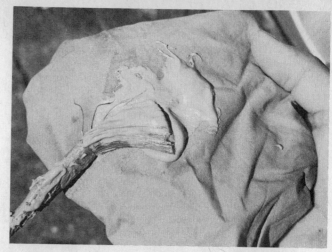

1 Hand rubbing compound can be used just as it comes from the can. Apply a small amount to a clean, dry cloth.

4 Compounding smoothes the surface, giving it a high shine. The headlight well has been compounded. The rest of the car has not.

5 Apply polish to the compounded surface to protect it somewhat until it can be waxed. Squirt the polish onto the surface and let it dry to a haze.

## Wax and cleaner-wax

Paste wax makes a surface shine and protects it from weather conditions. Wax is used on a new finish after it has cured for 90 days and on an old finish after it has been compounded. Wax is never applied or buffed with a machine because the machine creates too much heat.

Cleaner-wax is a wax with a polishing compound added. It will smooth a surface and wax it in one operation. It is used to restore a dull, older finish needing more than wax but less than compounding.

Wax should be applied to one small area at a time. Cleaner-wax can be applied to an entire panel. Wax is rubbed off immediately. Cleaner-wax is allowed to dry to a haze before being rubbed off.

### Applying wax

1 Use a soft, slightly damp cloth to apply paste wax to one small area at a time, about two feet square.

2 Wipe off the wax immediately with a clean cloth. Do not allow it to dry or it will be extremely difficult to rub off.

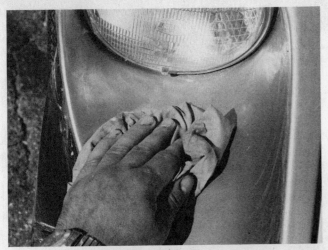

**2** Rub the compound into the surface using considerable force initially and then easing up gradually as the compound dries and a gloss develops.

**3** Clean up the area with a soft, clean, dry cloth. If the area is large and flat, you can dry-buff it with a polishing disc or lamb's wool bonnet.

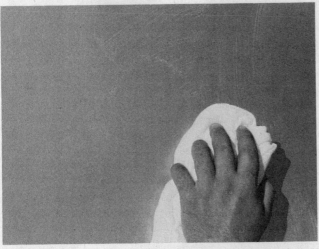

**6** Rub off the polish with a clean rag. Keep turning the rag and shaking out the dried polish so you are always rubbing with a clean cloth.

**7** If you want to polish by machine, make sure the polish you buy is made to be applied by either hand or machine.

## Applying cleaner-wax

**1** After the surface has been washed and dried thoroughly, apply cleaner-wax with its own applicator, a clean rag, or a sponge in a circular motion to one panel at a time.

**2** Let the cleaner-wax dry slightly until it forms a haze. The length of drying time will be specified by the manufacturer.

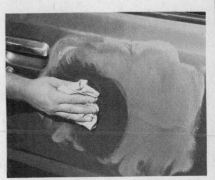

**3** Wipe it off with a clean cloth. Turn the cloth frequently and shake it out so you don't rub dried cleaner-wax into the surface.

# When your lights don't work: common problems and cures

## Headlights

| Symptom | Probable cause | Remedy |
|---|---|---|
| One headlight inoperative or intermittent. | 1. Loose connection. | 1. Secure connections to sealed beam, including ground. |
| | 2. Defective sealed beam. | 2. Replace sealed beam. |
| One or more headlights dim. | 1. Open ground connection at headlight. | 1. Repair ground wire connection between sealed beam and body ground. |
| | 2. Ground wire mislocated in headlight connector (Number 2 sealed beam). | 2. Relocate ground wire in connector. |
| One or more headlights have short life. | 1. Voltage regulator maladjusted. | 1. Readjust regulator to specifications. |
| All headlights inoperative or intermittent. | 1. Loose connection. | 1. Check and secure connections at dimmer switch and light switch. |
| | 2. Defective dimmer switch. | 2. Check voltage at dimmer switch with test light. If test light bulb goes on only at switch "Hot" wire terminal, replace dimmer switch. |
| | 3. Open wiring—light switch to dimmer switch. | 3. Check wiring with test light. If bulb goes on at light switch wire terminal, but not at dimmer switch, repair open wire. |
| | 4. Open wiring—light switch to battery. | 4. Check "Hot" wire terminal at light switch with test light. If light does not go on, repair open wire circuit to battery (possible open fusible link). |
| | 5. Shorted ground circuit. | 5. If, after a few minutes of operation, headlights flicker on and off, and/or a thumping noise can be heard from the light switch (circuit breaker opening and closing), repair short to ground in circuit between light switch and headlights. After repairing short, check for headlight flickering after one minute of operation. If flickering still occurs, the circuit breaker has been damaged and light switch must be replaced. |
| | 6. Defective light switch. | 6. Check switch, replace if necessary. |
| Upper or lower beam will not light or intermittent. | 1. Open connection or defective dimmer switch. | 1. Check dimmer switch terminals with test light. If bulb lights at all wire terminals, repair open wiring between dimmer switch and headlights. If bulb will not light at one of these terminals, replace dimmer switch. |
| | 2. Short circuit to ground. | 2. Follow remedy above for all headlights inoperative or intermittent. |

## Side marker lights

| Symptom | Probable cause | Remedy |
|---|---|---|
| One light inoperative. | 1. Turn signal bulb burned out (front light). | 1. Switch turn signals on. If signal bulb does not light, replace it. |
| | 2. Side marker bulb burned out. | 2. Replace bulb. |
| | 3. Loose connection or open wiring. | 3. Using test light, check "Hot" wire terminal at bulb socket. If test light goes on, repair open ground circuit. If light does not go on, repair open "Hot" wire circuit. |
| Front or rear lights inoperative. | 1. Loose connection or open ground connection. | 1. If associated tail or parking lights do not operate, secure all connectors in "Hot" wire circuit. If tail and parking lights operate, repair open ground connections. |
| | 2. Multiple bulbs burned out. | 2. Replace bulbs. |

## Side marker lights, continued:

| Symptom | Probable cause | Remedy |
| --- | --- | --- |
| All lights inoperative. | 1. Blown fuse. | 1. If parking and taillights do not operate, replace blown fuse. If new fuse blows, check for short to ground between fuse panel and lights. |
| | 2. Loose connection. | 2. Secure connector to light switch. |
| | 3. Open wiring. | 3. Check taillight fuse with test light. If test light goes on, repair open wiring between fuse and light switch. If not, repair open wiring between fuse and battery (possible open fusible link). |
| | 4. Defective light switch. | 4. Check light switch, replace if necessary. |

## Tail, parking, and license plate lights

| Symptom | Probable cause | Remedy |
| --- | --- | --- |
| One side inoperative. | 1. Bulb burned out. | 1. Replace bulb. |
| | 2. Open ground connection at bulb socket or ground wire terminal. | 2. Jump bulb base socket connection to ground. If light goes on, repair open ground circuit. |
| Both sides inoperative. | 1. Taillight fuse has blown. | 1. Replace fuse. If new fuse blows, repair short to ground in "Hot" wire circuit between fuse panel through light switch to lights. |
| | 2. Loose connection. | 2. Secure connector at light switch. |
| | 3. Open wiring. | 3. Using test light, check circuit on both sides of fuse. If neither light goes on, repair open circuit between fuse panel and battery (possible open fusible link). If test light goes on at light switch terminal, repair open wiring between light switch and lights |
| | 4. Multiple bulbs burned out. | 4. If test light goes on at light socket "Hot" wire terminal, replace bulbs. |
| | 5. Defective light switch. | 5. Check light switch, replace if necessary. |

## Turn signal and hazard warning lights

| Symptom | Probable cause | Remedy |
| --- | --- | --- |
| Turn signals inoperative on one side. | 1. Bulb(s) burned out (flasher cannot be heard). | 1. Turn hazard warning system on. If one or more bulbs are inoperative, replace them. |
| | 2. Open wiring or ground connection. | 2. Turn hazard warning system on. If one or more bulbs are inoperative, use test light and check circuit at light socket. If test light goes on, repair open ground connection. If not, repair open wiring between bulb socket and turn signal switch. |
| | 3. Defective bulb or turn signal switch. | 3. Turn hazard warning system on. If all front and rear lights operate, check for defective bulb. If bulbs are OK, replace turn signal switch. |
| | 4. Short to ground (flasher can be heard, no bulbs operate). | 4. Locate and repair short to ground by disconnecting front and rear circuits separately. |
| Turn signals inoperative on both sides. | 1. Blown turn signal fuse. | 1. Turn hazard warning system on. If all lights operate, replace blown fuse. If new fuse blows, repair short to ground between fuse and lights. |
| | 2. Defective flasher. | 2. If turn signal fuse is OK and hazard warning system will operate lights, replace flasher. |
| | 3. Loose connection. | 3. Secure steering column connector. |

# When your lights don't work (continued)

## Turn signal and hazard warning lights, continued:

| Symptom | Probable cause | Remedy |
|---|---|---|
| Hazard warning lights inoperative. | 1. Blown fuse. | 1. Switch turn signals on. If lights operate, replace fuse if blown. If new fuse blows, repair short to ground (could be in stoplight circuit). |
| | 2. Defective hazard warning flasher. | 2. If fuse is OK, switch turn signals on. If lights operate, replace defective flasher. |
| | 3. Open wiring or defective turn signal switch. | 3. Using a test light, check hazard switch feed wire in turn signal steering column connector. If light does not operate on either side of connector, repair open circuit between flasher and connector. If light goes on only on feed side of connector, clean connector contacts. If light operates on both sides of connector, replace defective switch assembly. |

## Stoplights

| Symptom | Probable cause | Remedy |
|---|---|---|
| One bulb inoperative. | 1. Bulb burned out. | 1. Replace bulb. |
| One side inoperative. | 1. Loose connection, open wiring, or defective bulb. | 1. Turn on directional signal. If light does not operate, check bulbs. If bulbs are OK, secure all connections. If light still does not operate, use test light and check for open wiring. |
| | 2. Defective directional signal switch or cancelling cam. | 2. If light will operate by turning directional signal on, switch is not centering properly during cancelling operation. Replace defective cancelling cam or directional signal switch. |
| All lights inoperative. | 1. Blown fuse. | 1. Replace fuse. If new fuse blows, repair short to ground in circuit between fuse and lights. |
| | 2. Stop switch maladjusted or defective. | 2. Check stop switch. Adjust or replace if required. |
| Lights will not turn off. | 1. Stop switch maladjusted or defective. | 1. Readjust switch. If switch still malfunctions, replace it. |

## Backup lights

| Symptom | Probable cause | Remedy |
|---|---|---|
| One light inoperative or intermittent. | 1. Loose or burned out bulb.<br>2. Loose connection.<br>3. Open ground connections. | 1. Secure or replace bulb.<br>2. Tighten connectors.<br>3. Repair bulb ground circuit. |
| Both lights inoperative or intermittent. | 1. Neutral start or backup light switch maladjusted.<br>2. Loose connection or open circuit. | 1. Readjust switch.<br>2. Secure all connectors. If OK, check continuity of circuit from fuse to lights with test light. If light does not operate on either side of fuse, correct open circuit from battery to fuse. |
| | 3. Blown fuse. | 3. Replace fuse. If new fuse blows, repair short to ground in circuit from fuse through neutral start switch to backup lights. |
| | 4. Defective neutral start or backup light switch.<br>5. Defective ignition switch. | 4. Check switch, replace if necessary.<br>5. If test light operates at ignition switch battery terminal but not at output terminal, replace ignition switch. |
| Lights will not turn off. | 1. Neutral start or backup switch maladjusted.<br>2. Defective neutral start or backup light switch. | 1. Readjust switch.<br>2. Check switch, replace if necessary. |

# GLOSSARY

**Abrasive** a gritty substance which can be used to make a surface either rough or smooth depending on its coarseness.

**Acetylene** one of the two gasses (the other is oxygen) used in combination in welding and brazing.

**Acrylic** a clear chemical added to lacquer and enamel paint to provide durability and to retain color and gloss.

**Adhesion** the term used to describe how well paint sticks to the surface to which it is applied. Surface preparation has a strong influence on adhesion.

**Adhesive** a substance which causes two surfaces to stick together.

**Adhesive caulking** a substance used for lining and sealing seams and joints.

**Adjustable part** an auto body section whose fasteners permit some movement as an aid to alignment.

**Aging** the deterioration of a painted surface caused by long exposure to weather and pollution.

**Air compressor** a machine which supplies air under pressure for spray painting and pneumatic tools.

**Air dry** the ability of paint to reach its complete hardness under normal atmospheric conditions.

**Air transformer** a device used with an air compressor to prevent oil and water from getting into the air line. It also regulates pressure.

**Align** to correct panel or section spacing. For example, between the trunk lid and the trunk opening.

**Alignment gap** the space between panels.

**Aluminum oxide** an abrasive frequently used in auto bodywork.

**Arcing** in spray painting, moving the gun in a semicircular path, resulting in a coat of uneven thickness.

**Atomize** to break up paint into fine particles by forcing air into it. This is done at the nozzle of the spray gun.

**Attachments** parts such as drill bits and grinding cones used with a source of power.

**Automatic cutoff** a device which shuts off an air compressor when it has reached a pre-set pressure.

**Base** the non-coloring component of paint in which the pigment is suspended.

**Base coat** the coat of paint upon which the final coats will be applied.

**Bleeding** an older color showing through after a new topcoat has been applied. It occurs mostly with reds and maroons and can be prevented by using a special bleeder-sealer.

**Bleedthrough** the showing through of the old finish after the final coat has dried.

**Blistering** raising of a paint finish because of dirt or moisture remaining on the original surface.

**Blushing** a milky, misty or dull appearance in lacquer and acrylic paint occuring immediately after spraying. It is caused by the condensation of moisture on the wet paint.

**Body spoons** hand tools used in bodywork either alone for prying or with a hammer for dent work.

**Bolt-on-panels** auto body panels fastened with screws or bolts as opposed to welded sections.

**Bond** adhesion; or the power of the adhesion of two surfaces which are stuck together.

**Bonding strips** reinforcement strips used in fiberglass repair.

**Bond strength** the exertion required to break a bond.

**Buckles** high places associated with dents in a metal panel.

**Bumper brackets** supports joined to the body frame to which the bumper is attached.

**Bumping hammer** a tool used for rough pounding of body panels.

**Butyl rubber** a synthetic used in strips as an adhesive.

**Catalyst** a) a hardening additive for plastic body filler; b) a resin-hardening agent in fiberglass work.

**Caulking compound** a sealing substance used on cracks and air and water leaks.

**CFM** cubic feet per minute, referring to air.

**Channels** the slots in which window glass goes up and down.

**Clear** a finish with no pigment or color in it.

**Clearance** the amount of space between adjacent panels.

**Closed style door** a sedan door, one having a full window frame.

**Combination body-and-frame construction** a type of construction with a separate body and frame bolted together.

**Compound** to bring up the luster of a car's body surface by rubbing with an abrasive paste.

**Consistency** the viscosity of a liquid or the thickness of a paste.

**Contours** rounded areas on a car's surface.

**Coverage** the area a given amount of paint will cover.

**Cowl panels** panels forward of the passenger compartment to which the fenders, hood, and dashboard are bolted.

**Crazing** small cracks in the paint surface.

**Curing** the final drying stage where a paint achieves its full strength and durability through chemical change.

**Direct damage** the damage suffered by the part of the car which is struck. See Indirect damage.

**Disc grinder** a rotating, portable power tool used to remove a finish down to bare metal.

**Dolly block** one of various portable anvils used to straighten dents.

**Door lock assembly** all of the parts of a door lock.

**Door trim** the cloth or plastic attached to the passenger compartment side of the door.

**Double coat** a single coat of paint followed immediately by a second coat without allowing any drying time in between. The second coat is often applied in the opposite direction to the first. One is sprayed horizontally and the other vertically.

**Drier** a catalyst added to paint to speed up the drying time.

**Drip molding** the metal molding which serves as a rain gutter over side glass.

**Drying time** the length of time required for the evaporation of solvent from a paint coat.

**Dry sanding** a method of sanding which does not use water. See Wet sanding.

**Dry spray** in painting, an imperfect coat resulting from premature drying of the solvent.

**Elasticity** the capacity of a substance or material to return to its original form when external pressures are removed.

**Enamel** a type of paint that dries in two stages: first by evaporation of the solvent and then by oxidation of the paint film.

**Epoxy resin** a liquid used in fiberglass panel repair.

**Evaporation** the transformation of solvents from liquid into gas and the escape of the gas from the paint into the air.

**External-mix cap** a spray-gun air cap which mixes air with the liquid-paint outside the cap.

**Featheredge** tapering the edges of any broken area on the surface with sandpaper or special solvents.

**Fiberglass** a spun-glass material used on some cars instead of sheet metal.

**Filing** using a metal tool with cutting edges to smooth a surface.

**Filler rod** metal wire used in welding.

**Filling** bringing surface depressions up to the level of surrounding areas with body filler or primer-surfacer.

**Finishing hammer** the type of hammer used to bring metal to its original smoothness.

**Fish eyes** depressions in the paint film caused by silicones remaining on the surface.

**Flash** the first stage of drying where some of the solvents have evaporated, causing the paint film to look slightly duller than the wet gloss.

**Flash time** the time it takes for a coat of paint to become dry to the touch.

**Frame** the heavy metal structure which supports the auto body and other external components.

**Fusion welding** welding in which the two metal panels are brought together and heated to a fluid state.

**Gauge** a measure of the thickness of sheet metal.

**Glazing putty** a substance similar to but thicker than primer-surfacer. It is used to fill surface flaws.

**Gloss** surface luster or brightness due to the reflection of light.

**Grinding** using a rotating power tool with abrasive disc attachments to remove the finish on metal.

**Grit** a measure of the size of particles on sandpaper or discs.

**Hammer-off-dolly** the method of using a hammer and dolly in which the dolly is held away from the area of the metal being tapped by the hammer.

**Hammer-on-dolly** a method of using a hammer and dolly in which the dolly is held directly under the area where the hammer is tapping.

**Hardtop** an auto body style having a rigid roof and a convertible-type door.

**Headlining** the cloth or plastic material covering the ceiling area in the passenger compartment.

**Hiding** the ability of paint to cover or obscure the surface to which it is applied.

**Holdout** the ability of an undercoat to resist penetration by the topcoat.

**Humidity** the amount of moisture in the air.

**Impact tool** a tool combining hammering and rotating action used for cutting sheet metal as well as removing nuts.

**Indirect damage** damage occuring somewhere other than at the point of impact. See Direct damage.

**Inner panels** reinforcing metal panels connected to outer panels.

**Internal mix cap** in spray painting, an air cap which mixes the air and paint within the spray gun.

**Joint** the point where or line along which two pieces are connected.

**Lacquer** a type of paint that dries by evaporation only. A quick-drying paint.

**Lamination** joining layers of like material.

**Lifting** the loss of adhesion of a paint coat by the action of the solvents of a new paint coat placed over it.

**Line pressure** the pressure in the air hose coming from the compressor.

**Locking pliers** a tool which holds parts together so the bodyworker can join them by pop riveting or welding.

**Lock pillar** the door post containing the lock striker.

**Mallet** a large hammer with a non-metallic head, often made of wood or plastic.

**Masking** the covering of areas on the car not to be painted.

**Mechanism** the moving parts of an assembly.

**Metal bumping** returning damaged metal to its original shape.

**Metal conditioner** a chemical cleaner that removes rust and corrosion from bare metal and helps to prevent further rusting.

**Metal finishing** restoring damaged metal by bumping out and grinding.

**Metallic paint** paint in which flakes of metal are suspended in the binder.

**Misaligned** having uneven spacing, as between body panels.

**Mist coat** a final coat of paint that has been thinned considerably with solvent and is very wet.

**Molding clips** fasteners which hold metal trim to a panel.

**Orange peel** a pebbly surface looking like the skin of an orange. Caused by paint applied so dryly and thinly that the droplets won't flow together.

**Original finish** the paint applied to the car at the factory.

**Orbital sander** a power tool which fine sands by means of an oscillating action.

**Outer panels** sheet metal sections which, when attached to the inner panels, form the auto's exterior.

**Overlap** that part of the spray applied over paint applied in the previous stroke.

**Overspray** sprayed paint which falls on an area next to the one being painted.

**Oxidation** the combining of oxygen from the air with the paint. This is the chemical process by which enamel paint continues to dry and harden.

**Paint film** the layer of paint on the surface.

**Paper-taper** a machine found in auto painting shops which applies tape to the edge of masking paper to make an apron.

**Peeling** in spray painting, the condition in which the topcoat does not adhere to the underlying surface.

**Pick hammer** a metal-working tool having a point at one side of the head and a flat face at the other.

**Pinholing** small holes or pock marks that form in the topcoat or undercoat.

**Plastic body filler** a putty-like compound used for filling depressions in metal up to the level of the surrounding surface.

**Plastic filler file** a grating tool made for filing plastic body filler. A cheese grater file.

**Pneumatic tool** a power tool driven by compressed air.

**Polisher** a low-speed power tool used for compounding.

**Pop-off valve** an air compressor valve which releases excessive pressure.

**Portable power tools** electric or pneumatic drills, polishers, and the like which are light enough to use as hand tools.

**Power tools** tools, either portable or stationary, which are powered by electricity or pneumatic pressure.

**Prime coat** an application of primer or primer surfacer to a bare metal surface.

**Primer** an undercoat applied to bare metal to promote the adhesion of the topcoat.

**Primer-sealer** an undercoat applied over the old finish to promote adhesion of the new coat and to provide holdout, the ability to prevent the topcoat from sinking into the old finish.

**Primer-surfacer** an undercoat promoting the adhesion of the new paint and also filling in minor scratches and nicks to bring surface areas up to the level of the adjacent painted surface.

**Psi** pounds per square inch of pressure.

**Quarter panel** the outer panel, including the wheel well.

**Rear compartment lid** luggage compartment cover; trunk lid or deck lid.

**Rear wheelhouse panel** an inner panel attached over the rear wheel which keeps out mud and water, part of the quarter panel.

**Reducer** the solvent used to thin enamel.

**Reduction** the amount of thinner specified for a particular paint.

**Resilience** the capacity of a substance or material to return to its original shape when a deforming force has been removed.

**Resin** a substance used when working on fiberglass bodies.

**Respirator** a mask incorporating a filter. Recommended for spray painting, grinding, and power sanding work.

**Retaining clips** fasteners which hold trim to a panel; molding clips.

**Retarder** a solvent that slows down the rate of evaporation and hence the drying time of a coat of paint.

**Riveter, pop** a tool used to join metal panels together.

**Rocker panel** the narrow, outer panel attached below the car door.

**Roughing hammer** a bumping tool used during the initial stages of repairing sheet metal damage.

**Round spray** in spray painting, the pattern which results from turning the spread control clockwise.

**rpm** revolutions per minute.

**Rubber adhesive** the liquid bonding agent used to apply rubber to metal.

**Running** in spray painting, the overlay liquid condition associated with various mistakes in application, such as improper use of solvents or a too heavy spray.

**Safety goggles** impact resistant glasses that fit snugly against the head for protection, especially when working with power tools or metal.

**Sagging** in spray painting, the sliding of paint on the surface, caused by one of a number of mistakes in application. See Chapter 13, Painting.

**Sand scratches** the marks made in bare metal or on the old finish caused by using too coarse a grit sandpaper. Also, marks in the finish coat due to improper filling or sealing.

**Scribe** to mark a line on metal using a pointed tool, usually for the purpose of lining up when reassembling parts.

**Sealant** caulking used to prevent leaks around joints, windshields, and rear glass.

**Sealer** in painting, a protective coating which inhibits bleeding between the old coat and the fresh one.

**Setting time** the time it takes for a new coat of paint to achieve firmness.

**Shelf life** the time beyond which a substance, even though its container has never been opened, is no longer usable.

**Shrinkage** automobile paint contracts or shrinks as it dries. If surface flaws such as scratches have not been properly filled, the paint shrinks into them and they show in the topcoat.

**Shrinking dolly** a type of dolly having a flat or slightly curved face.

**Silicone** an ingredient used in polish and wax, making them water resistant, heat resistant, and smooth and sleek to the touch.

**Silicone carbide** a common type of sanding or grinding grit in bodywork.

**Single coat** to paint a surface in individual strokes, with each stroke overlapping the previous one by 50 percent.

**Siphon gun** a spray gun in which the paint is drawn up to mix with the air by means of the vacuum created by the rapid passage of air over the pickup tube.

**Skimming** a flawed paint coat resulting from the drying of the surface while underlying layers remain fluid.

**Solids** the part of the paint that stays on the surface after evaporation, thus forming the coat.

**Solvent** a liquid added to paint which dilutes it enough so it can be applied to the surface. The term includes reducers and thinners.

**Spot putty** a special fast drying substance for filling dings and small imperfections.

**Spray gun** a tool using compressed air to atomize sprayable material and apply it to a surface.

**Stability** resistance to chemical change.

**Stationary sections** welded, as opposed to bolted-on, panels.

**Straight-in damage** damage resulting from a direct hit, a collision for example, rather than from a glancing hit.

**Striker** the stationary side of a lock assembly.

**Stripping** using a chemical solvent to remove one or more coats of paint.

**Stroke** in spray painting, a single, complete sweep of the gun.

**Superstructure** the frame and inner panels of an auto body.

**Tack** stickiness.

**Tack cloth** a cheesecloth that has been dipped in diluted varnish to make it tacky. It is used to pick up dust and lint from the car's surface.

**Tacking** using a tack cloth.

**Tack range** the length of time a substance remains tacky when exposed to drying.

**Tape print** the mark caused by applying tape to a surface not totally dry.

**Thinner** the solvent used to thin lacquer and acrylic.

**Tilting** in painting, holding the gun at an angle other than 90° to the surface to be painted, resulting in a heavier accumulation near the gun than farther away.

**Toxic fumes** fumes associated with painting procedures which can harm the eyes, skin or breathing tract.

**Triggering** manipulating the spray gun trigger for optimum results.

**Trim** decorative metal pieces on a car body.

**Trim cement** a liquid cement for use with upholstery trim.

**Twist damage** damage which distorts the cross members of the frame.

**Undercoat** a protective coat which resists the development of rust in the most vulnerable places.

**Unitized construction** auto body construction in which the body and frame are welded together as one unit.

**Vehicle** the binder and thinner of a paint in which the pigment and filler are suspended.

**Ventilator window assembly** the mechanism and parts which make up the small window in the front door.

**Vertical spray** in spray painting, the pattern obtained from turning the spread control counter-clockwise.

**Vinyl cover** a synthetic material frequently used on auto tops.

**Viscosity** the thickness of a liquid.

**Volatile** evaporating at a relatively low temperature.

**Water-and-oil extractor** an attachment for air compressors which removes moisture and impurities from the air line.

**Water trap** a U-shaped fitting in a pressure hose which collects any moisture passing through it.

**Weathering** the deterioration of a car's painted surface due to exposure to environmental conditions.

**Weatherstripping** the rubber molding which prevents water and dirt from entering the passenger compartment or trunk.

**Welding** joining metals by bringing them to the melting point.

**Wetcoat** in spray painting, a heavy application.

**Wet sanding** dousing the surface with water while sanding.

**Window channels** the slots in which window glass goes up and down.

**Window regulator** the mechanism governing the movement of windows. It is found inside the door.

**Wrinkling** imperfections in a painted surface caused by exposing a wet coat to excessive heat.

**Zebra effect** in spray painting, a streaky look resulting from uneven application.

# INDEX